ENDORSEMENTS

"Have you ever wanted Christian theology made simple? R.C. Sproul has the gift of making things simple without dumbing them down. Like a father teaching his child to swim, he can bring us into waters too deep for us touch bottom, but he won't let us drown. So I invite you to jump into this pool of the knowledge of God. Whether you want to learn more about what makes the Bible different, who God is, why Christ died, how the Holy Spirit works in a person's soul, or what happens on judgment day, in these pages you will find clear answers from a wise teacher."

—Dr. Joel R. Beeke
President and Professor of Systematic Theology and Homiletics
Puritan Reformed Theological Seminary, Grand Rapids, Michigan

"A young man once told me that one night he dreamed he saw an army of theologians coming over the horizon toward him. At the front, leading the charge, was R.C. Sproul. Read this book and you will understand the dream. For here is theology rooted in Scripture, nourished by the best of the church's theologians, and expounded with the clarity and simplicity that is the hallmark of a master theologian-communicator.

"Do you need to be a theologian to read this book? Of course. But that's the point of the title: you are—the real question is whether you are a good one or not! So, read, mark, learn, and inwardly digest *Everyone's a Theologian*. By the time you are finished you will almost certainly be a healthier and happier one."

—Dr. Sinclair B. Ferguson
Teaching Fellow
Ligonier Ministries

"R.C. Sproul is a consummate teacher, especially skilled at explaining difficult theological concepts in uncomplicated terms. Here, he tackles every major category of systematic theology in a succinct, lucid, even-handed fashion. This is a tremendously valuable resource for everyone from the newest believer to the most seasoned pastor. It is quite true that we are all theologians. Dr. Sproul helps us all be *better* theologians."

—DR. JOHN MACARTHUR
Pastor-Teacher, Grace Community Church
President, The Master's University and Seminary
Sun Valley, California

"R.C. Sproul has written a brief, comprehensive summary of systematic theology that I intend to recommend to my classes for years to come. It is biblically faithful, solidly Reformed, grounded in the two-thousand-year-old Christian tradition, and up to date on questions crucial to the minds of people in our secularized culture. He writes with his typical clarity and economy of words. As always, he holds the reader's attention. For a long time I have recommended to students Berkhof's *Summary of Christian Doctrine* as a reliable and succinct source of Reformed systematic theology. It is still very useful, but I suspect I shall now be recommending Sproul's *Everyone's a Theologian* more than anything else in this category. Trinity, predestination, creation, sin, the extent of the atonement, justification, speaking in tongues, angels and demons, heaven and hell: all of these, and many another topic, are fairly and responsibly set forth in a way that honors the Word of God written, and will edify those who are open to its truth."

—DR. DOUGLAS F. KELLY
Professor of Theology Emeritus
Reformed Theological Seminary, Charlotte, North Carolina

R.C. SPROUL

EVERYONE'S A THEOLOGIAN

AN INTRODUCTION
to SYSTEMATIC THEOLOGY

ℝ *Reformation Trust*   A DIVISION OF LIGONIER MINISTRIES, ORLANDO, FL

Everyone's a Theologian: An Introduction to Systematic Theology
© 2014 by R.C. Sproul

Adapted from the teaching series *Foundations: An Overview of Systematic Theology* (1999), published by Ligonier Ministries.

Published by Reformation Trust Publishing
a division of Ligonier Ministries
421 Ligonier Court, Sanford, FL 32771
Ligonier.org   ReformationTrust.com

Printed in Ann Arbor, Michigan
Cushing-Malloy, Inc.
0000419
Second edition, first printing

ISBN 978-1-64289-202-4 (Paperback)
ISBN 978-1-56769-369-0 (ePub)
ISBN 978-1-56769-370-6 (Kindle)

Cover design: Gearbox Studios
Interior design and typeset: Katherine Lloyd, The DESK

Scripture quotations are from the ESV® Bible (The Holy Bible, English Standard Version®), copyright © 2001 by Crossway, a publishing ministry of Good News Publishers. Used by permission. All rights reserved.

Library of Congress Cataloging-in-Publication Data

Sproul, R.C. (Robert Charles), 1939-2017
    Everyone's a theologian : an introduction to systematic theology /
R.C. Sproul.
    pages cm
ISBN-13: 978-1-56769-365-2 (hardcover)
ISBN-10: 1-56769-365-2 (hardcover)
1. Theology, Doctrinal--Popular works. I. Title.
BT77.S7183 2014
230--dc23
                                                      2013037126

To my family,
who has been so loving and supportive
through the years of my ministry

CONTENTS

Part One

INTRODUCTION

———

Chapter 1

WHAT IS THEOLOGY?

Several years ago, a well-known Christian school invited me to address the faculty and administration on this question: "What is a Christian college or university?" Upon my arrival, the dean gave me a tour of the campus. During the tour, I noticed this inscription on a set of office doors: "Department of Religion." When it came time to address the faculty that evening, I mentioned the inscription I had seen, and I asked whether the department had always been called by that name. An older faculty member replied that years ago the department had been called the "Department of Theology." No one could tell me why the department name had been changed.

"Religion" or "theology"—what difference does it make? In the academic world, the study of religion has traditionally come under the broader context of either sociology or anthropology, because religion has to do with the worship practices of human beings in particular environments. Theology, by contrast, is the study of God. There is a big difference between studying human apprehensions of religion and studying the nature and character of God Himself. The first is purely natural in its orientation. The second is supernatural, dealing with what lies above and beyond the things of this world.

After explaining this in my lecture to the faculty, I added that a true Christian college or university is committed to the premise that the ultimate truth is the truth of God, and that He is the foundation and source of all other truth. Everything we learn—economics, philosophy, biology, mathematics—has to be understood in light of the overarching reality of the character of God. That is why, in the Middle Ages, theology was called "the queen of the sciences" and philosophy "her handmaiden." Today the queen has been deposed from her throne and, in many cases, driven into exile, and a supplanter now reigns. We have replaced theology with religion.

THEOLOGY DEFINED

In this volume, we are concerned with theology, specifically with systematic theology, which is an orderly, coherent study of the principal doctrines of the Christian faith. In this chapter, I will give a brief introduction to the science of systematic theology and some basic definitions.

The word *theology* shares a suffix, *-ology*, with the names of many disciplines and sciences, such as *biology*, *physiology*, and *anthropology*. The suffix comes from the Greek word *logos*, which we find in the opening of John's gospel: "In the beginning was the Word, and the Word was with God, and the Word was God" (John 1:1). The Greek word *logos* means "word" or "idea," or, as one philosopher translated it, "logic" (it is also the term from which we get the English word *logic*). So when we study biology, we are looking at the word or logic of life. Anthropology is the word or logic about humans, *anthrōpos* being the Greek word for *man*. The primary part of the word *theology* comes from the Greek *theos*, which means "god," so theology is the word or logic of God Himself.

Theology is a very broad term. It refers not only to God but to all that God has revealed to us in sacred Scripture. Included in the discipline of theology is the study of Christ, which we call "Christology." It also includes the study of the Holy Spirit, which we call "pneumatology," the study of sin, which is called "hamartiology," and the study of future things, which we call "eschatology." These are subdivisions of theology. Theologians also speak of "theology proper," which has specific reference to the study of God Himself.

Many are comfortable with the word *theology* but cringe when they

4

hear the qualifying term *systematic*. This is because we live in a time of widespread aversion to certain kinds of systems. We respect inanimate systems—computer systems, fire alarm systems, and electrical circuitry systems—because we understand their importance for society. However, when it comes to systems of thought or to understanding life and the world in a coherent manner, people are uncomfortable. Part of the reason for that has to do with one of the most influential philosophies to emerge in Western history—existentialism.

THE INFLUENCE OF PHILOSOPHY

Existentialism is a philosophy of existence. It presupposes that there is no such thing as essential truth; rather, there is distinctive existence—not essence, but existence. By definition, existentialism abhors a generic system of reality. It is an anti-system that holds to truths but not to *truth* and to purposes but not to *purpose*. Existentialists do not believe that reality can be understood in an orderly fashion because they see the world as ultimately chaotic and without meaning or purpose. One simply confronts life as it happens; there is no overarching viewpoint to make sense of it all, because ultimately life does not make sense.

Existentialism has had a tremendous impact in Western culture along with its offspring, relativism and pluralism. The relativist says, "There is no absolute truth except the absolute truth that there is absolutely no absolute truth. All truth is relative. What is true for one may be false for another." There is no effort to bring opposing views into harmony (something a system would seek to do) because, according to relativists, there is no possibility of a systematic understanding of truth.

Such philosophy has also had a strong impact on theology, even in the seminaries. Systematic theology is rapidly becoming a forgotten discipline, not only because of the impact of existential thought and of relativism and pluralism, but also because some people misunderstand systematic theology as an attempt to force the Bible into a philosophical system. Some *have* attempted to force the Bible into a philosophical system, as was the case with René Descartes and his rationalism and with

John Locke and his empiricism. Those who make such attempts do not hear the Word of God or seek to understand it on its own terms; rather, they seek to bring a preconceived system to bear on the Scriptures.

In Greek mythology, a bandit named Procrustes attacked people and cut off their legs to fit them into the dimensions of an iron bed rather than simply enlarging the bed. Attempts to force Scripture into a preconceived system of thought are similarly misguided, and the result has been an aversion to systematic theology. However, systematic theology does not attempt to force Scripture into a philosophy or system, but instead it seeks to draw out the teachings of Scripture and understand them in an orderly, topical way.

ASSUMPTIONS OF SYSTEMATIC THEOLOGY

Systematic theology is based on certain assumptions. The first assumption is that God has revealed Himself not only in nature but also through the writings of the prophets and the Apostles, and that the Bible is the Word of God. It is theology *par excellence*. It is the full *logos* of the *theos*.

The second assumption is that when God reveals Himself, He does so according to His own character and nature. Scripture tells us that God created an orderly cosmos. He is not the author of confusion because He is never confused. He thinks clearly and speaks in an intelligible way that is meant to be understood.

A third assumption is that God's revelation in Scripture manifests those qualities. There is a unity to the Word of God despite the diversity of its authors. The Word of God was written over many centuries by many authors, and it covers a variety of topics, but within that diversity is unity. All the information found in Scripture—future things, the atonement, the incarnation, the judgment of God, the mercy of God, the wrath of God—have their unity in God Himself, so that when God speaks and reveals Himself, there is a unity in that content, a coherence.

God's revelation is also consistent. It has been said that consistency is the hobgoblin of little minds, but if that were true, we would have to say that God has a small mind, because in His being and character, He is utterly consistent. He is the same yesterday, today, and forever (Heb. 13:8).

These assumptions guide the systematic theologian as he goes about his task of considering the whole scope of Scripture and inquiring how it all fits together. At many seminaries, the systematic theology department is separate from the New Testament department and the Old Testament department. This is because the systematic theologian has a different focus than the Old Testament professor and the New Testament professor. Biblical scholars focus on how God has revealed Himself at various points over time, while the systematician takes that information, puts it all together, and shows how it fits into a meaningful whole. This is a daunting task, to be sure, and I am convinced that no one has ever done it perfectly.

As I engage in systematic theology, I never cease to be amazed by the specific, intricate coherence of the scope of divine revelation. Systematic theologians understand that each point in theology addresses every other point. When God speaks, every detail He utters has an impact on every other detail. That is why our ongoing task is to see how all the pieces fit together into an organic, meaningful, and consistent whole. That is what we will be doing in this volume.

Chapter 2

———

THE SCOPE AND
PURPOSE OF THEOLOGY

Theology is a science. Many disagree vociferously and claim that there is a big gap between science and theology. Science, they say, is that which we learn through empirical inquiry and investigation, whereas theology springs from those inflamed by religious emotions. Historically, however, systematic theology has been understood to be a science.

THEOLOGY AND SCIENCE

The word *science* comes from the Latin word that means "knowledge." Christians believe that through God's divine revelation, we have real knowledge of God. Theology could not rightly be called a science if knowledge of God were impossible. The quest for knowledge is the essence of science. The science of biology is a quest to gain a knowledge of living things, the science of physics is an attempt to gain knowledge about physical things, and the science of theology is an attempt to gain a coherent, consistent knowledge of God.

All sciences use paradigms or models that change or shift over time. A *paradigm shift* is a significant change in the scientific theory of a given discipline. If you were to come across a high school physics textbook from the 1950s, you would see that some of the theories presented then have been demolished. No one takes them seriously because there have been significant shifts in the theories of physics in the years since then. The same thing happened when Newtonian physics replaced earlier theories of physics. Then Albert Einstein came along and created a new revolution, and we had to adjust our understanding of physics again. A paradigm shift occurs when a new theory replaces an old one.

That which usually provokes paradigm shifts in the natural sciences is the presence of anomalies. An anomaly is a detail or a minor point that does not fit into a particular theory; it is something for which the theory cannot account. If one attempts to fit ten thousand details into a coherent picture, much like working with a ten-thousand-piece jigsaw puzzle, and can make all the pieces fit except for one, most scientists consider that to be a good paradigm. The assembled structure that fits together in 9,999 ways will make sense of and account for almost every bit of data explored. However, if there are too many anomalies— if a significant amount of data cannot be tied into the structure—the theory falls apart.

When anomalies become too numerous or too weighty, the scientist is forced to go back to the drawing board, to challenge the assumptions of previous generations, and to construct a new model that will make sense of the new discoveries or pieces of information. That is one of the reasons why we see constant change and significant progress in the sciences.

When it comes to understanding the Bible, the approach is different. Theological scholars have been working with the same information for two thousand years, which is why a dramatic paradigm shift is unlikely. Of course, we do gain new nuggets of precise understanding, such as the nuance of a Greek or a Hebrew word that earlier generations of scholars did not have at their disposal. Yet most of the shifts in theology today are not driven by new discoveries from archaeology or from the study of ancient languages; they are most often driven by new philosophies that appear in the secular world and by attempts to achieve syntheses or integration between those modern philosophies and the ancient religion revealed in Scripture.

That is why I tend to be a conservative theologian. I doubt I will ever come up with an insight that has not already been worked over in great detail by greater minds than mine. In fact, when it comes to theology, I am not interested in novelty. If I were a physicist, I would try constantly to come up with new theories to satisfy nagging anomalies, but I consciously refrain from doing that when it comes to the science of theology.

Sadly, many are quite willing to pursue novelty. In academia, there is always pressure to come up with something new and creative. I recall a man who sought to prove that Jesus of Nazareth never existed, but was instead the mythological creation of members of a fertility cult while they were under the influence of psychoactive mushrooms. His thesis certainly was novel, but it was as absurd as it was new.

Of course, this fascination with novelty is not unique to our era. The Apostle Paul encountered it among the philosophers at Mars Hill in Athens (Acts 17:16–34). We do want progress in our knowledge and growth in our understanding, but we have to be careful not to be lured into the temptation to come up with something new just to be novel.

THE SOURCES OF SYSTEMATIC THEOLOGY

The principal source for the systematic theologian is the Bible. In fact, the Bible is the primary source for all three theological disciplines: biblical theology, historical theology, and systematic theology. The task of biblical theology is to consider the data of Scripture as it unfolds over time, and this work serves as a source for the systematic theologian. A biblical scholar goes through the Scriptures and studies the progressive development of terms, concepts, and themes in both the Old and New Testament to see how they are used and understood over the course of the history of revelation.

A problem in seminaries today is a method of doing biblical theology called "atomism," in which every "atom" of Scripture stands alone. One scholar might decide to limit himself to studying only Paul's doctrine of salvation in Galatians, while another focuses exclusively on Paul's teaching on salvation in Ephesians. The result is that each comes up with a different view of salvation—one from Galatians and another from Ephesians—but there is a failure to examine how the two views harmonize. The presupposition is that Paul was not inspired by God when he wrote Galatians and Ephesians, so there is no overarching unity, no coherence, to the Word of God. In recent years, it has been common to hear theologians claim that we find not only differences in theology between "early" Paul and "late" Paul, but also as many theologies in the Bible as there are authors. There is Peter's theology, John's theology, Paul's theology, and Luke's theology, and they do not fit together. That is a negative view of the coherence of Scripture, and it is the danger when one focuses only on a narrow piece of the Bible without at the same time considering the whole framework of the biblical revelation.

The second discipline, another source for systematic theology, is historical theology. Historical theologians look at how doctrine has developed in the life of the church historically, primarily at crisis points—when heresies emerged and the church responded. Theologians today become frustrated when so-called brand-new controversies arise in churches and seminaries, because the church has experienced each of these seemingly fresh theological disputes time and time again in the past. The church historically has met in councils to settle disputes, such as at the Council of Nicea (AD 325) and the Council of Chalcedon (AD 451). Studying those events is the function of historical theologians.

The third discipline is systematic theology. The systematician's job is to look at the source of biblical data; the sources of the historical developments that come through controversies and church councils and their subsequent creeds and confessions; and the insights of the great minds with which the church has been blessed over the centuries. The New Testament tells us that God in His grace has given teachers to the church (Eph. 4:11–12). Not all teachers are as astute as Augustine, Martin Luther, John Calvin, or Jonathan Edwards. Such men do not have Apostolic authority, but the sheer magnitude of their research and the depth of their understanding profit the church in every age. Thomas Aquinas was called "the doctor angelicus," or "the angelic doctor," by the Roman Catholic Church. Roman Catholics do not believe that Aquinas was infallible, but no Roman Catholic historian or theologian ignores his contributions.

The systematician studies not only the Bible and the creeds and the confessions of the church, but also the insights of the master teachers that God has given throughout history. The systematician looks at all the data—biblical, historical, and systematic—and brings it together.

THE VALUE OF THEOLOGY

The real question concerns the value of all such study. Many people believe that theological study holds little value. They say, "I don't need theology; I just need to know Jesus." Yet theology is unavoidable for every Christian. It is our attempt to understand the truth that God has revealed to us—something every Christian does. So it is not a question of whether we are going to engage in theology; it is a question of whether our theology is sound or unsound. It is important to study and learn because God has taken great pains to reveal Himself to His people. He gave us a book, one that is not meant to sit on a shelf pressing dried flowers, but to be read, searched, digested, studied, and chiefly to be understood.

An important text in the writings of the Apostle Paul is found in his second letter to Timothy: "All Scripture is breathed out by God and profitable for teaching, for reproof, for correction, and for training in righteousness, that the man of God may be complete, equipped for every good work" (2 Tim. 3:16–17). That text should put an end to claims that we do not need doctrine or that doctrine has no value. There is profit from a careful study of the Bible. Because the Bible is inspired by almighty God, it gives us a valuable and profitable asset, and that asset is doctrine.

The Bible is profitable also for reproof. The academic world devotes much energy to biblical criticism, sometimes called higher criticism, which is an analytical critique of Scripture. However, the biblical criticism in which we ought to engage renders us the object rather than the subject of the criticism. In other words, the Bible criticizes *us*. When we come to the Word of God, the Word of God exposes our sin. The biblical doctrine of man includes us, as does the biblical doctrine of sin, and we are reproved for our sinfulness when we come to the text of Scripture. We may not listen to the criticism of our peers, but we are wise to heed the criticism of God as it comes to us in sacred Scripture.

Scripture is also profitable for correction from both false living and false belief. Some time ago, at the request of a friend, I read a *New York Times* best seller about how to become a medium and communicate with the dead. I got about halfway through the book and had to stop reading. There was so much spiritual filth in that book, so much falsehood, that those with even a simple understanding of the law of God in the Old Testament would have been able to detect the lies. Such is the profit of correction from false teaching and false living that we can gain from Scripture.

Finally, Scripture is profitable "for training in righteousness, that the man of God may be complete, equipped for every good work." The purpose of theology is not to tickle our intellects but to instruct us in the ways of God, so that we can grow up into maturity and fullness of obedience to Him. That is why we engage in theology.

———

Chapter 3

GENERAL REVELATION AND NATURAL THEOLOGY

We have already seen that Christianity is not based on speculative philosophy; it stands or falls as a revealed faith. The fundamental assertion of the Christian faith is that the truth we embrace as Christians has come to us from God Himself. We cannot see Him with our eyes, but we can know Him by means of revelation, He has removed the veil that hides Him from us. A *revelation* is a making plain or an unfolding of that which is hidden.

In theology, we make a distinction between kinds of revelation. An important distinction is that between *general revelation* and *special revelation*. In this chapter, I want to concentrate on general revelation. The Scriptures tell us that God is the source of all truth. Everything flows from Him, just as a spring, small as it might be, can be the source of a mighty river. God is the source, the spring of all truth. In other words, not only religious truth but *all* truth is dependent upon God's work of revelation.

The principle taught by Augustine and later by Thomas Aquinas is that we as creatures could not know anything were it not that God has made knowledge possible for us. Augustine illustrated the idea by means of physical sight. He said that even those with perfect vision, if they were placed in a room filled with beautiful objects, could not see any of the beauty if the room were immersed in darkness. Although they might have the necessary equipment to see the beautiful objects in the room, unless those things were set in the light, even people's most acute vision would be inadequate to perceive them. In the same way, Augustine said, the light of divine revelation is necessary for us to know any truth whatsoever. Aquinas quoted Augustine verbatim, saying that all truth and all knowledge, in the final analysis, rest on God as the source of truth and as the One who makes it possible for us to know anything at all. So, when scientists seek to discern truth in their laboratories while belittling us for our claim to trust in revelation for the content of our religious faith, we can simply point out that they could learn nothing from a test tube were it not for the Creator's revelation and His gift of the ability to learn through a study of nature.

GOD'S UNVEILING

God's unveiling of Himself in all truth is called "general" for two reasons. First, this revelation is general because it is knowledge that is given to everyone. Divine general revelation is available to all people in the world. God does not simply reveal Himself to specific individuals; His self-revelation is manifested to every human being. The entire world is His audience. The Bible says, for example, "The heavens declare the glory of God, and the sky above proclaims his handiwork" (Ps. 19:1). Anyone with physical vision can walk in the theater of nature and see the glory of God through the stars, the moon, and the sun. It is a grand theater.

The physically blind are not shut out, however, because the Bible also speaks about the knowledge that God plants in human souls. He gives man a conscience, through which He reveals Himself to people inwardly. God has given all human beings a sense of right and wrong, so even those born blind have an interior knowledge of God (Rom. 1:19–20).

So, in sum, the term *general* means that everyone is in the audience; every human being is exposed to God's revelation. Millions have never seen a Bible or heard Scripture preached, but they have lived in the theater of nature, where God manifests Himself.

The second reason the term *general* is applied to this type of revelation is that the content of it is of a general sort; that is, it does not give us the details of God's work in redemptive history, such as the atonement or the resurrection of Christ. One cannot study a sunset and see the heavens declaring God's plan of salvation; one must go to the Bible for that. Scripture has specific information that no one can gain from a study of nature.

We must understand the difference between general and special revelation. General revelation is given to everyone and supplies us with a general knowledge of God. It is different from the revelation of Scripture. The Bible is special revelation, and only those who have access to the Bible or its content receive it. Special revelation gives much more detailed information about the work and the plans of God.

NATURAL REVELATION

Sometimes, general revelation is called "natural revelation," a term that can be confusing. In theological parlance, the term *natural revelation* is a synonym for *general revelation* because general revelation comes to us in and through nature.

In general revelation, God does not simply give us planet earth and then expect us to use the naked power of our reason to figure out who He is on the basis of what He has placed here. We can study a painting carefully and figure out who the artist is by means of the style of brush strokes or the paint pigments, but that is not how general revelation works. Creation is a medium through which God actively reveals Himself. Nature is not independent of God; rather, God communicates Himself through the medium of the world. He communicates Himself through the glory and majesty of the heavens, the world, and all that He made.

The revelation of God that comes through nature is what we call natural revelation. The term *natural revelation*, simply stated, refers to the work or actions by which God reveals Himself in and through nature.

LEARNING THROUGH NATURE

There is another category of study called "natural theology." Natural (or general) revelation and natural theology are not the same. Natural revelation is something God does, whereas natural theology is what humans do with natural revelation.

For quite some time now, there has been controversy among theologians as to whether we can arrive at true knowledge about God through nature, that is, whether *natural theology* is a fruitful endeavor. Some vigorously oppose the idea that man has any ability to know anything about God without being saved. Paul says in 1 Corinthians 2:14 that the natural man does not and cannot know God, so it seems that the Apostle does indeed preclude the possibility that we can get any knowledge of God by means of nature apart from the Holy Spirit illuminating us. However, in Romans 1, which is the classic scriptural text regarding natural theology, the Apostle says that we *do* gain knowledge of God through nature.

The atomists claim that Paul believed one thing when he wrote Romans and something different when he wrote 1 Corinthians. In other words, they say that God, speaking through Paul, changed His mind. Others say that the differences indicated by 1 Corinthians 2 and Romans 1 are a clear example of a contradiction in the Bible. However, the verb "to know," in both Greek and Hebrew, is used in more than one way. There is knowledge that we call "cognitive knowledge," which indicates an intellectual awareness of something, and then there is personal, intimate knowledge. By way of illustration, when the Bible speaks of a man "knowing" his wife, the verb "to know" is used to indicate the most intimate human relationship between a man and a woman. Likewise, Paul writes to the Corinthians about a spiritual discernment of the things of God, saying that, in our fallen condition, we do not have that spiritual discernment. There he is writing about a knowledge that goes beyond mere intellectual cognition.

In Romans 1, Paul writes, "The wrath of God is revealed from heaven against all ungodliness and unrighteousness of men, who by their unrighteousness suppress the truth" (v. 18). Paul is concerned here to show why it is necessary for us to be saved. He brings the entire world before the tribunal of God to demonstrate that everyone needs the gospel because everyone has been judged guilty—not for rejecting Jesus, of whom many have never heard, but for rejecting God the Father, who has revealed Himself plainly to every human being. It is our nature as sinners to suppress that truth in unrighteousness (other translations say "to repress," "to hinder," or "to stifle"). Paul says that God is angry about what human beings do with His revelation.

Paul continues, "For what can be known about God is plain to them, because God has shown it to them" (v. 19). The Greek word translated "plain" is *phaneros*; in Latin it is *manifestum*, from which we get the word *manifest,* meaning that which is clear. The idea is that God has not planted esoteric clues around the world so that man needs a guru to explain that God exists; rather, the revelation He gives of Himself is *manifestum*—it is clear. Paul adds, "For his invisible attributes . . . have been clearly perceived, ever since the creation of the world" (v. 20a). That might seem to be a contradictory statement— how can anyone see what is invisible? Yet there is no contradiction. We see clearly but not directly. We do not see the invisible God, but we do see the visible world, and that carries to us the revelation of God. God's unseen character is revealed through things that can be seen.

Man has no excuse for missing God's revelation: "For his invisible attributes, namely, his eternal power and divine nature, have been clearly perceived, ever since the creation of the world, in the things that have been made. So they are without excuse" (v. 20). Those who refuse to come to God attempt to excuse their refusal by claiming that God has failed to provide sufficient proof of His existence, but Paul wipes away that excuse here in Romans with a harsh reality: "For although they knew God, they did not honor him as God or give thanks to him, but they became futile in their thinking, and their foolish hearts were darkened" (v. 21). The Bible is clear that God's revelation of Himself in nature provides us with true and clear knowledge of His character.

MEDIATE AND IMMEDIATE REVELATION

We must also note the distinction between *mediate* and *immediate* general revelation. These terms *mediate* and *immediate* have to do with the function or use of something that stands between two points. God is transcendent and we are on earth. That which mediates God's revelation is nature; in other words, nature is the medium of revelation, just as a newspaper or a television broadcast is a medium of communication, which is why such methods of communication are collectively called "media." In like manner, the principal medium of general revelation is nature.

Immediate general revelation is the term used to describe another way God reveals Himself to us. In Romans 2:15, Paul says that the law of God has been written on our hearts, something John Calvin called the *sensus divinitatis*, or the sense of the divine. It is an awareness of God that He has planted in man's soul, and this awareness is manifested in our conscience and in our knowledge of God's law. We do not glean that knowledge through a medium; rather, it comes directly from God to us, which is why such revelation is called "immediate."

God's eternal power and deity are made clear to the whole world through general revelation. Our sinful suppression of that revelation does not erase the knowledge of God that He has given to us through nature and in our hearts.

———•

Chapter 4

SPECIAL REVELATION

While God reveals Himself in some ways to all people everywhere through what is called general revelation, there is another kind of revelation, special revelation, that not everyone in the world has the opportunity to receive. Special revelation discloses God's plan of redemption. It tells us of the incarnation, the cross, and the resurrection—things that cannot be learned through a study of the natural realm. It is found primarily (though not exclusively) in sacred Scripture. The Bible bears witness to how God has revealed Himself in a special way:

> Long ago, at many times and in many ways, God spoke to our fathers by the prophets, but in these last days he has spoken to us by his Son, whom he appointed the heir of all things, through whom also he created the world. He is the radiance of the glory of God and the exact imprint of his nature, and he upholds the universe by the word of his power. After making purification for sins, he sat down at the right hand of the Majesty on high. (Heb. 1:1–3)

We receive distinct information from God Himself, and that astonishing fact lies at the root of a Christian understanding of knowledge.

Epistemology, a subdivision of philosophy, is the science of knowing. It analyzes the ways in which human beings are able to acquire knowledge. Great debates rage over whether humans learn primarily through the mind—the *rational* approach to knowledge—or through the five senses of sight, sound, taste, touch, and smell—the *empirical* approach. Even within Christian circles, the debate goes on as to whether reason or the senses is primary. As Christians, however, we should all agree that Christianity is based ultimately on knowledge that comes to us from God Himself. Holding to that conviction is vitally important for our determination of truth, because knowledge that comes from God is far superior to anything we can deduce from an analysis of our situation, from introspection, or from observation of the world around us.

In Old Testament times, God spoke to people directly on occasion. There were also occasions when He revealed Himself through dreams and particular signs, as He did for Gideon. There were times when God revealed Himself through the casting of lots, through the use of the Urim and Thummim by the priests, and through theophanies. The word *theophany* comes from the Greek words *theos*, which means "God," and *phaneros*, which means "manifestation," so a theophany was simply a visible manifestation of the invisible God.

Perhaps the best-known Old Testament theophany is the burning bush that Moses encountered in the Midianite wilderness. When Moses saw a bush on fire but not consumed by the flames, he approached the bush, and God spoke audibly to Moses from the bush, saying, "I AM WHO I AM" (Ex. 3:14). The bush was a visible manifestation of the invisible God. The pillar of cloud and the pillar of fire that led the people of Israel through their wanderings in the wilderness after the exodus were also visible manifestations of the invisible God.

PROPHETS AND APOSTLES

The primary way in which God communicated with the people of Israel was through the prophets, whom we call "agents of revelation." The prophets were human beings just like us. They used human language, but because they received information from God, their words functioned as vessels or conduits of divine revelation. That is why they began their prophecies with the words, "Thus says the Lord." The words of the prophets were set down in writing and became the inscripturated Word of God. Thus, the Old Testament was produced by people like us, who, unlike us, were designated by God to be His spokesmen to His people.

Of course, not everyone in ancient Israel who claimed to be a prophet was, in fact, a prophet; indeed, Israel's biggest struggle was not with hostile nations but with false prophets in the camp or within the gates of the city. False prophets were known for teaching what people wanted to hear rather than true revelation from God. Throughout his ministry, Jeremiah was plagued by false prophets. When Jeremiah attempted to warn the people of the impending judgment of God, the false prophets opposed Jeremiah's prophecy and did everything they could to stifle his message.

There were ways to distinguish between a true prophet and a false prophet. The Israelites were to apply three tests to determine who was a true vehicle for divine revelation. The first test was a divine call, which is why the prophets were zealous to show that they had been called directly by God and commissioned for the task. In the Old Testament, we see several of the prophets, including Amos, Isaiah, Jeremiah, and Ezekiel, recount for their audience the circumstances by which they were specifically called and anointed to prophesy.

In the New Testament, the counterpart to the prophet was the Apostle. The prophets and the Apostles together form the foundation of the church (Eph. 2:20). The chief mark of an Apostle was that he had received a direct call by Christ. The term *Apostle* refers to one who is sent or commissioned with the authority of the one doing the sending. Jesus said to His Apostles, "Whoever receives you receives me, and whoever receives me receives him who sent me" (Matt. 10:40). Controversially, one of the most important Apostles in the New Testament, Paul, was not one of the original Twelve. Paul presumably did not know Jesus during Jesus' earthly ministry, and he was not an eyewitness of the resurrection as the rest of them were. Paul seemed to lack the credentials necessary to be an Apostle, which is why the New

Testament recounts, both through Paul's own testimony and through the testimony of Luke, the circumstances of Paul's call on the road to Damascus. Additionally, the other Apostles confirmed the authenticity of Paul's Apostleship.

The second test of a true prophet in the Old Testament was the presence of miracles. Not all the prophets in the Old Testament performed miracles, but their ministry was authenticated at the outset by an outburst of miracles that began with Moses and continued in the days of Elijah, and the other prophets followed in that line. Distinguishing a true miracle from a false one was a critical matter, because there were imitation miracles, such as those performed by the magicians in the court of Pharaoh. Their so-called miracles were only deceptive tricks.

The third test of a true prophet was fulfillment; in other words, did the things that the prophets announced come to pass? False prophets attempted to predict what was going to happen, but when their predictions failed to come true, their messages were proven to be false.

Through both the prophets of the Old Testament and the Apostles of the New Testament, we have been given a written record of special revelation. It has come to us by the agents of Christ, His authorized agents of revelation. Jesus left no manuscript bearing His signature; He was the author of no book. Everything we know about Him is contained in the New Testament record that has come to us through the work of His Apostles. They are His emissaries, who were given His authority to speak on His behalf.

THE INCARNATE WORD

The author of Hebrews points out another dimension of special revelation, the supreme revelation, which is the incarnate Word. We have the written Word, which gives us special revelation, but we also have the Word of God incarnate, the One about whom the written Word speaks. The One who embodies the very Word of God is Jesus Himself, as the author of Hebrews declares, saying, "Long ago, at many times and in many ways, God spoke to our fathers by the prophets, but in these last days he has spoken to us by his Son, whom he appointed the heir of all things, through whom also he created the world" (Heb. 1:1–2).

When the disciples were gathered with Jesus in the upper room, Philip said to Him, "Lord, show us the Father, and it is enough for us." Jesus responded: "Have I been with you so long, and you still do not know me, Philip? . . . Do you not believe that I am in the Father and the Father is in me?" (John 14:8–10). The chief of all Apostles, the One whom God chose as His ultimate vehicle of self-disclosure, is Christ Himself. In Christ we meet the fullness of the revelation of the Father, and it is only through Scripture that we meet Christ.

Chapter 5

———

THE INSPIRATION AND AUTHORITY
OF SCRIPTURE

The material cause of the sixteenth-century Reformation was the doctrine of justification by faith alone, but lurking behind the scenes was another important issue—authority.

When Martin Luther engaged in debate with the leaders of the Roman Catholic Church over the doctrine of justification, he was maneuvered into a position in which he had to confess publicly that his views did not agree with previous statements made by the church and with certain statements that had been issued by former popes. That provoked a crisis for Luther; questioning the authority of the church or of the pope was unacceptable in Luther's day. Luther held his ground, however, and finally, at the Diet of Worms in 1521, he said:

> Unless I am convinced by the testimony of the Scriptures or by clear reason (for I do not trust either in the pope or in councils alone, since it is well known that they have often erred and contradicted themselves), I am bound by the Scriptures I have quoted and my conscience is captive to the Word of God. I cannot and I will not recant anything, since it is neither safe nor right to go against conscience. I cannot do otherwise, here I stand, may God help me, Amen.[*]

---

[*] *Luther's Works*, vol. 32, ed. George W. Forell (Philadelphia: Fortress, 1958), 113.

Out of that conflict came the Reformation slogan *sola Scriptura*, which means "Scripture alone." Luther and the other Reformers said that only one authority ultimately has the absolute right to bind our consciences. Luther did not demean the lesser authority of the church or the importance of historic church councils such as Nicea and Chalcedon. His point was that even church councils do not have the same level of authority that the Bible has. This focused attention on the nature of and basis for biblical authority.

AUTHORSHIP AND AUTHORITY

Fundamental to the Reformers' view of the primacy and authority of Scripture was the Bible's authorship. Notice the closeness between these two words, *authority* and *authorship*. Both contain the word *author*. The Reformers said that although the Bible appeared one book at a time and was written by human beings, the ultimate author of the Bible was not Paul, Luke, Jeremiah, or Moses, but God Himself. God exercised His authority through the writings of human authors who served as His spokesmen to the world.

How was it possible for human authors to be invested with the authority of God? The prophets, as we observed in the last chapter, claimed that their messages came from God, and that is why two Latin phrases have historically been used to refer to the nature of sacred Scripture. One phrase is *verbum Dei*, which means "the Word of God," and the other is *vox Dei*, which means "the voice of God." The Reformers believed that although God did not personally write down the words that appear on the pages of the Bible, they are no less His words than if they had been delivered to us directly from heaven.

In his second letter to Timothy, Paul writes, "All Scripture is breathed out by God" (2 Tim. 3:16a). The Greek word that is translated here as "Scripture," *graphē*, simply means "writings." For the Jewish people, however, *graphē* had specific reference to the Old Testament. Additionally, the phrase "It is written" was a technical term that they understood to have specific reference to the biblical writings. This text in 2 Timothy is very significant, because the term *Scripture* here has

26

specific reference to the Old Testament and, by extension, incorporates the writings of the Apostles in the New Testament, as the Apostles were conscious of their own authority to deliver the New Testament Word of God communicated to them by the Holy Spirit. (For example, the Apostle Peter includes Paul's writings with the rest of the Scripture; see 2 Peter 3:16. Paul is conscious of His own authority to issue binding revelation; see 1 Cor. 7:10–16.) Paul makes an astonishing claim when he says that all of these writings, all of the *graphē*, are given by divine inspiration.

BREATHED OUT

The word translated "breathed out" in the English Standard Version is translated as "given by inspiration" in the King James Version and other translations. Given the long history of the doctrine of inspiration, we must make a distinction between the meaning of 2 Timothy 3:16 and the way that the term *inspiration* has been understood throughout the history of the church.

B.B. Warfield once pointed out that the real meaning of 2 Timothy 3:16 has to do not so much with the way in which God communicated His information (through human writers) as with the source of that information. Literally, Paul writes here that all Scripture is *theopneustos*, that is, "God-breathed," which has to do with what God breathes out rather than into what God breathes. The force behind Paul's words is that all of Scripture is breathed out from God. To breathe out is *expiration*, whereas to breathe in is *inspiration*, so technically we ought to translate this phrase as saying that all Scripture is given by "expiration of God" rather than by "inspiration." The point is that when Paul insists that all Scripture has been breathed out by God, he is saying that its ultimate origin is God. God is the source of these writings.

When we speak of inspiration as a concept, we are talking about the work of the Holy Spirit, who came upon people at various times and anointed them by His power, so that they were inspired to write the true Word of God. The Holy Spirit's work in this regard is nowhere defined in Scripture, but the Bible is clear that Scripture is not of human initiation. In sum, the doctrine of inspiration concerns the way in which God superintended the writing of sacred Scripture.

Some have charged orthodox Christians with teaching a mechanical view of inspiration, sometimes called "the dictation theory," which is the idea that the authors of Scripture merely took dictation from God, just as a secretary writes down word for word a letter as it is verbally dictated. The church has historically distanced herself from this simplistic view of inspiration, although there have been times when some in the church seemed to imply that this view was true. John Calvin, for example, said that, in a certain sense, the prophets and the Apostles served as *amanuenses* (secretaries) for God. Insofar as they were agents to communicate God's words, they were *amanuenses*, but that does not explain the mode of inspiration.

We do not know how God superintended the recording of sacred Scripture, but the salient point for the church today is that what we have in Scripture, though it reflects the personalities, the vocabularies, and the concerns of the human writers, was written under the supervision of God, and the authors were not writing under their own power. If they had been writing under their own power, we would expect to find many errors.

EVERY LAST WORD

Additionally, the church has historically believed that the inspiration of the Bible was verbal; in other words, inspiration extends not simply to a broad outline of the information communicated by the earthly authors but to the very words of Scripture themselves. That is one of the reasons the church has been zealous to reconstruct as carefully as possible the original manuscripts of the Bible and has given such care to studying the meanings of ancient Hebrew and Greek terms. Every word carries divine authority.

When Jesus talked with Satan in the wilderness during His temptation, they debated citations from Scripture. Jesus regularly made a case against the devil or the Pharisees by the turn of a single word. He also said that not a jot or a tittle of the law shall pass away until all is fulfilled (Matt. 5:18). He meant that there is not a superfluous word in the law of God or a word that is open to negotiation. Every word carries the weight of the binding authority of its ultimate author.

In our day, with the avalanche of criticism against the Bible, there have been attempts to get out from under the concept of inspiration. The German scholar Rudolf Bultmann (1884–1976) rejected the idea of the divine origin of Scripture wholesale. Neoorthodox theologians are concerned to restore the preaching of the Bible to the church and to give a higher view of the Bible than that which was left from nineteenth-century liberalism, but they also reject verbal inspiration and propositional revelation. Karl Barth (1886–1968), for example, said that God reveals Himself through events, not propositions. However, the Bible is not merely a narrative record of events in which we are told what happened and then left to ourselves to interpret their meaning. Rather, the Bible gives us both the record of what happened and the authoritative, Apostolic, and prophetic interpretation of the meaning of those events.

Jesus' death on the cross, for example, was both recorded for us and explained in the Gospels and Epistles. People viewed Jesus' death in different ways. For many of His followers, it caused tragic disillusionment; for Pontius Pilate and for Caiaphas, it was a matter of political expediency. The Apostle Paul, when he expounds on the meaning of the cross, frames it as a cosmic act of redemption, as an atonement offered to satisfy the justice of God, a truth not immediately apparent from simply viewing the event.

Neoorthodox theologians also say that the Bible is not revelation but a *Zeugnis*, or "witness," to revelation, which reduces the level of the Bible's authority significantly. They claim that while Scripture has some historical significance and bears witness to the truth, it is not necessarily itself the revelation. Conversely, orthodox Christianity claims that Scripture not only bears witness to the truth but *is* the truth. It is the actual embodiment of divine revelation. It does not simply point beyond itself; it gives us nothing less than the veritable Word of God.

Chapter 6

———

INFALLIBILITY AND INERRANCY

A ny discussion of the nature of sacred Scripture that includes the issue of inspiration has to tackle the issues of infallibility and inerrancy. Throughout church history, the traditional view has been that the Bible is infallible and inerrant. However, with the rise of so-called higher criticism, particularly in the nineteenth and twentieth centuries, not only has the inspiration of Scripture come under widespread attack, but the concepts of infallibility and inerrancy in particular have been sharply criticized.

Some critics say that the doctrine of inerrancy was the creation of Protestants in the seventeenth century, which is sometimes called "the age of Protestant scholasticism," corresponding to the era of secular philosophy called "the age of reason." These critics claim that inerrancy as a rational construct was foreign to the biblical writers and even to the magisterial Reformers of the sixteenth century. However, the Reformers did declare the Scriptures to be without error, as did the church fathers, including Tertullian, Irenaeus, and particularly Augustine. Even more important is the Bible's own claim to divine origin. It is significant to the church that the Bible claims to have come about through divine inspiration.

DEFINING THE TERMS

The church historically has seen that the Bible alone, of all the written literature in history, is uniquely infallible. The word *infallible* may be defined

30

as "that which cannot fail"; it means something is incapable of making a mistake. From a linguistic standpoint, the term *infallible* is higher than the term *inerrant*. By way of illustration, a student can take a test made up of twenty questions and get twenty correct answers, giving him an inerrant test. However, the student's inerrancy in this restricted arena does not make him infallible, as mistakes on subsequent tests would verify.

Much of the controversy surrounding the issue of inspiration involves a certain amount of confusion about the terms *inerrancy* and *infallibility*, specifically, the extent to which they apply. To illustrate, note the difference in the following two statements:

A. The Bible is the only infallible rule of faith and practice.

B. The Bible is infallible only when it speaks of faith and practice.

The two statements sound similar, but they are radically different. In the first statement, the term *only* sets Scripture apart as the one infallible source with authoritative capacity. In other words, Scripture is the rule of our faith, which has to do with all that we believe, and it is the rule of our practice, which has to do with all that we do.

These words change their orientation in the second statement. Here the word *only* restricts a portion of the Bible itself, saying that it is infallible only when it speaks of faith and practice. This is a view called "limited inerrancy," and this way of viewing Scripture has become popular in our day. The terms *faith* and *practice* capture the whole of the Christian life, but in this second statement, "faith and practice" are reduced to a portion of the teaching of Scripture, leaving out what the Bible says about history, science, and cultural matters. In other words, the Bible is authoritative only when it speaks of religious faith; its teachings on anything else are considered fallible.

THE AUTHORITY OF CHRIST

In the final analysis, the question of the authority of the Bible rests on the authority of Christ. During the 1970s, Ligonier Ministries sponsored a conference on the topic of the authority of Scripture.* Scholars from around the world came together to discuss the question of inerrancy, and with no collusion, every scholar there considered the issue from a christological standpoint: what was Jesus' view of Scripture? The desire of these scholars was to hold a view of the Bible that reflected the view of Scripture taught by Jesus Himself.

The only way we know of Jesus' view of the Bible is by reading the Bible, which is a fact that leads to a circular argument: Jesus taught inerrancy in the Bible, yet we know what Jesus said only by virtue of the Bible. However, there is widespread agreement even among the critics that the least-disputed portions of Scripture with regard to historical authenticity are those that contain Jesus' statements about Scripture. There is no serious dispute among theologians about Jesus' view of the Bible. Scholars and theologians of all backgrounds, liberals and conservatives alike, agree that the historical Jesus of Nazareth believed and taught the high, exalted view of Scripture that was common to first-century Judaism, namely, that the Bible is nothing less than the inspired Word of God. Jesus' view of Scripture is revealed in the Gospels: "Until heaven and earth pass away, not an iota, not a dot, will pass from the Law until all is accomplished" (Matt. 5:18); "Scripture cannot be broken" (John 10:35); and "Your word is truth" (John 17:17). Additionally, Jesus frequently rested His case on the Old Testament, saying simply, "It is written," to settle a theological dispute.

There are few, if any, scholars who challenge the view that Jesus of Nazareth taught what the church for two thousand years has been teaching. However, many of those same scholars turn around and say that Jesus was wrong in His view of Scripture. One must wonder at the arrogance of such a statement from Christian theologians. They make this claim by reasoning that Jesus was influenced by the prevailing view of Scripture held by the Jewish community of His age, which, in His human nature, He did not know was erroneous. They are quick to

---

* See *God's Inerrant Word: An International Symposium on the Trustworthiness of Scripture*, ed. John Warwick Montgomery (Calgary, Alberta: Canadian Institute for Law, Theology, and Public Policy, 1974).

point out to their detractors that there were things the human Jesus, despite His divine nature, did not know. When pressed about the day and the hour of His return, for example, Jesus told His disciples that no one knows the day or hour except for the Father (Matt. 24:36), and in so saying, Jesus expressed a limit to His own knowledge. This, the critics claim, excuses Jesus for giving us a false view of Scripture.

In response, orthodox scholars say that while Jesus' human nature did not have the attribute of omniscience, it was not necessary for Him to be omniscient in order to be our Redeemer. The divine nature did have omniscience, but the human nature did not. However, the deeper issue here is the sinlessness of Christ. It would have been sinful for One claiming to teach nothing except what He received from God to teach an error. The Scriptures have an ethic about teaching, that not many ought to become teachers because they will be judged more strictly (James 3:1). I have a moral responsibility as a teacher not to lie to my students. If my students ask me a question to which I do not know the answer, I am obliged to tell them that I do not know. If my thinking is tentative on the matter, I must let them know that I am unsure of the answer. Such caution is necessary because a teacher has power to influence the thinking of those studying at his feet.

No teacher in history has had greater influence and authority than Jesus of Nazareth. If He told people that Moses wrote of Him, that Abraham rejoiced to see His day, that the Word cannot be broken, and that the Scripture is true, but He was wrong, He is culpable for that; He was responsible to put a limit on His own certainty where that limit actually fell.

If Jesus was wrong in His teaching about a matter as crucial as the authority of the Bible, I cannot imagine anyone taking Him seriously about anything else He taught. Jesus said, "If I have told you earthly things and you do not believe, how can you believe if I tell you heavenly things?" (John 3:12), yet there is now a generation of theologians who say that although Jesus was right about heavenly things, He was wrong about earthly things.

However, since the Bible gives us enough reliable historical information to conclude that Jesus was a prophet, and since Jesus Himself tells us that the source of this information is absolutely reliable, we have moved not in a circular argument but in a progressive one. We have moved from a starting point of historical openness, to criticism, to historical reliability, to historical knowledge of the teaching of Jesus, to the teaching of Jesus, who tells us that this source is not just somewhat reliable but absolutely reliable because it is nothing less than the Word of God.

When we say that the Bible is the only rule of faith and practice, it is because we believe this rule has been delegated by the Lord, whose rule it is. Therefore, we say that Bible is inerrant and infallible. Of the two terms we have considered in this chapter, *inerrancy* and *infallibility*, *inerrancy* is the lesser term; it flows naturally from the concept of infallibility—if something cannot err, then it does not err. In order to pass the test of criticism, the Bible has only to be consistent with its own claims, and if we define *truth* the way the New Testament does, then there is no valid reason for anyone to dispute the inerrancy of the Bible. If the Word of God cannot fail, and if it cannot err, it does not fail or err.

Chapter 7

———

CANONICITY

The word *Bible* comes from the Greek word *biblos*, which means "book." However, although the Bible is bound up in one volume, it is not a single book but rather a collection of sixty-six individual books. It is a library of books. Since there are so many books that together make up the sacred Scriptures, how do we know that the right books have been included in this collection or library of books? That question falls under the issue of *canonicity*.

We get the word *canon* from another Greek word, *kanōn*, which means "measuring rod" or "norm." To call the Bible "the canon of Scripture" is to say that its sixty-six books together function as the supreme measuring rod or authority for the church. The Bible often has been described as *norma normans et sine normativa*. A form of the word *norm* appears three times in that expression. *Norma normans* means "the norm of norms," and *sine normativa* means "without norm." The Bible is the norm or the standard of all standards, and it is judged by no other standard.

EXTENT OF THE CANON

In our examination of the nature of Scripture, we have looked at the issues of inspiration, infallibility, and inerrancy. In this chapter, we are considering not the nature of Scripture but rather the scope of it; that is, how far does the canon of Scripture extend?

There are many misconceptions about the canon. Critics argue that, given the large number of books—more than two thousand, they claim—that could have been included in the Bible, it seems probable that some books should have been included but were not, while other books that were not qualified for inclusion made their way in. However, the overwhelming majority of the books considered for inclusion in the canon were quickly and easily dismissed by the early church because they were so obviously fraudulent.

In the second century, Gnostic heretics, claiming Apostolic authority, wrote their own books and disseminated them widely. However, these books were never seriously considered for inclusion in the canon, which is why it is misleading to say that there were more than two thousand potential candidates. If we consider the historical selection process undertaken by the church, a process governed by great caution and careful investigation, we see that only three of the excluded documents were given serious consideration for inclusion in the New Testament: the Didache, the Shepherd of Hermas, and the First Letter of Clement of Rome. These documents originate from the late first or early second century, and it becomes clear if one reads them that the writers were conscious that their work was subapostolic and postapostolic. They thus submitted to the authority of the Apostles and of their writings.

The excluded documents are important and useful for the church, and they have been so throughout church history, but there was never a struggle over whether to include them in the canon. Most of the controversy over the canon in the earlier centuries concerned not what was excluded but what was actually included. Debate went on for some time about whether to include Hebrews, 2 Peter, 2 and 3 John, Jude, and Revelation.

THE CANON ESTABLISHED

Others take exception to the authority of the canon because it was not established until the fourth century, long after the life and death of Christ. Establishing the canon was a process that took place over a period of time; however, that does not mean the church was without a New Testament until the end of the fourth century. From the very beginning of the church, the basic books of the New Testament, those that we read and observe today, were in use, and they functioned as a canon because of their Apostolic authority.

The issue that provoked the establishment of the canon was the appearance of a heretic named Marcion, who issued his own canon. Under the influence of Gnosticism, Marcion believed that the God portrayed in the Old Testament is not the ultimate God of the universe but rather a lesser deity called a "demiurge" who has a nasty disposition, and that Christ came to reveal the true God and to deliver us from this mean-spirited deity. As a result, Marcion expurgated everything in the New Testament that could link Christ in a positive way to Yahweh, the God of the Old Testament. The gospel of Matthew and much material from the other gospels were cut out, as was any reference that Christ made to God as His Father. Marcion also eliminated some of Paul's writings. He ended up producing a small, abridged, and edited version of the New Testament. This heresy spurred the church to give an authoritative, formal list of actual biblical books.

THE MARKS OF CANONICITY

In order to determine canonical authenticity, the church applied a threefold test. Some are troubled by the fact that there was a selection process, but the thoroughness of the process should reassure us.

The first mark or test used to verify a book's authority was its Apostolic origin, a criterion that had two dimensions. To be of Apostolic origin, a document had to have been written either by an Apostle or under the direct and immediate sanction of an Apostle. The book of Romans, for example, was not in question because everyone conceded that it had been written by the Apostle Paul and thus bore Apostolic authority. Likewise, neither the gospel of Matthew nor the gospel of John was questioned because they were written by Apostles of Jesus. The gospel of Luke was not questioned because Luke was an associate of Paul and traveled with him on his missionary journeys. Likewise, Mark was seen as the spokesman for the Apostle Peter, so the authority of Peter stood behind the gospel of Mark. From the very beginning, there was no doubt about the Apostolic authority and biblical canonicity of the four Gospels or of the basic corpus of Paul's writings.

The second mark for acceptance into the canon was reception by the primitive church. The epistle to the Ephesians is an example that fits this criterion. The assumption is that Paul intended this letter for an audience broader than just the church at Ephesus. It was written as a circular letter, one designed to be disseminated to all the churches in the region around Ephesus. Not only was that true of the Ephesian epistle but also of the other epistles of Paul. The Gospel writings were widely circulated among first-century congregations as well. As a matter of historical reconnaissance, the church, when considering what to include in the canon, took into account how a particular document had been received and quoted as authoritative from early on. In the First Letter of Clement, which was not recognized as canonical, Clement cites Paul's letter to the Corinthians, showing that 1 Corinthians had been received by the early Christian community as authoritative. In the Bible itself, the Apostle Peter makes mention of Paul's letters as being included among the category of Scripture (2 Peter 3:16).

The third mark of canonicity was the cause of most of the controversy. The books deemed to be Apostolic or sanctioned by an Apostle, and also received by the early church, made up the basic core of the New Testament and were accepted into the canon without any real controversy, but there was a second level of books about which there was some debate. One of the issues concerned the compatibility of the doctrine and teaching of these books with the core books. This is the issue that provoked some of the questions about the book of Hebrews. A portion of this epistle, Hebrews 6, has often been interpreted as indicating that those redeemed by Christ can lose their salvation, a teaching out of sync with the rest of biblical teaching on that subject. However, that chapter may be interpreted in such a way that it is not out of sync with the rest of the Scripture. What finally swung the debate over Hebrews was the argument that Paul was its author. The church in the early centuries believed that Paul was the author of Hebrews, and that landed the epistle in the canon. Ironically, there are few scholars today who believe that Paul wrote it, but there are even fewer who would deny that it belongs in the canon.

THE SCOPE OF THE CANON

A dispute arose in the sixteenth century between the Roman Catholic Church and Protestants over the scope and extent of the Old Testament Scriptures, specifically over the Apocrypha, a group of books produced during the intertestamental period. The Roman Catholic Church embraced the Apocrypha; the Reformation churches, for the most part, did not. The dispute centered on what the first-century church and Jesus Himself had accepted as canonical. All the evidence from Palestine indicates that the Jewish Palestinian canon did not include the Apocrypha, whereas many in Alexandria, the cultural center for Hellenistic Jews, did include it. However, more recent scholarship suggests that even the Alexandrian canon recognized the Apocrypha only at a secondary level, not at the full level of biblical authority. So the question remains as to who was right—the Roman Catholic Church or the Protestants? In other words, by what authority do we determine what is canonical?

According to the Protestants, each book found in the Bible is an infallible book, but the process undertaken by the church as to which books to include was not infallible. We believe that the church was providentially guided by the mercy of God in the process of determining the canon and thereby made the right decisions, so that every book that should be in the Bible is in the Bible. However, we do not believe that the church was inherently infallible, then or now. By contrast, the Roman Catholic formula says that we have the correct books because the church is infallible and anything the church decides is an infallible decision. In the Roman Catholic understanding, the formation of the canon rests on the authority of the church, whereas in the Protestant understanding, it rests upon the providence of God.

I would commend to you further study of the development of the canon. Let me emphasize in conclusion that even though there was a historical investigation, I believe that the church did exactly what God wanted it to do, and that we have no reason to be anything but fully assured that the right books were included in the canon of sacred Scripture.

Chapter 8

SCRIPTURE AND AUTHORITY

A few years ago, I encountered an old friend. We had gone to college together, and during those years he and I had met nightly for Bible study and prayer. We lost touch with each other after college, so I was delighted to see him. During our conversation, he told me that since college his view of Scripture had changed; he no longer believed in the inspiration of the Bible. Instead, he said, he had come to believe that spiritual authority lies with the church.

HISTORICAL DEBATE

In the final analysis, is the ultimate, unquestionable authority for the church found in the Apostolic words of sacred Scripture or in the body of teachers who currently serve as overseers of God's flock? That was the issue debated in the sixteenth century, at which time the Reformers determined that Scripture alone is the ultimate, authoritative revelation of God; the church does not have authority on an equal footing with Scripture. However, when the Roman Catholic Church convened at the Council of Trent in the middle of the sixteenth century to respond to the Reformation, the fourth session of that council addressed the relationship of the authority of the church and the authority of Scripture. In that session, the church professed confidence in the inspiration and authority of the Bible while also claiming that God reveals Himself through the tradition of the church.

We can find the truth of God in places besides the Bible. We can find it in sound books on theology, insofar as they *are* sound, but they are not the original source of that special revelation. However, the Roman Catholic Church holds to a "dual-source theory" in which there are two sources of special revelation, one of which is Scripture and the other of which is the tradition of the church. This theory has the effect of placing the church on an equal footing with the Bible itself in terms of authority.

The fourth session of the Council of Trent was dismissed abruptly when war broke out on the Continent, so some of the records of what actually occurred at the council are unclear. In the original draft of the fourth session, the decree read that "the truths . . . are contained partly [*partim*] in Scripture and partly [*partim*] in the unwritten traditions." But at a decisive point in the council's deliberations, two priests rose in protest against the "*partim . . . partim*" formula. They protested on the grounds that this view would destroy the uniqueness and sufficiency of Scripture. All we know from that point on is that the words "partly . . . partly" were removed from the text and replaced by the word "and" (*et*). Did this mean that the council responded to the protest and perhaps left the relationship between Scripture and tradition purposely ambiguous? Was the change stylistic, meaning that the council still maintained two distinct sources of revelation? We do not know the answer to those questions strictly from the record of the Council of Trent, but we do know the answer from subsequent decrees and decisions of the church, most recently in the papal encyclical *Humani Generis* (1950), in which Pope Pius XII put forth with no ambiguity that the church embraces two distinct sources of special revelation.

So, the Roman Catholic Church appeals to both the tradition of the church and the Bible for its doctrine, which is what makes ecumenical dialogue very difficult. When a particular doctrine falls under scrutiny, Protestants want to establish their position strictly on the authority of the Bible, whereas Rome wants to include the renderings of church councils or papal encyclicals. We see this with issues such as the immaculate conception of Mary. Although no such doctrine is found anywhere in the Scriptures, Roman Catholics establish the doctrine on the basis of tradition.

In response to those who uphold *sola Scriptura*, the Roman Catholic Church argues that since it was by the church's decision that certain books were formally included in the canon, the authority of the Bible is subject to the authority of the church and, in a very real sense, the Bible derives its abiding authority from the even greater authority of the church itself. Protestants reject that for biblical, theological, and historical reasons. The Reformers restricted binding authority to the Scriptures because they were convinced that the Scriptures are the Word of God, and that God alone can bind the conscience and has absolute authority.

The Roman Catholic Church does claim that God alone is the ultimate authority, but it argues that He has delegated that authority to the church, which is what they believe happened when Jesus said to Peter, "You are Peter, and on this rock I will build my church, and the gates of hell shall not prevail against it" (Matt. 16:18). The authority of Peter and the Apostles then passed to their successors in what is called "Apostolic succession." The Roman Catholic formulation of this belief asserts that the bishop of Rome, the pope, sits in Peter's place as his successor and so exercises the authority of Peter as Christ's representative on earth.

Whether the Bible clearly affirms Apostolic succession is open to dispute, and controversy continues as to exactly what Jesus meant at Caesarea Philippi when He said that He would build His church on the rock. We do know that there was a delegation process. Christ is the delegated Apostle *par excellence*, as was shown when He said, "I have not spoken on my own authority, but the Father who sent me has himself given me a commandment—what to say and what to speak" (John 12:49). Christ claimed to speak with nothing less than the authority of God, so when the church embraces Christ as Lord, it is recognizing that Christ has authority as the head of the church and is therefore superior to any other part of the church.

In the process of finalizing the canon of Scripture, the church used a Latin term, *recipemus*, which means "we receive." This indicates that the church was not so arrogant as to claim that it was creating the canon or that the canon received its authority from the church. Rather, the church recognized that the books of the canon have binding authority over all. If God were to appear before me today and I were to ask Him to verify His identity as God, and if He were to do so in such a way that I could not help but bow before His authority, my acquiescence to His authority would not bestow on Him any authority that He did not already have. I would merely be recognizing the authority that is already there and bowing before it. That is exactly what the church did during the early centuries when it was involved in the process of formally recognizing the canon of Scripture.

The church is always subordinate to the authority of the Bible. This does not mean that the church has no authority. State government and parents have authority, but those authorities have been delegated by God. They do not have the absolute authority that goes with God's own Word. So any authority held by the church is subordinate to the authority of Scripture.

THE CONTENT OF SCRIPTURE

We have covered this portion of our study of systematic theology rather quickly. We began with the doctrine of revelation, and over the past few chapters we have covered the concept of Scripture. Thus far, we are still focused on the abstract—the nature of Scripture, the origin of Scripture, the authority of Scripture, the relationship of biblical authority to ecclesiastical authority, the scope of the canon, and so on. Yet if we have an accurate concept of the nature of the Bible, and if we are orthodox in our confession of its authority and of the scope of the canon but have no mastery of the content of sacred Scripture, what have we gained? Scripture is given to us not merely as an abstract doctrine; it comes to us as God's divine Word, designed for edification, reproof, correction, and instruction, that we may be fully equipped as men and women of God.

The crisis in our day is not simply over the issue of whether the

Bible is infallible, inerrant, or inspired; the crisis is over the content of the Bible. We spend so much time looking at the academic issues of what we call "prolegomena"—the dating, the culture, and the language of Scripture—that pastors can make it through seminary without ever coming to grips with the content of sacred Scripture.

Do you know what is in the Bible? This volume on systematic theology is ambitious in that it covers many issues, yet far more important than studying systematic theology is that the people of God come to a knowledge of the content of Scripture. However, even if we deal with the content of Scripture and hold to sound doctrine, we are still left with the question of how to be responsible interpreters of the Bible. We are not infallible, and at some point we might distort the Scriptures. That is why we need to learn something about the basic principles of biblical interpretation.*

This chapter concludes part 1 of our study. We have covered revelation and the Bible, which prepares us for part 2, where we will begin a study of the character of God.

---

* R.C. Sproul, *Knowing Scripture*, rev. ed. (Downers Grove, Ill.: InterVarsity, 2009), provides a layman's guide to the fundamental principles of how to interpret the Bible in such a way as to avoid misunderstanding, misinterpretation, or distortion of the Word of God.

Part Two

THEOLOGY PROPER

Chapter 9

———

KNOWLEDGE OF GOD

God has plainly revealed His existence to every creature on earth; all people know that He exists, whether or not they acknowledge it. However, we need to move beyond the knowledge that God exists and come to a deeper understanding of who He is—His character and nature—because no aspect of theology defines everything else as comprehensively as our understanding of God. In fact, only as we understand the character of God can we understand every other doctrine properly.

GOD INCOMPREHENSIBLE

Historically, the first undertaking for systematic theologians is the study of the incomprehensibility of God. At first glance, such an undertaking appears contradictory; how can one study something that is incomprehensible? However, this pursuit makes sense when we grasp that theologians use the term *incomprehensible* in a narrower and more precise way than it is used in everyday speech. Theologically speaking, *incomprehensible* does not mean that we cannot know anything about God but rather that our knowledge of Him will always be limited. We can have an apprehensive, meaningful knowledge of God, but we can never, not even in heaven, have an exhaustive knowledge of Him; we cannot totally comprehend all that He is.

One reason for that was articulated by John Calvin in the phrase *finitum non capax infinitum*, which means "the finite cannot grasp the infinite." The phrase can be interpreted in two distinct ways because the word *capax* can be translated either as "contain" or as "grasp." An eight-ounce glass cannot possibly contain an infinite amount of water because it has only a finite volume; the finite cannot contain the infinite. But when Calvin's phrase is translated with the other meaning of *capax*, "grasp," it indicates that God cannot be grasped in His totality. Our minds are finite, lacking the capacity to grasp or understand all that God is. His ways are not our ways. His thoughts are not our thoughts. He surpasses our ability to comprehend Him in His fullness.

GOD REVEALED

Since the finite cannot grasp the infinite, how can we, as finite human beings, learn anything about God or have any significant or meaningful knowledge of who He is? Calvin said that God in His graciousness and mercy condescends to lisp for our benefit. In other words, He addresses us on our terms and in our own language, just as a parent might coo when talking to an infant. We call it "baby talk"; nevertheless, something meaningful and intelligible is communicated.

Anthropomorphism

We find this idea in the Bible's anthropomorphic language. *Anthropomorphic* comes from the Greek word *anthrōpos*, which means "man," "mankind," or "human," and *morphology* is the term for the study of forms and shapes. Therefore, we can easily see that *anthropomorphic* simply means "in human form." When we read in Scripture that the heavens are God's throne and the earth is His footstool (Isa. 66:1), we imagine a massive deity seated in heaven and stretching out His feet on the earth, but we do not really think that is what God actually does. Likewise, we read that God owns the cattle on a thousand hills (Ps. 50:10), but we do not interpret that to mean that He is a great cattle rancher who comes down and has a shootout with the devil every now and then. To the contrary, that image communicates to us that God is powerful and self-sufficient just like a human rancher who owns vast herds of cattle.

The Scriptures tell us that God is not a man—He is spirit (John 4:24) and therefore not physical—yet He is often described with physical attributes. There are mentions of His eyes, His head, His strong right arm, His feet, and His mouth. Scripture speaks of God having not only physical attributes but also emotional attributes. We read in places of God repenting, yet elsewhere in the Bible we are told that God does not change His mind. God is described in human terms in certain instances in the Bible because it is the only way man knows to speak about God.

We must be careful to understand what the Bible's anthropomorphic language conveys. On the one hand, the Bible affirms what these forms communicate about God; on the other hand, in a more didactic way, it warns us that God is not a man. However, this does not mean that abstract, technical, theological language is superior to anthropomorphic language, so that we are better off saying, "God is omnipotent," rather than "God owns the cattle on a thousand hills." The only way we can understand the word *omni* or *all* is by our human ability to understand what *all* means. Similarly, we do not conceive of power in the same way God conceives of power. He has an infinite understanding of power, whereas we have a finite understanding of it.

For all these reasons, God does not speak to us in His language; He speaks to us in ours, and because He speaks to us in the only language we can understand, we are able to grasp it. In other words, *all* biblical language is anthropomorphic, and *all* language about God is anthropomorphic, because the only language we have at our disposal is anthropomorphic language, and that is because we are human beings.

God Described

Because of these limits imposed by the gulf between the infinite God and finite human beings, the church has had to be careful in how it seeks to describe God.

One of the most common ways to describe God is called the *via negationis.* A *via* is a "road" or "way." The word *negationis* simply means "negation," which is a primary way we speak about God. In other words, we describe God by saying what He is not. For example, we have noted that God is infinite, which means "not finite." Similarly, human beings change over time. They undergo mutations, so they are called "mutable." God, however, does not change, so He is immutable, which means "not mutable." Both terms, *infinite* and *immutable*, describe God by what He is not.

There are two other ways that systematic theologians speak of God. One is called the *via eminentiae*, "the way of eminence," in which we take known human concepts or references to the ultimate degree, such as the terms *omnipotence* and *omniscience*. Here, the word for "power," *potentia*, and the word for "knowledge," *scientia*, are taken to the ultimate degree, *omni*, and applied to God. He is all-powerful and all-knowing, whereas we are only partially powerful and knowing.

The third way is the *via affirmationis*, or "way of affirmation," whereby we make specific statements about the character of God, such as "God is one," "God is holy," and "God is sovereign." We positively attribute certain characteristics to God and affirm that they are true of Him.

THREE FORMS OF SPEECH

In considering God's incomprehensibility, it is important to note three distinct forms of human speech that the church has delineated: univocal, equivocal, and analogical.

Univocal language refers to the use of a descriptive term that, when applied to two different things, renders the same meaning. For example, to call a dog "good" and a cat "good" is to say they both are obedient.

Equivocal speech refers to the use of a term that changes radically in its meaning when used for two different things. If you went to hear a dramatic poetry reading but were disappointed with the performance, you might say, "That was a bald narrative." You certainly would not mean that the narrator had no hair on his head; you would mean that something was lacking. There was no pizzazz or passion. Just as something is lacking on the head of a bald person—namely, hair—so there was something lacking in the dramatic reading. You are employing a metaphorical use of the word *bald*, and in so doing you are moving far away from the meaning of the word when it is applied to hair.

In between univocal speech and equivocal speech is analogical speech. An analogy is a representation based on proportion. The meaning changes in direct proportion to the difference of the things being described. A man and a dog may both be good, but their goodness is not exactly the same. When we say that God is good, we mean that His goodness is like or similar to our goodness, not identical but enough like ours that we can talk meaningfully with each other about it.

The fundamental principle is that even though we do not know God exhaustively and comprehensively, we do have meaningful ways of speaking about Him. God has addressed us in our terms, and, because He has made us in His image, there is an analogy that opens for us an avenue of communication with Him.

Chapter 10

———

ONE IN ESSENCE

When we look at the cultures of antiquity, we cannot help but notice a highly developed system of polytheism. We think, for example, of the Greeks, who had their pantheon of deities, and of the Romans, who had their corresponding gods and goddesses covering every sphere of human concern and endeavor. In the midst of that ancient Mediterranean world, one culture—the Jews—stands out for its uniquely developed commitment to monotheism.

Some critical scholars argue that the Jewish religion as reflected in the Old Testament was not really monotheistic but was a subtle blending of forms of polytheism. These critics claim that the Scriptures as we have them today were worked over by later editors who wrote a more modern view of monotheism back into the patriarchal accounts in the biblical record. Those critical theories notwithstanding, from the first page of Scripture we find an unambiguous declaration that there are no limits on the reign and authority of the Lord God. He is the God of heaven and earth, the One who creates and rules all things.

UNITY AND UNIQUENESS

Great emphasis was placed on God's uniqueness in the Old Testament community of Israel. We think, for example, of the *Shema* in the book of Deuteronomy. The *Shema* was recited in Israelite liturgy and was deeply rooted in the consciousness of the people: "Hear, O Israel: The

LORD our God, the LORD is one. You shall love the LORD your God with all your heart and with all your soul and with all your might" (Deut. 6:4–5). Those words also comprise the Great Commandment (Matt. 22:37). After declaring the *Shema*, Moses adds:

> And these words that I command you today shall be on your heart. You shall teach them diligently to your children, and shall talk of them when you sit in your house, and when you walk by the way, and when you lie down, and when you rise. You shall bind them as a sign on your hand, and they shall be as frontlets between your eyes. You shall write them on the doorposts of your house and on your gates. (Deut. 6:6–9)

This announcement of the nature of God—His unity and uniqueness—was so central to the religious life of the people that this point was to be given by way of instruction to the children on a daily basis. The people were to put it on their wrists, on their foreheads, and on their doorposts; in other words, they were to think and talk about it all the time. Israelite parents were to make sure that their children understood the uniqueness of God so that this truth would permeate the community in each generation. The polytheism in the false religions of the nations all around them was seductive, as the Old Testament reveals. The greatest threat to Israel was the corruption that came from pursuing false gods. Israel needed to remember there was no God except its God.

The uniqueness of God is also exhibited in the first of the Ten Commandments: "You shall have no other gods before me" (Ex. 20:3). The commandment does not mean that God's people can have other gods so long as Yahweh is ranked first. "Before me" means "in my presence," and the presence of Yahweh extends throughout the entire creation. So when God said, "You shall have no other gods before me," He was saying that there are no other gods because He alone reigns as deity.

THE TRINITY

The Old Testament stresses monotheism, yet we confess our faith in a triune God. The doctrine of the Trinity, one of the most mysterious doctrines of the Christian faith, has caused no small amount of controversy throughout church history. Some of the controversy stems from misunderstanding the Trinity as three distinct gods—Father, Son, and Holy Spirit. This idea is called "tritheism," which is a form of polytheism.

How can the Christian church affirm the Trinity, that God is Father, Son, and Holy Spirit? The doctrine of the Trinity is established by the New Testament itself. The New Testament speaks of God in terms of the Father, the Son, and the Holy Spirit. No text expresses this concept more clearly than the opening chapter of John's gospel, the prologue of which sets the stage for the church's confession of faith in the Trinity:

> In the beginning was the Word, and the Word was with God, and the Word was God. He was in the beginning with God. All things were made through him, and without him was not any thing made that was made. In him was life, and the life was the light of men. The light shines in the darkness, and the darkness has not overcome it. (John 1:1–5)

We translate the Greek word *logos* as "word," so the actual Greek reads: "In the beginning was the *logos*, and the *logos* was with God, and the *logos* was God." John makes a distinction between God and the *logos*. The Word and God are together yet distinct—"the Word was with God."

The word *with* may seem insignificant, but in the Greek language there are at least three terms that can be translated by the English *with*. There is *sun*, which comes across as the English prefix *syn-*. We find that prefix in *synchronize*, which means "to occur at the same time"; we synchronize our watches to gather at the same time. The Greek word *meta* is also translated as "with." In the term *metaphysics*, *meta* is used in the sense of being alongside of. A third word for "with" used by the Greeks is *pros*, which forms the basis of another Greek word, *prosōpon*, which means "face." This use of *with* connotes a face-to-face relationship, which is the most intimate way in which people can be together. It is this term John uses when he writes, "In the beginning was the Word, and the Word was *with* God." By using *pros*, John is indicating that the *logos* was in the closest possible relationship to God.

So we see that the *logos* was with God from the beginning in an intimate relationship, but the next clause seems to confuse that: "and the Word [the *logos*] was God." Here John uses a common form of the Greek verb "to be," a linking verb used here in the copulative sense. This means that what is affirmed in the predicate is found in the subject, such that they are reversible: "The Word was God and God was the Word." This a clear ascription of deity to the Word. The Word is differentiated from God, but the Word is also identified with God.

The church developed the doctrine of the Trinity not only from this New Testament text but also from many others. Of all the descriptive terms used for Jesus in the New Testament, the one that dominated the thinking of theologians during the first three hundred years of church history was *logos,* because it gives such an exalted view of the nature of Christ.

John also gives us the response of Thomas in the upper room. Thomas was skeptical about the reports he had received from the women and from his friends of the resurrection of Christ, and he said, "Unless I see in his hands the mark of the nails, and place my finger into the mark of the nails, and place my hand into his side, I will never believe" (John 20:25). When Christ appeared and showed His wounded hands to Thomas and invited Thomas to put his hand into His wounded side, Thomas cried out, "My Lord and my God!" (v. 28).

The New Testament writers, particularly the Jewish ones, were acutely conscious not only of the first commandment of the Old Testament but also of the second commandment, the warning against making graven images. The prohibition against all forms of idolatry— creature worship—is deeply rooted in the Old Testament. Because of that, the New Testament writers were aware that Christ could be worshiped only if He is divine, and the fact that Jesus accepted the worship of Thomas is significant.

When Jesus healed on the Sabbath and forgave sin, some of the scribes objected and said, "Who can forgive sins but God alone?" (Mark 2:7). Every Jew understood that the Lord of the Sabbath was God, the One who had instituted the Sabbath, so when Jesus explained that He had healed the man "that you may know that the Son of Man has authority on earth to forgive sins," He was declaring His deity (v. 10). Many reacted in anger because Jesus was claiming authority that belongs only to God.

When John writes, "He was in the beginning with God. All things were made through him, and without him was not any thing made that was made," the *logos* is identified with the Creator. John also says, "In Him was life." To say that life is in the *logos*, that the *logos* is the source of life, is clearly to attribute deity to this One called "the Word."

In a similar fashion, the New Testament attributes deity to the Holy Spirit. This is often done by ascribing to the Spirit attributes that pertain to God alone, including holiness (Matt. 12:32), eternality (Heb. 9:14), omnipotence (Rom. 15:18–19), and omniscience (John 14:26). The divinity of the Holy Spirit is also demonstrated when He is placed on the same level with the Father and Son, as in the baptismal formula in Matthew 28:18–20 or Paul's benediction in 2 Corinthians 13:14.

Chapter 11

———

THREE IN PERSON

Some time ago, a professor of philosophy shared with me his view that the doctrine of the Trinity is a contradiction and that intelligent people do not embrace contradictions. I agreed with him that intelligent people should not embrace contradictions. I was surprised, however, that he classified the doctrine of the Trinity as a contradiction, because, as a philosopher, he had been trained in the discipline of logic and therefore knew the difference between a contradiction and a paradox.

A PARADOX

The formula for the Trinity is paradoxical, but it is by no means contradictory. The law of non-contradiction states that something cannot be what it is and not be what it is at the same time and in the same relationship. For instance, I can be a father and a son at the same time, but not in the same relationship. The historic formula is that God is one in essence and three in person; He is one in one way and three in another way. To violate the law of non-contradiction, one would have to say that God is one in essence and at the same time three in essence, or that God is one in person and at the same time three in person. Therefore, when we look at the formal categories of rational thought, we see, objectively, that the formula of the Trinity is not contradictory.

The church struggled with this profoundly in the first four centuries in order to be faithful to the clear teaching of Scripture that God is one and also that the Father, the Son, and the Holy Spirit are all divine. Resolving this apparent contradiction was no mean feat. At first glance, it looks as if the Christian community was confessing faith in three gods, which would violate the principle of monotheism that was so deeply entrenched in the Old Testament.

However, as I said above, the concept of the Trinity is paradoxical but not contradictory. The word *paradox* is based on both a Greek prefix and a Greek root. The prefix *para* means "alongside of." When we refer to parachurch ministries, paramedics, or paralegals, we have in mind organizations and people who work alongside of others. In like manner, a parable was something that Jesus gave alongside of His teaching to illustrate a point. The root of the word *paradox* comes from the Greek word *dokeō*, which means "to seem," "to think," or "to appear." So the word *paradox* refers to something that, when placed alongside of something else, appears to be contradictory until closer examination reveals it is not so.

The Christian formula for the Trinity—God is one essence in three persons—may seem to be contradictory because we are accustomed to seeing one being as one person. We cannot conceive of how one being could be contained in three persons and still be only one being. To that extent, the doctrine of the Trinity in this formulation is mysterious; it boggles the mind to think of a being who is absolutely one in His essence yet three in person.

ESSENCE AND PERSON

When my wife and I were living in Holland, we learned that people vacuum their houses with a *stofzuiger*, which literally means "stuff sucker." They could have used a more sophisticated metaphysical term, but the word *stuff* explains much.

What is the stuff that distinguishes a human being from an antelope, an antelope from a grape, or a grape from God? It is the essence of the thing, its *ousios*, a Greek word that means "being" or "substance." The stuff of deity, the essence—the *ousios*—is what God is in Himself. When the church declared that God is one essence, it was saying that God is not partly in one place and partly in another. God is only one being.

Part of the problem we have with explaining how God is one in being but three in person is that this formula was derived from the Latin *persona*, from which we get our word "person." Its primary function in the Latin language was as a legal term or as a term used in the dramatic arts. It was customary for highly trained actors to play more than one role in a play, and the actors distinguished their characters by speaking through masks, the Latin word for which was *persona*. So when Tertullian first spoke of God as one being, three *personae*, he was saying that God simultaneously exists as three roles or personalities—Father, Son, and Holy Spirit. However, the idea of "person" in that formula does not correspond exactly to our English concept of personality, in which one person means one distinct being.

SUBSISTENCE AND EXISTENCE

In order to make a distinction among the persons of the Trinity, other terms have been used. One is *subsistence*. We are familiar with that term because it is often used to describe those who live beneath standard economic levels. A subsistence in the Godhead is a real difference but not an essential difference in the sense of a difference in being. Each person in the Trinity subsists or exists *under* the presence of deity. Subsistence is a difference within the scope of being, not a separate being or essence. All persons in the Godhead have all the attributes of deity.

Another important term for understanding the distinction among the persons of the Trinity is *existence*. The term *exist* in English is derived etymologically from the Latin *existere*, from *ex* ("out of") and *stere* ("to stand"). From a philosophical standpoint, going back before Plato, the concept of *existence* refers to pure being that depends on nothing for its ability to be. It is eternal. It has the power of being within itself. It is by no means creaturely. Creaturely existence is characterized not by *being* but by *becoming*, because the chief character trait of all creatures is that they change. Whatever you are today, you will be ever so slightly different tomorrow, and today you are different from what you were yesterday.

God does not exist in the way human beings do, because that would make Him a creature, giving Him a dependent and derived existence. We say, rather, that God *is*. God is being, not becoming or changing. He is eternally the same, so we say He is one being. Theologians speak of the Trinity not as three *existences* but as three *subsistences*; that is, within the one underived being of God, at a lower dimension, we must distinguish among these subsistences, which the Bible calls Father, Son, and Holy Spirit. There are not three existences or beings but rather three subsistences within that one eternal being.

That we distinguish among the three persons is necessary because the Bible makes the distinction. It is a real distinction but not an essential distinction, and by "not essential" I do not mean unimportant. I mean that although there are real differences within the Godhead, there are not within the essence of the deity Himself. One being, three persons—Father, Son, and Holy Spirit.

Chapter 12

———

INCOMMUNICABLE ATTRIBUTES

When I go to the bank to cash a check, the teller requests some form of identification. I usually open my wallet and show my Florida driver's license. One side of the license lists my eye and hair color and my age. These characteristics define some of my human attributes.

In the study of the doctrine of God, a primary concern is to develop an understanding of His attributes. We seek to look at specific characteristics of God, such as His holiness, His immutability, and His infinity, to gain a coherent understanding of who He is.

A DISTINCTION

At the outset, we must make a distinction between God's *communicable* attributes and His *incommunicable* attributes. A communicable attribute is one that can be transferred from one person to another. For example, the Centers for Disease Control and Prevention in Atlanta studies contagious diseases. Such diseases are also known as communicable diseases because they are easily transmitted from one person to another. In like manner, God's communicable attributes are those that can be transferred to His creatures.

By contrast, an incommunicable attribute is one that cannot be transferred. God's incommunicable attributes, therefore, cannot be attributes of human beings. Even God cannot communicate certain characteristics of His being to the creatures He has made. Sometimes theologians are asked whether it is possible for God to create another god, and the answer is no. If God were to create another god, the result would be a creature, which, by definition, would lack the necessary attributes that describe God, such as independence, eternality, and immutability.

As we examine the distinction between God's communicable and incommunicable attributes, it is important to note that God is a simple being; in other words, He is not made up of parts. We have distinctive body parts—toes, intestines, lungs, and so forth. God is a simple being in the sense that He is not complex. Theologically speaking, God *is* His attributes.

God's simplicity also means that His attributes define one another. We say, for example, that God is holy, just, immutable, and omnipotent, but His omnipotence is always a holy omnipotence, a just omnipotence, and an immutable omnipotence. All the character traits that we can identify in God also define His omnipotence. By the same token, God's eternality is an omnipotent eternality, and His holiness is an omnipotent holiness. He is not one part holiness, another part omnipotence, and another part immutability. He is altogether holy, altogether omnipotent, and altogether immutable.

The distinction between God's communicable and incommunicable attributes is important because it helps us come to a clear understanding of the difference between God and any creature. No creature can ever possess an incommunicable attribute of almighty God.

ASEITY

The ultimate difference between God and other beings lies in the fact that creatures are derived, conditional, and dependent. However, God is not dependent. He has the power of being in and of Himself; He does not derive it from something else. This attribute is called God's *aseity*, from the Latin *a sei*, meaning "from oneself."

Scripture tells us that in God "we live and move and have our being" (Acts 17:28), but nowhere are we told that God has His being in man. He has never needed us to survive or to be, and yet we cannot survive for an instant without the power of His being upholding our being. God created us, which means that from our first breath we are dependent upon Him for our very existence. What God creates, He also sustains and preserves, so we are as dependent upon God for our continuing existence as we were for our original existence. This is the supreme difference between God and us; God has no such dependence upon anything outside of Himself.

In an essay, John Stuart Mill rebutted the classical cosmological argument for the existence of God, which holds that every effect must have a cause, the ultimate cause being God Himself. Mill said that if everything has to have a cause, then God had to have a cause, so to carry the argument all the way through, we cannot stop with God but have to ask who caused God. Bertrand Russell was convinced by the cosmological argument until he read Mill's essay. The argument Mill put forth was an epiphany for Russell, and he used it in his book *Why I Am Not a Christian.**

Mill was wrong, however. His insight was based on a false understanding of the law of causality. This law affirms that every *effect* must have a cause, not that everything that *is* must have a cause. The only thing that requires a cause is an effect, and an effect requires a cause by definition because that is what an effect is—something caused by something else. But does God require a cause? He does not, because He has His being in and of Himself; He is eternal and self-existent.

> An inquisitive boy went for a walk in the woods with his friend and asked, "Where'd that tree come from?"
>
> His friend replied, "God made that tree."
>
> "Oh. Well, where did those flowers come from?"
>
> "God made those flowers."
>
> "Well, where did you come from?"
>
> "God made me."

---

* See Bertrand Russell, *Why I Am Not a Christian and Other Essays on Religion and Related Subjects*, 39th ed. (New York: Touchstone, 1967).

"All right, where did God come from?"
The friend said, "God made Himself."

The friend was trying to be profound, but he was profoundly wrong, because even God cannot make Himself. For God to have made Himself, He would have had to be before He was, which is impossible. God is not self-created; He is self-existent.

The aseity of God is what defines the supremacy of the Supreme Being. Human beings are fragile. If we go a few days without water or a few minutes without oxygen, we die. Likewise, human life is susceptible to all kinds of diseases that can destroy it. But God *cannot* die. God is not dependent on anything for His being. He has the very power of being in and of Himself, which is what human beings lack. We wish we had the power to keep ourselves alive forever, but we do not. We are dependent beings. God and God alone has aseity.

Reason compellingly demands a being who possesses aseity; without it, nothing could exist in this world. There never could have been a time when nothing existed, because if there ever was such a time, nothing could exist now. Those who teach that the universe came into being seventeen billion years ago think in terms of self-creation, which is nonsense, because nothing can create itself. The fact that there is something now means that there has always been being.

A blade of grass screams of the aseity of God. The aseity is not in the grass itself. Aseity is an incommunicable attribute. God cannot impart His eternality to a creature, because anything that has a beginning in time is, by definition, not eternal. We can be given eternal life going forward, but we cannot get it retroactively. We are not eternal creatures.

Eternality, as such, is an incommunicable attribute. God's immutability is linked with His aseity because God is eternally what He is and who He is. His being is incapable of mutation or change. We, as creatures, are mutable and finite. God could not create another infinite being because there can be only one infinite being.

WORTHY OF PRAISE

God's incommunicable attributes point to the way in which God is different from us and the way in which He transcends us. His incommunicable attributes reveal why we owe Him glory, honor, and praise. We stand up and give accolades to people who excel for a moment and then are heard no more, and yet the One who has the very power of being in and of Himself eternally, upon whom every one of us is absolutely dependent and to whom we owe our everlasting gratitude for every breath of air that we take, does not receive the honor and glory from His creatures that He so richly deserves. The One who is supreme deserves the obedience and the worship of those whom He has made.

—●

Chapter 13

COMMUNICABLE ATTRIBUTES

God's incommunicable attributes, those not shared by creatures, include His infinity, eternality, omnipresence, and omniscience. There are other attributes, however, that can be reflected in created beings, as the Apostle Paul makes clear: "Therefore be imitators of God, as beloved children. And walk in love, as Christ loved us and gave himself up for us, a fragrant offering and sacrifice to God" (Eph. 5:1–2).

Paul calls the believer to imitate God. We can imitate God only if there are certain things about God that we have the ability to reflect. This text in Ephesians assumes that God possesses certain attributes that are communicable; that is, attributes that we have the ability to possess and manifest.

HOLINESS

The Scriptures say that God is holy. The term *holy*, as it is used in the Bible to describe God, refers to both His nature and His character. Primarily, God's holiness refers to His greatness and His transcendence, to the fact that He is above and beyond anything in the universe. In that regard, the holiness of God is incommunicable. He alone in His being transcends all created things. Secondarily, the word *holy*, as it is applied to God, refers to His purity, His absolute moral and ethical excellence. This is what God has in mind when He commands holiness from His creatures: "Be holy, for I am holy" (Lev. 11:44; 1 Peter 1:16).

When we are grafted into Christ, we are renewed inwardly by the Holy Spirit. The third person of the Trinity is called "holy" in part because His primary task in the Trinitarian work of redemption is to apply the work of Christ to us. He is the One who regenerates us and the One who works for our sanctification. The Holy Spirit works in us and through us to bring us into conformity with the image of Christ, that we might fulfill the mandate for holiness that God has imposed upon us.

In our fallen state, we are anything but holy; nevertheless, through the ministry of the Holy Spirit, we are being made holy, and we look toward our glorification, when we will be completely sanctified, purified of all sin. In that sense, we are imitators of God. Even in our glorified state, however, we will still be creatures; we will not be divine beings.

LOVE

When Paul speaks of our responsibility to be imitators of God, he mentions that we are called to manifest love (Eph. 5:2). The Scriptures tell us that God is love (1 John 4:8, 16). The love of God is descriptive of His character; it is one of His moral attributes, and therefore it is a quality that does not belong to God alone but is communicated to His creatures. God is love, and love is of God, and all who love in the sense of the *agapē* of which the Scriptures speak are born of God. His love is an attribute that can be imitated, and we are called to do just that.

GOODNESS

The goodness of God is another moral attribute that we are called to emulate, though the Scriptures give a grim description of our ability in this regard. A rich young ruler asked Jesus, "Good Teacher, what must I do to inherit eternal life?" Jesus responded, "Why do you call me good? No one is good except God alone" (Mark 10:17–18). Jesus was not denying His deity here, but simply asserting the ultimate goodness of God. Elsewhere, the Apostle Paul, quoting the psalmist, says, "None is righteous, no, not one" (Rom. 3:10). In our fallen condition, we do not imitate or reflect this aspect of God's character. Yet believers are called to a life of good works, so with the help of the Holy Spirit, we can grow in goodness and reflect this aspect of God's nature.

JUSTICE AND RIGHTEOUSNESS

There are other communicable attributes of God that we are to imitate. One is justice. When justice is spoken of in biblical categories, it is never as an abstract concept that exists above and beyond God, and to which God Himself is bound to conform. Rather, in the Scriptures, the concept of justice is linked with the idea of righteousness, and it is based on the internal character of God. The fact that God is just means that He always acts according to righteousness.

Theologians make a distinction between the internal righteousness or justice of God and the external righteousness or justice of God. When God acts, He always does what is right. In other words, He always does that which is in conformity with justness. In the Bible, justice is distinguished from mercy and grace. I used to tell my students never to ask God for justice, because they might get it. If we were to be treated by God according to His justice, we would all perish. That is why, when we stand before God, we plead that He would treat us according to His mercy and grace.

Justice defines God's righteousness; He never punishes people more severely than the crimes they have committed deserve, and He never fails to reward those to whom a reward is due. He always operates justly; never does God do anything that is unjust.

There are two universal categories: justice and nonjustice. Everything outside the circle of justice is in the category of nonjustice, but there are different kinds of nonjustice. The mercy of God is outside the circle of justice and is a kind of nonjustice. Also in this category is injustice. Injustice is evil; an act of injustice violates the principles of righteousness. If God were to do something unfair, He would be acting unjustly. Abraham knew the impossibility of that when he said to God, "Shall not the Judge of all the earth do what is just?" (Gen. 18:25). Because God is a just judge, all His judgments are according to righteousness, so that He never acts in an unjust way; He never commits an injustice.

People get confused, however, when considering this alongside of God's mercy and grace, because grace is not justice. Grace and mercy are outside the category of justice, but they are not inside the category of injustice. There is nothing wrong with God's being merciful; there is nothing evil in His being gracious. In fact, in one sense, we have to extend this. Even though justice and mercy are not the same thing, justice is linked to righteousness, and righteousness may at times include mercy and grace. The reason we need to distinguish between them is that justice is necessary to righteousness, but mercy and grace are actions God takes freely. God is never required to be merciful or gracious. The moment we think that God owes us grace or mercy, we are no longer thinking about grace or mercy. Our minds tend to trip there so that we confuse mercy and grace with justice. Justice may be owed, but mercy and grace are always voluntary.

In terms of God's external righteousness or justice and His internal righteousness or justice, God always does what is right. His actions, His external behavior, always correspond to His internal character. Jesus put it simply when He told His disciples that a corrupt tree cannot produce good fruit; corrupt fruit comes from a corrupt tree, and good fruit comes from a good tree (Matt. 7:17–18). Just so, God always acts according to His character, and His character is righteous altogether. Therefore, everything He does is righteous. There is a distinction between His internal righteousness and His external righteousness, between who He is and what He does, though they are connected.

The same is true of us. We are not sinners because we sin; we sin because we are sinners. There is something flawed about our inner character. When the Holy Spirit changes us inwardly, that change is evidenced in an outward change of behavior. We are called to conform outwardly to the righteousness of God because we have been made as creatures in the image of God, with the capacity for righteousness. We have been made with the capacity to do what is right and to act in a just fashion. The prophet Micah wrote, "What does the Lord require of you but to do justice, and to love kindness, and to walk humbly with your God?" (Mic. 6:8). God's justice and righteousness are communicable attributes that we are called to emulate.

WISDOM

I want to make reference to one more of God's communicable attributes—wisdom. God is seen as not only wise but as all-wise, and we are told to act according to wisdom. The body of Old Testament literature that falls between the Historical Books and the Prophets is called the Wisdom Literature, and it includes Job, Psalms, Proverbs, Ecclesiastes, and Song of Solomon.

Proverbs tells us that the fear of the Lord is the beginning of wisdom (Prov. 9:10). For the Jew, the very essence of biblical wisdom was found in godly living, not in clever knowledge. In fact, the Old Testament makes a distinction between knowledge and wisdom. We are told to get knowledge, but above all we are told to get wisdom. The purpose of gaining knowledge is to become wise in the sense of knowing how to live in a way that is pleasing to God. God Himself never makes foolish decisions or behaves in a foolish manner. There is no foolishness in His character or activity. We, on the other hand, are filled with foolishness. Yet wisdom is a communicable attribute, and God Himself is the fountainhead and source of all wisdom. If we lack wisdom, we are called to pray that God, in His wisdom, would illuminate our thinking (James 1:5). He gives us His Word that we might be wise.

Chapter 14

———

THE WILL OF GOD

Several years ago, Ligonier Ministries hosted a short question-and-answer radio program called "Ask R.C.," and the question I was asked more than any other was, "How can I know the will of God for my life?" Those who are earnest in their Christian faith and want to live in obedience to Him desire to know what God wants them to do.

Whenever we find ourselves struggling over the will of God for our lives, we do well to begin with these words from Scripture: "The secret things belong to the LORD our God, but the things that are revealed belong to us and to our children forever, that we may do all the words of this law" (Deut. 29:29). The location of that verse in Scripture is important. The book of Deuteronomy is the second book of the law; its title means "second law." It contains a recapitulation of the entire law that Moses delivered from God to the people. Near the conclusion of this account of the giving of the law, we find this text that makes a distinction between the hidden will of God and the revealed will of God.

THINGS SECRET AND THINGS REVEALED

The Reformers, Martin Luther in particular, talked about the difference between the *Deus absconditus* and the *Deus revelatus*. There are limits to our knowledge of God; as we have seen, we do not have a comprehensive knowledge of Him. God has not revealed to us everything that could possibly be known about Him or about His intentions for the world; much of that is unrevealed. This hiddenness of God is called the *Deus absconditus*, that which God has concealed from us. At the same time, we are not left totally in the dark to grope after an understanding of God. It is not as if God has run away and failed to disclose anything about Himself. On the contrary, there is also what Luther referred to as the *Deus revelatus*, that part of God that He has revealed. That principle is revealed in Deuteronomy 29:29. "The secret things" refers to what we call "the hidden will" of God.

One aspect of the will of God is His decretive will, which refers to the fact that God sovereignly brings to pass whatsoever He wills. Sometimes this is called the absolute will of God, the sovereign will of God, or the efficacious will of God. When God decrees sovereignly that something should come to pass, it must indeed come to pass. Another way to speak of this is the "determinate forecounsel" of God. One example of this is the crucifixion. When God decreed that Christ should die on the cross in Jerusalem at a particular time in history, it had to come to pass at that place and time. It came to pass through the determinate counsel or will of God. It was irresistible; it *had* to happen. Likewise, when God called the world into existence, it came into existence.

There is also the preceptive will of God. Whereas the decretive will of God cannot be resisted, we not only can resist the preceptive will of God but we do resist it all the time. The preceptive will of God refers to God's law, to His commandments. The first commandment, "You shall have no other gods before me" (Ex. 20:3), for example, is part of the preceptive will of God.

When people ask me how they can know the will of God for their lives, I ask them which will they are talking about—the hidden, decretive will of God or the preceptive will of God. If they are talking about the hidden will of God, they must understand that it is hidden. Most of those who ask the question are struggling with what to do in particular situations. When I am asked about God's will in such cases, I reply that I cannot read God's mind. However, I can read God's Word, which gives me His revealed will, and learning and conforming to that will is enough of a task to last me a lifetime. I can help people with that, but not with knowing His hidden will. John Calvin said that when God "closes his holy mouth, let us also stop the way, that we may not go farther."* Translating that into modern nomenclature, we would say, "The hidden will of God is none of our business." That is why it is hidden.

It is indeed a virtue to desire to know what God wants you to do. He has a secret plan for your life that is absolutely none of your business, but He may lead you and direct your paths. So there is nothing wrong with seeking the illumination of the Holy Spirit, or the leading of God, in our lives, and that is usually what people are concerned with when they ask about God's will. However, we tend to have an ungodly desire to know the future. We want to know the end from the beginning, which is indeed none of our business. It is God's business, which is why He is so severe in His warnings in Scripture against those who try to find out the future through illicit means such as Ouija boards, fortune tellers, and tarot cards. Those things are off-limits for Christians.

LIVING GOD'S WILL

What does the Bible say about God's leading? It says that if we acknowledge God in all our ways, He will direct our paths (Prov. 3:5–6). We are encouraged by Scripture to learn the will of God for our lives, and we do so by focusing our attention not on the decretive will of God but on the preceptive will of God. If you want to know God's will for your life, the Bible tells you: "This is the will of God, your sanctification" (1 Thess. 4:3). So when people wonder whether to take a job in Cleveland or in San Francisco, or whether to marry Jane or Martha, they should study closely the preceptive will of God. They should study the law of God to learn the principles by which they are to live their lives from day to day.

The psalmist writes, "Blessed is the man who walks not in the counsel of the wicked, nor stands in the way of sinners, nor sits in the seat of scoffers; but his delight is in the law of the LORD, and on his law he meditates

---

* John Calvin, *Commentaries on the Epistle of Paul the Apostle to the Romans*, trans. and ed. John Owen (repr., Grand Rapids: Baker, 2003), 354.

day and night" (Ps. 1:1–2). The godly man's delight is in the preceptive will of God, and one so focused will be like "a tree planted by streams of water that yields its fruit in its season" (v. 3). The ungodly, however, are not like that but "are like chaff that the wind drives away" (v. 4).

If you want to know which job to take, you have to master the principles. As you do, you will discover that it is God's will that you make a sober analysis of your gifts and talents. Then you are to consider whether a particular job is in keeping with your gifts; if it is not, you should not accept it. In that case, the will of God is that you look for a different job. The will of God is also that you match your vocation—your calling—with a job opportunity, and that requires a lot more work than using a Ouija board. It means applying the law of God to all the various things in life.

When it comes to deciding whom to marry, you look at everything Scripture says with respect to God's blessing on marriage. Having done that, you might discover that there are several prospects who meet the biblical requirements. So which one do you marry? The answer to that is easy: whichever one you *want* to marry. As long as the one you choose falls within the parameters of the preceptive will of God, you have complete liberty to act according to whatever pleases you, and you do not need to lose any sleep wondering whether you are outside the hidden or decretive will of God. First, you cannot be outside the decretive will of God. Second, the only way you are going to know the hidden will of God for you today is to wait until tomorrow, and tomorrow will make it clear to you because you can look back on the past and know that whatever happened in the past is the outworking of the hidden will of God. In other words, we only know God's hidden will after the fact. We usually want to know the will of God in terms of the future, whereas the emphasis in Scripture is on the will of God for us in the present, and that has to do with His commands.

"The secret things" belong to God, not to us. "The secret things" are not our business because they are not our property; they are His. However, God has taken some of the secret plans of His mind and removed the secrecy, and such things *do* belong to us. He has taken the veil away. This is what we call revelation. A revelation is a disclosure of that which once was hidden.

The knowledge that is ours through revelation properly belongs to God, but God has given it to us. That is what Moses was saying in Deuteronomy 29:29. The secret things belong to God, but that which He has revealed belongs to us, and not only to us but to our children. God has been pleased to reveal certain things to us, and we have the unspeakable blessing of sharing those things with our children and others. The priority of passing that knowledge on to our children is one of the main emphases in Deuteronomy. God's revealed will is given in and through His preceptive will, and this revelation is given that we might be obedient.

As I said earlier, many people ask me how they can know the will of God for their lives, but rarely does anyone ask me how he can know the law of God. People do not ask because they know how to understand the law of God—they find it in the Bible. They can study the law of God in order to know it. The more difficult question is how we can *do* the law of God. Some are concerned about that, but not too many. Most people who inquire about the will of God are seeking knowledge of the future, which is closed. If you want to know the will of God in terms of what God authorizes, what God is pleased with, and what God will bless you for, again, the answer is found in His preceptive will, the law, which is clear.

One of the chief values of the Old Testament law for the New Testament Christian is that it reveals the character of God and what is pleasing to Him. We can study the Old Testament law when we are trying to find out what pleases God, and even though some of that legislation is not repeated in the New Testament, the unveiling of the character of God is there, and in it we have a lamp for our feet and a light for our path (Ps. 119:105). If we are looking for our way and groping in darkness as we seek to know the will of God for our lives, we need a lamp to show us where to go, a light to show us the pathway for our feet. It is found in the preceptive will of God. The will of God is that we obey every word that proceeds from His mouth.

Chapter 15

———

PROVIDENCE

Most Christians are familiar with Paul's words in Romans: "We know that for those who love God all things work together for good, for those who are called according to his purpose" (8:28). What jumps out is the strength of conviction the Apostle expresses here. He does not say, "I sure hope that everything will come out well in the end," or, "I believe that things will work out according to the will of God." Instead, he says, "*We know* that for those who love God all things work together for good, for those who are called according to his purpose." He writes with such an Apostolic assurance about something so basic to the Christian life that we can derive great comfort from this verse.

However, I fear that today, the strength of conviction Paul expresses is very much absent from our churches and Christian communities. There has been a striking change in our understanding of the way in which our lives relate to the sovereign government of God.

I once watched a television miniseries about the Civil War. One of the most moving segments of that series occurred when the narrator read letters sent from soldiers on both sides of that conflict. As these soldiers wrote home to their loved ones, they mentioned their concerns and their fears, yet they made frequent mention of their trust in a good and benevolent God. When people settled this country, they named a Rhode Island city "Providence." That would not happen in our culture today. The idea of divine providence has all but disappeared from our culture, which is tragic.

GOD FOR US

One way in which the secular mind-set has made inroads into the Christian community is through the worldview that assumes that everything happens according to fixed natural causes, and God, if He is actually there, is above and beyond it all. He is just a spectator in heaven looking down, perhaps cheering us on but exercising no immediate control over what happens on earth. Historically, however, Christians have had an acute sense that this is our Father's world and that the affairs of men and nations, in the final analysis, are in His hands. That is what Paul is expressing in Romans 8:28—a sure knowledge of divine providence. "And we know that for those who love God all things work together for good, for those who are called according to his purpose."

Immediately thereafter, Paul moves into a predestination sequence: "For those whom he foreknew he also predestined to be conformed to the image of his Son, in order that he might be the firstborn among many brothers. And those whom he predestined he also called, and those whom he called he also justified, and those whom he justified he also glorified" (vv. 29–30). Then Paul concludes: "What then shall we say to these things?" (v. 31a). In other words, what should be our response to the sovereignty of God and to the fact that He is working out a divine purpose in this world and in our lives? The world repudiates that truth, but Paul answers this way:

> If God is for us, who can be against us? He who did not spare his own Son but gave him up for us all, how will he not also with him graciously give us all things? Who shall bring any charge against God's elect? It is God who justifies. Who is to condemn? Christ Jesus is the one who died—more than that, who was raised—who is at the right hand of God, who indeed is interceding for us. Who shall separate us from the love of Christ? Shall tribulation, or distress, or persecution, or

famine, or nakedness, or danger, or sword? . . . No, in all these things we are more than conquerors through him who loved us. (vv. 31b–37)

One of the oldest sayings of the ancient church summarizes the essence of the relationship between God and His people: *Deus pro nobis*. It means "God for us." That is what the doctrine of providence is all about. It is God's being for His people. "What then shall we say to these things?" Paul asks. If God is for us, who can be against us, and who can separate us from the love of Christ? Is it going to be distress, peril, the sword, persecution, suffering, sickness, or human hostility? Paul is saying that no matter what we have to endure in this world as Christians, nothing has the power to sever the relationship we have to a loving and sovereign providence.

I have written a good bit on the doctrine of providence, but I cannot cover all of that in one chapter. * A brief introduction is all we have space for here. The word *providence* is made up of a prefix and a root. The root comes from the Latin *videre*, from which we get the English word *video*. Julius Caesar famously said, "*Veni, vidi, vici*"—"I came, I saw, I conquered." The *vidi* in that statement, "I saw," comes from *videre*, which means "to see." That is why we call television "video." The Latin word *provideo*, from which we get our word *providence*, means "to see beforehand, a prior seeing, a foresight." However, theologians make a distinction between the foreknowledge of God and the providence of God. Even though the word *providence* means the same thing etymologically as the word *foreknowledge*, the concept covers significantly more ground than the idea of foreknowledge. In fact, the closest thing to this Latin word in our language is the word *provision*.

Consider what the Bible says about the responsibility of the head of a family: "If anyone does not provide for his relatives, and especially for members of his household, he has denied the faith and is worse than an unbeliever" (1 Tim. 5:8). The responsibility is given to

---

* For a fuller treatment on the doctrine of providence, see R.C. Sproul, *The Invisible Hand: Do All Things Really Work for Good?* (Phillipsburg, N.J.: P&R, 2003).

the head of the household to be the one who provides and makes provision; that is, that person has to know in advance what the family is going to need in terms of the essentials of life, then meet those needs. When Jesus said, "Do not be anxious about your life, what you will eat or what you will drink, nor about your body, what you will put on" (Matt. 6:25), He was not advocating a careless approach to life. He was talking about anxiety. We are not to be frightened; we are to put our trust in the God who will meet our needs. At the same time, God entrusts a responsibility to heads of households to be provident, that is, to consider tomorrow and to make sure there is food and clothing for the family.

The first time we find the word *providence* in the Old Testament is in the narrative of Abraham's offering of Isaac upon the altar. God called Abraham to take his son Isaac, whom he loved, to a mountain and offer him as a sacrifice. Quite naturally, Abraham anguished under a great internal struggle with God's command, and as Abraham prepared to obey, Isaac asked him, "Behold, the fire and the wood, but where is the lamb for a burnt offering?" (Gen. 22:7). Abraham replied, "God will provide for himself the lamb for a burnt offering, my son" (v. 8). Abraham spoke here of *Jehovah jireh*, "God will provide." That is the first time the Bible speaks of God's providence, which has to do with God's making a provision for our needs. And of course, this passage looks forward to the ultimate provision He has made by virtue of His divine sovereignty, the supreme Lamb who was sacrificed on our behalf.

PROVIDENCE AND ASEITY

The doctrine of providence covers several areas. First, it covers the sustenance of creation. When we read the creation narrative in Genesis, that God created all things, the Hebrew word translated "create," *bara*, means more than God's simply making things and stepping out of the picture. It means that what God creates and brings into being, He then sustains and preserves. Therefore, not only are we dependent on God for our origin, but we also are dependent on God for our moment-by-moment existence.

We noted in an earlier chapter that the chief incommunicable attribute of God is His aseity, His self-existence. God alone has the power of being within Himself. Systematic theology comes into play when we consider God's aseity alongside His power of creation. The fact that God sustains what He makes reveals the relationship between the doctrine of providence and the doctrine of aseity. In Him we live and move and have our being (Acts 17:28). We are dependent upon God, who sustains and preserves us.

Our culture has been heavily influenced by the pagan view that nature operates according to fixed independent laws, as if the universe were an impersonal machine that somehow came together through chance. There is the law of gravity, the laws of thermodynamics, and other powers that keep everything operating; there is an infrastructure to the universe that makes it continue. However, the biblical view is that there could not be a universe in the first place apart from the divine act of creation, and when God created the universe, He did not step out of the picture and let it operate on its own. What we call "the laws of nature" merely reflect the normal way in which God sustains or governs the natural world. Perhaps the most wicked concept that has captured the minds of modern people is the belief that the universe operates by chance. That is the nadir of foolishness.

Elsewhere, I have written more extensively on the scientific impossibility of assigning power to chance, because *chance* is simply a word that describes mathematical possibilities.* Chance is not a thing. It has no power. It cannot do anything, and therefore it cannot influence anything, yet some have taken the word *chance*, which has no power, and diabolically used it as a replacement for the concept of God. But the truth, as the Bible makes clear, is that nothing happens by chance and that all things are under the sovereign government of God, which is exceedingly comforting to the Christian who understands it.

I worry about tomorrow, and that is a sin. I worry about my health,

---

* See R.C. Sproul, *Not a Chance: The Myth of Chance in Modern Science and Cosmology* (Grand Rapids, Mich.: Baker, 1999).

and that, too, is a sin. We are not supposed to worry, but it is natural to worry about painful things and about the loss of things we value. We do not want to lose our loved ones, our health, our safety, or our possessions, but even if we do, God is working all things for our good. Even our sicknesses and losses in this world come under the providence of God, and it is a good providence.

We find that hard to believe because we are shortsighted. We feel the pain and loss now, and we do not see the end from the beginning, as God does, yet God tells us that the sufferings we have to endure in this world are not worthy to be compared with the glory He has laid up for His people in heaven (Rom. 8:18). Knowledge of divine providence brings comfort in our suffering. God is in control not only of the universe and its operations but also of history. The Bible tells us that God raises up kingdoms and brings them down, and our individual station in life has to do, in the final analysis, with what God in His providence has ordained for us. Our lives are in His hands, our vocations are in His hands, as are our prosperity or our poverty—He governs all these things in His wisdom and goodness.

CONCURRENCE

Perhaps the most difficult aspect of providence is the doctrine of concurrence, which, in one sense, is the fact that everything that happens, *even our sin*, is the will of God. As soon as we say that, we could be guilty of making God the author of evil and blaming Him for our wickedness. God is not the author of sin, yet even my sin is worked out under the sovereign authority of God.

We see a clear example of this doctrine in the story of the patriarch Joseph in Genesis. As a young man, he was radically violated by his jealous brothers, who sold him to a caravan of traders making their way down to Egypt. Joseph was purchased at the slave market and then falsely accused of attacking his master's wife, which landed him in prison for many years. He was eventually released, however, and because of his great abilities and by the hand of God upon him, he was elevated to the level of prime minister over all of Egypt.

Then came a great famine. Back in Canaan, Joseph's brothers, the sons of Jacob, were starving, so Jacob sent his sons to Egypt to try to purchase food. The brothers encountered Joseph, but Joseph concealed his identity from them for a period. Eventually the truth came out, and the brothers realized that the prime minister of Egypt from whom they needed aid was the brother they had wronged years ago. They were terrified that Joseph would enact vengeance upon them, but Joseph did not. Instead he said:

> I am your brother, Joseph, whom you sold into Egypt. And now do not be distressed or angry with yourselves because you sold me here, for God sent me before you to preserve life. For the famine has been in the land these two years, and there are yet five years in which there will be neither plowing nor harvest. And God sent me before you to preserve for you a remnant on earth, and to keep alive for you many survivors. So it was not you who sent me here, but God. He has made me a father to Pharaoh, and lord of all his house and ruler over all the land of Egypt. (Gen. 45:4–8)

Later, after the death of Jacob, Joseph reassured his brothers again, once more stressing the divine intent behind their evil actions:

> Do not fear, for am I in the place of God? As for you, you meant evil against me, but God meant it for good, to bring it about that many people should be kept alive, as they are today. (50:19–20)

That is the great mystery of providence—a concurrence. In the mystery of divine providence, God works His will even through our intentional decisions. When Joseph said, "You meant evil against me, but God meant it for good," he meant that although his brothers had intended something evil, the good providence of God stood above that, and God was working through their wickedness for the good of the people. We see the same thing in the New Testament with Judas. Judas betrayed Jesus for evil, but God was using the sin of Judas to bring about our salvation.

That is the great comfort of the doctrine of providence, that God stands over all things and works them together for the good of His people (Rom. 8:28), and He is the ultimate source of our comfort.

Part Three

ANTHROPOLOGY
AND CREATION

Chapter 16

———

CREATIO EX NIHILO

The doctrine of creation is the central issue that separates Christianity and other religions from all forms of secularism and atheism. Proponents of secularism and atheism have aimed their guns at the Judeo-Christian doctrine of creation, because if they can undercut the concept of divine creation, the Christian worldview collapses. Primary to Judeo-Christian faith is the concept that the world did not emerge by means of a cosmic accident; it came about by the direct, supernatural work of a Creator.

IN THE BEGINNING

The first sentence of sacred Scripture sets forth the affirmation upon which everything else is established: "In the beginning, God created the heavens and the earth" (Gen. 1:1). Three fundamental points are affirmed in that first sentence of Scripture: (1) there was a beginning; (2) there is a God; and, (3) there is a creation. One would think that if the first point can be established firmly, the other two would follow by logical necessity. In other words, if there was indeed a beginning to the universe, then there must be something or someone responsible for that beginning; and if there was a beginning, there must be some kind of creation.

For the most part, although not universally, those who adopt secularism acknowledge that the universe had a beginning in time.

Advocates of the big bang theory, for example, say that fifteen to eighteen billion years ago, the universe began as a result of a gigantic explosion. However, if the universe exploded into being, what did it explode out of? Did it explode from nonbeing? That is an absurd idea. It is ironic that most secularists grant that the universe had a beginning yet reject the idea of creation and the existence of God.

Virtually all agree that there is such a thing as a universe. Some may plead the case that the universe or external reality—even our self-consciousness—is nothing but an illusion, yet only the most recalcitrant solipsist tries to argue that nothing exists. One must exist in order to make the argument that nothing exists. Given the truth that something exists and that there is a universe, philosophers and theologians historically have asked, "Why is there something rather than nothing?" That is perhaps the oldest of all philosophical questions. Those who have sought to answer it have realized that there are only three basic options to explain reality as we encounter it in our lives.

EX NIHILO NIHIL FIT

The first option is that the universe is self-existent and eternal. We have already noted that the overwhelming majority of secularists believe that the universe did have a beginning and is not eternal. The second option is that the material world is self-existent and eternal, and there are those who, in the past and even today, have made this argument. These options have one important common element: both argue that something is self-existent and eternal.

The third option is that the universe was self-created. Those who hold to this option believe that the universe came into being suddenly and dramatically by its own power, although proponents of this view do not use the language of self-creation because they understand that this concept is a logical absurdity. In order for anything to create itself, it must be its own creator, which means that it would have to exist before it was, which means it would have to be and not be at the same time and in the same relationship. That violates the most fundamental law of reason—the law of noncontradiction. Therefore, the concept of self-creation is manifestly absurd, contradictory, and irrational. To hold to such a view is bad theology and equally bad philosophy and science, because both philosophy and science rest upon the ironclad laws of reason.

One of the main aspects of the eighteenth-century Enlightenment was the assumption that "the God hypothesis" had become an unnecessary way to explain the presence of the external universe. Up until that time, the church had enjoyed respect in the philosophical realm. Throughout the Middle Ages, philosophers had not been able to gainsay the rational necessity of an eternal first cause, but by the time of the Enlightenment, science had advanced to such a degree that an alternative explanation could be used to explain the presence of the universe without an appeal to a transcendent, self-existent, eternal first cause or to God.

The theory was spontaneous generation—the idea that the world popped into existence on its own. There is no difference between this and the self-contradictory language of self-creation, however, so when spontaneous generation was reduced to absurdity in the scientific world, alternative concepts arose. An essay by a Nobel Prize–winning physicist acknowledged that while spontaneous generation is a philosophical impossibility, that is not the case with gradual spontaneous generation. He theorized that given enough time, nothingness can somehow work up the power to bring something into being.

The term usually used in place of *self-creation* is *chance creation*, and here another logical fallacy is brought into play—the fallacy of equivocation. The fallacy of equivocation happens when, sometimes very subtly, the key words in an argument change their meaning. This happened with the word *chance*. The term *chance* is useful in scientific investigations because it describes mathematical possibilities. If there are fifty thousand flies in a closed room, statistical odds can be used to show the likelihood of a certain number of flies being in any given square inch of that room at any given time. So in the effort to predict things scientifically, working out complex equations of possibility quotients is an important and legitimate vocation.

However, it is one thing to use the term *chance* to describe a mathematical possibility and quite another to shift the usage of the term to refer to something that has actual creative power. For chance to have any effect on anything in the world, it would have to be a thing that possesses power, but chance is not a thing. Chance is simply an intellectual concept that describes mathematical possibilities. Since it has no being, it has no power. Therefore, to say that the universe came into being by chance—that chance exercised some power to bring the universe into being—merely takes us back to the idea of self-creation, because chance is nothing.

If we can eliminate this concept altogether, and reason demands that we do so, then we are left with one of the first two options: that the universe is self-existent and eternal or that the material world is self-existent and eternal. Both of those options, as we mentioned, agree that if anything exists now, then something somewhere must be self-existent. If that were not the case, nothing could exist at the present time. An absolute law of science is *ex nihilo nihil fit*, which means "out of nothing, nothing comes." If all we have is nothing, that is all we will ever have, because nothing cannot produce something. If there ever was a time when there was absolutely nothing, then we could be absolutely certain that today, at this very moment, there would still be absolutely nothing. Something has to be self-existent; something must have the power of being within it for anything to exist at all.

Both of these options pose many problems. As we have noted, nearly everyone agrees that the universe has not existed eternally, so the first option is not viable. Likewise, since virtually everything we examine in the material world manifests contingency and mutation, philosophers are loath to assert that this aspect of the universe is self-existent and eternal, because that which is self-existent and eternal is not given to mutation or change. So the argument is made that somewhere in the depths of the universe lies a hidden, pulsating core or power supply that is self-existent and eternal, and everything else in the universe owes its origin to that thing. At this point, materialists argue that there is no need for a transcendent God to explain the material universe because the eternal, pulsating core of existence can be found inside the universe rather than out there in the great beyond.

EX NIHILO

That is the point at which a linguistic error is made. When the Bible speaks of God as transcendent, it is not describing God's location. It is not saying that God lives "up there" or "out there" somewhere. When we say that God is above and beyond the universe, we are saying that He is above and beyond the universe in terms of His being. He is ontologically transcendent. Anything that has the power of being within itself and is self-existent must be distinguished from anything that is derived and dependent. So if there is something self-existent at the core of the universe, it transcends everything else by its very nature. We do not care where God lives. We are concerned about His nature, His eternal being, and the dependence of everything else in the universe upon Him.

The classical Christian view of creation is that God created the world *ex nihilo*, "out of nothing," which seems to contradict the absolute law of *ex nihilo nihil fit*, "out of nothing, nothing comes." People have argued against creation *ex nihilo* on those very grounds. However, when Christian theologians say that God created the world *ex nihilo*, it is not the same as saying that once there was nothing and then, out of that nothing, something came. The Christian view is, "In the beginning, God . . ." God is not nothing. God is something. God is self-existent and eternal in His being, and He alone has the ability to create things out of nothing. God can call worlds into existence. This is the power of creativity in its absolute sense, and only God has it. He alone has the ability to create matter, not merely reshape it from some preexisting material.

An artist can take a square block of marble and form it into a beautiful statue or take a plain canvas and transform it by arranging paint pigments into a beautiful pattern, but that is not how God created the universe. God called the world into being, and His creation was absolute in the sense that He did not simply reshape things that already existed. Scripture gives us only the briefest description of how He did it. We find therein the "divine imperative" or the "divine fiat," whereby God created by the power and authority of His command. God said, "Let there be . . . ," and there was. That is the divine imperative. Nothing can resist the command of God, who brought the world and everything in it into being.

Chapter 17

—•—

ANGELS AND DEMONS

I once asked the college students I was teaching if they believed in the devil. Only a few said they did. However, when I asked them if they believed in God, almost all said they did. I was surprised by the response, so I then asked, "Would you accept a definition of God as a supernatural being who has the ability to influence people for good?" They said yes.

Then I asked, "Would you accept a definition of the devil as a super-natural being who has the ability to influence people for evil?" Despite the similar definition, only the same few responded affirmatively.

What is it about Satan that makes him so unbelievable, given the pervasive presence of evil in the universe? As I probed that question with the students, I began to see that they viewed Satan as akin to goblins, witches, and things that go bump in the night. One student said, "I don't believe in some ridiculous-looking creature with horns, cloven feet, and a tail who runs around in a red suit causing people to do bad things."

That image of Satan originated during the Middle Ages, when the church was acutely conscious of the devil's reality. People then were much concerned about finding ways to resist Satan's evil impulses. Theologians were teaching that Satan had been a good angel before he fell, and that since his particular sin had been pride, people could resist him by mocking him. As a result, people invented ludicrous portrayals of Satan in order to attack his pride so that he would depart from them. No one in those days really believed that Satan carried a pitchfork and had horns and cloven feet, but subsequent generations came to believe that the people of the Middle Ages had actually believed in such a creature.

If we are going to be biblical in our theology, and if we are confident that the Bible is not simply a sourcebook of mythology but represents the sober, revealed truth of God, then we have to take seriously what Scripture says about angels and demons.

ANGELS AND CHRIST

The New Testament word for "angel," *angelos*, occurs more often than the word *hamartia*, which is the New Testament word for "sin," and more often than the word *agapē*, the word for "love." So since the Bible devotes that much space to angels, it behooves us to take them seriously.

Concern with the nature and function of angels became a matter of great urgency in the early church because of a heresy that claimed Jesus was an angel. Some said that Jesus was a supernatural being—more than a man but less than God. The author of Hebrews challenges such an assumption:

> Long ago, at many times and in many ways, God spoke to our fathers by the prophets, but in these last days he has spoken to us by his Son, whom he appointed the heir of all things, through whom also he created the world. He is the radiance of the glory of God and the exact imprint of his nature, and he upholds the universe by the word of his power. After making purification for sins, he sat down at the right hand of the Majesty on high, having become as much superior to angels as the name he has inherited is more excellent than theirs.
>
> For to which of the angels did God ever say, "You are my Son, today I have begotten you"? Or again, "I will be to him a father, and he shall be to me a son"? And again, when he brings

the firstborn into the world, he says, "Let all God's angels worship him." (Heb. 1:1–6)

The author of Hebrews is saying that God commands even the angels to give worship to Christ. He makes another contrast:

And to which of the angels has he ever said, "Sit at my right hand until I make your enemies a footstool for your feet"? Are they not all ministering spirits sent out to serve for the sake of those who are to inherit salvation? (vv. 13–14)

THE FUNCTION OF ANGELS

Here we get a clue into the nature of angels and their vocation. They are created beings and they are ministering spirits. They do not have natural bodies, or, at least, their substance is more ethereal than human flesh. When the Bible uses "spirit," it does not necessarily mean that which is totally unphysical. The word is used for such things as smoke and wind, which have physical particles but are so lacking in density as to rightly be called "spirit." Nevertheless, angels are creatures. Angels and demons alike are created beings. They are not equal with God.

Angels' first task is to minister. Scripture shows us several ways in which the angels function as ministers. First, some angels are created specifically for the purpose of ministering in the immediate presence of God. We encounter an example of this in Isaiah's prophecy:

In the year that King Uzziah died I saw the Lord sitting upon a throne, high and lifted up; and the train of his robe filled the temple. Above him stood the seraphim. Each had six wings: with two he covered his face, and with two he covered his feet, and with two he flew. And one called to another and said: "Holy, holy, holy is the Lord of hosts; the whole earth is full of his glory!" (Isa. 6:1–3)

One of the functions of angels is to be part of the heavenly court. The heavenly host includes angels and archangels, which indicates a hierarchy, an order of authority within the angelic world. The sera-phim minister in the immediate presence of God and are thus able to behold His presence daily.

Another function of the angels' ministry is to serve as messengers. Indeed, the Greek word *angelos* means "messenger." The angel Gabriel was sent to announce the birth of John the Baptist and then to Mary to announce the birth of Jesus. Angels in the field outside of Bethlehem announced, "Glory to God in the highest, and on earth peace among those with whom he is pleased!" (Luke 2:14).

Additionally, angels ministered to Jesus after He had endured forty days of temptation by Satan in the wilderness. One of the temptations Satan brought to Jesus was to jump from the pinnacle of the temple because He had been promised that angels would uphold him (Matt. 4:6). Satan challenged Jesus concerning the angelic care that had been promised to Him, but Jesus did not respond to that temptation. Imme-diately after Jesus successfully thwarted the temptation of Satan, we are told the angels appeared and ministered to Him (v. 11).

When Jesus was arrested, He claimed that He had the authority to call upon legions of angels who could come and rescue Him (Matt. 26:53), which is reminiscent of what happened to Elisha at Dothan, when chariots of fire came to his rescue. Those angels at Dothan were invisible to the naked eye, which is why Elisha prayed concerning his servant, "Open his eyes that he may see" (2 Kings 6:17).

For the most part, angels are invisible, but they can become visi-ble, as they did from time to time during the earthly ministry of Jesus. Jesus' resurrection was heralded by the angels at the tomb, and His ascension into heaven was heralded by the presence of angels. Addi-tionally, we are told that when Christ returns, He will come with His angels in glory (Mark 8:38). So we find angels all through the Scrip-tures ministering to the saints of God, but particularly to Jesus.

Elsewhere we are told, "Do not neglect to show hospitality to strangers, for thereby some have entertained angels unawares" (Heb. 13:2). In the Old Testament, angels sometimes appeared in the form of men and were not recognized immediately as visitors from the angelic realm or as God's messengers. Angels continue, even to this day, to minister to the saints in times of great jeopardy.

SATAN AND DEMONS

We must also look at the realm of fallen angels. As Adam and Eve were originally created good and holy, so the angels were created good, but a portion of the angelic realm fell with Lucifer. Lucifer became the supreme archangel of those fallen angels.

It is critical that Christians understand that Satan is not God. We are not dualists who believe in two equal and opposite powers, one good and one evil, one light and one dark. Satan is a creature. He does not have the power of God. He cannot do things that only God can do, yet he is more powerful and crafty than human beings. He is stronger than we are, but far weaker than God Himself, which is why anyone indwelt by the Holy Spirit does not have to fear being possessed by a demon. "He who is in you is greater than he who is in the world" (1 John 4:4).

We are warned against the crafty power of Satan because we are no different from Peter, who in his arrogance assumed that he could withstand any temptation and then went on to deny Jesus. Jesus knows the reality, which is why He said to Peter, "Satan demanded to have you, that he might sift you like wheat" (Luke 22:31). Peter was no match for Satan. At the same time, the Scriptures tell us that if we resist Satan, he will flee from us (James 4:7).

Scripture uses different images for Satan. We are told that he goes about as "a roaring lion, seeking someone to devour" (1 Peter 5:8). In my mind, I see two pictures. The first is a fierce and terrifying lion, and the second is that same lion running down a path with his tail between his legs after he has been resisted by one who possesses the Holy Spirit. Again, we must not attribute too much power to Satan, as if he were God Himself. Scripture also tells us that he is the tempter, the deceiver, and the accuser. He delights to entice people to sin, even as he sought to cause Christ to fall during the wilderness temptation. Perhaps more frequent than Satan's tempting people is his accusing them of sin. His goal is to drive us to despair rather than to repentance. Satan accuses us of sin but simultaneously hides the remedy. He would have us destroy ourselves, whereas Christ calls us to forgiveness and redemption.

I close this chapter with a warning. According to the New Testament, Satan's character is metamorphic. He has the ability to appear under the auspices of the good. We must get away from thinking of him as a diabolically ridiculous figure, because Satan has the ability to appear as an angel of light (2 Cor. 11:14). He will try to deceive us by coming to us not in an ugly state but as pious and pure, perhaps even quoting Scripture while causing us to go against the Word of God.

Chapter 18

———

THE CREATION OF MAN

In Western culture, we have seen a radical shift in the understanding of the origin of human beings. There has been an advance of various theories of evolution. Everything from microevolution to macroevolution and a host of nuances in between have significantly undermined human confidence in the dignity of our beginnings. We frequently hear ourselves described as "cosmic accidents" who emerged fortuitously out of the primordial soup, as it were, into our current evolutionary stage. It has been said that human beings are grown-up germs, sitting on one cog on one wheel of a vast cosmic machine that is destined for annihilation. Jean-Paul Sartre, the existentialist philosopher, defined man as "a useless passion," and his final comment on the significance of humanity was one word: "Nausea."

We have been bombarded with these sorts of pessimistic views of the nature, the origin, and the significance of human beings. Ironically, at the same time we have seen a renaissance of naive forms of humanism that celebrate the dignity of human beings. Humanists protest worldwide on behalf of human rights. Their naive view of the dignity of human beings rests ultimately on capital borrowed from Judeo-Christianity, which sees the dignity of the human species established by God's act of creation. The sanctity of human life is not inherent or intrinsic; rather, it is derived from God's ascribing worth to it, which we see in the creation narrative in Genesis.

THE *IMAGO DEI*

The creation narrative recounts the six days in which God formed various elements of the universe. At the conclusion of period, we are told:

> Then God said, "Let us make man in our image, after our likeness. And let them have dominion over the fish of the sea and over the birds of the heavens and over the livestock and over all the earth and over every creeping thing that creeps on the earth."
>
> So God created man in his own image, in the image of God he created him; male and female he created them.
>
> And God blessed them. And God said to them, "Be fruitful and multiply and fill the earth and subdue it, and have dominion over the fish of the sea and over the birds of the heavens and over every living thing that moves on the earth." (Gen. 1:26–28)

The world we live in today puts more value on sea turtle eggs than on the human embryo. We give more dignity to whales than to humanity, which is a reversal of the order of creation. God created mankind alone in His image. In a sense, God created man and woman as His vice-regents, as His deputy rulers over all creation. That is the status God accorded to humanity. That is what the Scriptures mean when they tell us man and woman were made in the *imago Dei*, or the image of God.

What is this distinctive dimension of human beings that makes them different from all other members of the animal kingdom? Historically, there have been many attempts to locate the distinctive characteristics of the image of God. We read in Genesis 1:26, "Then God said, 'Let us make man in our image, after our likeness.'" Two distinct words are used here: *image* and *likeness*. The Roman Catholic Church has said that the Bible is describing here not one specific characteristic of humans but two, so that there is a difference between the image and the likeness. The image, Roman Catholic theologians say, refers to certain aspects that we have in common with God, such as rationality and volition, and the likeness corresponds to an original righteousness that was added to human nature at creation.

The Protestant interpretation of Genesis 1:26 differs significantly. Protestant interpreters say that the two distinct words are a *hendiadys*, which is simply a grammatical structure in which two words both refer to the same thing. We find another instance of this structure in Romans 1, where we are told that God's wrath is revealed against "all ungodliness and unrighteousness of men" (Rom. 1:18). God's wrath is directed either at two distinct things—ungodliness and unrighteousness—or at one thing described by either term. The consensus among Protestants is that both Romans 1:18 and Genesis 1:26 contain a hendiadys. In whatever sense we were created in the image of God, that is the same sense in which we were made in His likeness.

DIFFERENT YET SIMILAR

So what does it mean to be made in the image of God? Medieval theologians introduced the idea of *analogia entis*, which came under sharp attack in the twentieth century by neoorthodox theologians, Karl Barth in particular. *Analogia entis* is "the analogy of being." Even though the Scriptures make clear that there is a wide gap between the nature of God and the nature of any creature, there is some way in which we are like God. We certainly are not God; we are creatures, and He has the power of being in Himself. However, it has become popular today, even among orthodox theologians, to refer to God as "wholly other." This expression is used in an effort to call attention to the majesty and transcendence of God, and to create a barrier against confusing God with anything in the created realm. However, to take that expression in a literal way is fatal to Christianity. If God were completely, totally, and entirely different from us, there would be no point of contact between the Creator and the creature; there would be no avenue of communication. It is crucial to Christian thought that there is some similarity between God and man that makes it possible for God to speak to us. Even though He speaks to us in human terms, what He says is meaningful because we share some similarity.

Throughout history, there have been attempts to pinpoint that similarity. The most popular view has been that the image is found in our rationality, our volition, and our affections. We are said to be rational in a way similar to God; in other words, God has a mind and we have minds. For centuries, people assumed that animals act solely by instinct, not by conscious decision. However, based on animal responses in a variety of ways, it does seem as though animals make conscious decisions, so, for the most part, the idea of rationality as limited to humans and instinct as defining animals has changed. People now say that what makes humans distinctive is our advanced reasoning capacities. God has knowledge and does complex reasoning, and we have minds and a power of contemplation that is unique in the animal world.

Additionally, we have the faculty of choosing. We are volitional creatures. In order to be a moral creature, one has to have a mind and a will, as God does. We do not put mice on trial or speak of an ethically developed sense of morality in our dogs, yet we hold human beings accountable for the choices they make. Humans are moral agents. They are volitional creatures. God gave human beings the directive to be holy even as He is holy and to reflect something of His righteousness, which we could not possibly do unless we were rational, moral creatures and unless we had some sense of feeling or affection. Historically, then, the church has seen these characteristics found both in God and in human beings as comprising the essence of the image.

Barth challenged that idea on the basis that our creation as image bearers is both "male and female." The word *man* is used generically in Genesis; it incorporates both male and female, such that all human beings participate in bearing God's image. Barth argued that "male and female" is not an analogy of being but an analogy of relationship. Just as God has interpersonal relationships within Himself in the Godhead, our uniqueness is our ability to have interpersonal relationships among ourselves. It is certainly true that we are able to have interpersonal relationships, but so do animals, and if that is the only point of the analogy, we would be unable to have a relationship with God, because there would be no means to communicate with Him.

Of all the creatures in the world, human beings are given a unique responsibility, and with that responsibility is a corresponding ability. Part of the uniqueness of the human race is the mission we have received from God to be His representatives to the rest of creation, to reflect the very character of God. This becomes clear when we reason back to Genesis from the New Testament picture of Christ Himself, the second Adam, in whom we see the perfect fulfillment of what it means to be made in the image of God. The author of Hebrews tells us that Christ is "the radiance of the glory of God and the exact imprint of his nature" (Heb. 1:3). In Christ's perfect obedience, we see the fulfillment of the human mandate to reflect the holiness and the righteousness of God. I am convinced that what we find in the image is a unique ability to mirror the character of God such that the rest of the world should be able to look at humans and say, "That gives us an idea of what God is like."

Unfortunately, when the world looks at us, they do not see much of what God is like, and for that reason, "the whole creation has been groaning together in the pains of childbirth" waiting for God's redemption (Rom. 8:22). The image of God in man has been so marred by the fall that the question persists: was the image of God in man obliterated by the fall so that we are no longer the image bearers of God? Orthodox Christianity insists that even though the image of God has been blurred, it has not been destroyed. Even sinful human beings are creatures made in the image of God, a fact that leads to the necessity of distinguishing between the image of God in the narrow or formal sense and the image of God in the broader or material sense. Even though we are fallen, we can think. Our minds have been infected by sin, but we still have minds, and we still can reason. We reason fallaciously, but we have the ability. We have a will, and we have the capacity to make choices.* Likewise, we have affections. Therefore, the image of God remains in human beings.

---

* For a fuller treatment of how we reflect God in our fallen condition, see R.C. Sproul's study guide *A Shattered Image: Facing Our Human Condition* (Sanford, Fla.: Ligonier Ministries, 1992).

Chapter 19

—◦—

THE NATURE OF SIN

When God finished each stage of His work in creation, He gazed upon it and pronounced it good. Today, however, we do not see all that goodness. The world exists in a fallen condition, and we observe it as fallen people. Much is desperately wrong with our world, and many of the problems we encounter are a direct result of the fall of mankind.

ALIENATION

The cosmic upheaval that came about as a result of the sin of Adam and Eve can be summarized as *alienation* or *estrangement*. Both words are important to the biblical understanding of salvation, because salvation is articulated in Scripture in terms of *reconciliation*. Reconciliation is necessary only when there is estrangement or alienation. Many of the early chapters of the Old Testament describe the historical roots of this alienation.

We are shown, first, that there is estrangement between man and nature after the fall. Sin is not merely a human problem; it brought upheaval to the entire cosmos: "We know that the whole creation has been groaning together in the pains of childbirth until now. And not only the creation, but we ourselves, who have the firstfruits of the Spirit, groan inwardly as we wait eagerly for adoption as sons, the redemption of our bodies" (Rom. 8:22–23). God gave Adam and Eve dominion over creation, so when they fell, their corruption affected everything within the boundaries of their domain. When God placed His curse upon Adam and Eve after the fall, that curse affected even the ground; the world became resistant to the hands of fallen mankind.

Second, there is alienation between man and God. As a result of the fall, we are by nature in a state of enmity with God. We hear people say that God loves everyone unconditionally, but such thinking ignores the the reality of this estrangement. In fact, much of Scripture is devoted to revealing to us the steps God has initiated to cure this problem. The goal of salvation is to bring about the reconciliation of estranged parties. If those parties are not reconciled, they remain estranged.

Third, there is the alienation of man from man. Much violence occurs between human beings, not only on the individual level of broken relationships but also on the grand scale of nations rising against nations. When we sin, we not only disobey and dishonor God, but we also violate each other with murder, theft, adultery, slander, hatred, and envy. The whole gamut of sin describes the way in which we injure other human beings and are injured by them in return.

Finally, we see the alienation of man from himself. People today focus much on self-esteem and human dignity, so much so that schools restrict punitive measures for wrongdoing to avoid injuring the fragile egos of children. This has gone to an extreme. Behind the self-esteem movement is a realization that human beings have a problem with self-esteem. The reason for that is sin. At the fall, we became alienated not only from God and from other people, but also from ourselves. It is not uncommon to hear people declare, "I hate myself." Underlying that attitude is the fact that we cannot completely deny the wickedness that resides in all mankind.

Karl Marx considered one of the biggest problems with the human race to be alienation from labor. While Marx was wrong about many things, he was on to something here, as pain and struggle of one sort or another accompany every vocation. We can trace the roots of that back to the garden of Eden, where the curse of God came upon man's work. We know that labor itself was not a curse, because man was put to work before the fall. Additionally, God works, and He finds fulfillment and blessedness in His labor, which was the original intent for us. Yet because of the fall, sin attends the workplace.

WHAT IS SIN?

Paul wrote in Romans, "All have sinned and fall short of the glory of God" (3:23). The Greek word translated as "sin" is *hamartia*. Etymologically, this word comes from the arena of archery, specifically when an archer missed the bull's-eye of his target. However, the biblical meaning goes deeper than that, as "missing the bull's-eye" might imply that the error is only minor. The truth is that the standard of righteousness, the bull's-eye, is God's law, and we are not even close to it. Our utter failure to meet God's standard of righteousness is the very definition of sin.

The Westminster Shorter Catechism defines sin as "any want of conformity to, or transgression of, the law of God" (Q&A 14). There is want of conformity on the one hand and transgression on the other hand. The word *want* is a negative expression, while *transgression* is an active or positive term. When I attended school in the Netherlands, I noted that Dutch society was governed by a vast number of laws that defined every aspect of life. I recall a frequent expression: "You have overstepped the law." That is the very nature of a transgression. It is to cross a line or step over a boundary that is defined by the law. That is the positive sense of a transgression. By contrast, the want of conformity calls attention to a lack or a failure to do what the law requires.

In a similar manner, theologians make a distinction between sins of commission and sins of omission. We are guilty of a sin of commission when we do something we are not allowed to do, and we commit a sin of omission when we fail to do something we are responsible to do. In that respect, sin has both a negative and a positive dimension. Those dimensions can be tied into historical theological and philosophical speculation on the nature of evil itself. It has been said that the origin of evil is the Achilles' heel of Judeo-Christianity because it raises some particularly difficult questions: How can a God who is altogether righteous and good bring into being a world that is now fallen? Did God

106

cause sin? From there, many wonder whether something is wrong with God Himself, since there is obviously something wrong with the world He made.

PRIVATIO AND NEGATIO

Philosophers and theologians have used two Latin words to define the nature of evil: *privatio*, from which we get our English word *privation*, and *negatio*, from which we get the word *negation*. Through these terms, sin is defined chiefly in negative categories.

A privation is a lack of something. In our present fallen condition, we are deprived of holiness and righteousness. We are born in a corrupt condition without the original righteousness that Adam and Eve possessed.

Likewise, evil is the negation of good. The Bible speaks of evil and sin using terms such as *ungodliness* and *unrighteousness*, such that sin is defined over against the positive norm by which it is measured. We cannot understand ungodliness until we have an understanding of godliness. We cannot understand unrighteousness until we have a clear understanding of righteousness. The term *antichrist* is meaningless apart from first understanding the meaning of the term *Christ*. So there is a sense in which evil is dependent upon the prior existence of the good for its very definition. Evil is like a leech, a parasite that is dependent upon its host for its life. That is why we cannot speak about the problem of evil without first affirming the existence of the good.

We must never conclude that sin is an illusion. Sin is real. Sin is mysterious, but there is a reality to the evil in which we participate. It does not simply intrude upon us from outside. It is something with which we are deeply, intimately, and personally involved in our hearts and souls.

Chapter 20

—•—

ORIGINAL SIN

When theologians talk of the fall of the human race and the nature and origin of sin, they are immediately pushed to contemplate the extent of sin and its impact upon us as human beings. This takes us to the doctrine of original sin.

A common misunderstanding of the concept of original sin is that it refers to the first sin committed by Adam and Eve. However, original sin does not refer to the first sin but to its consequences. Original sin describes our fallen, sinful condition, out of which actual sins occur. Scripture does not tell us that we are sinners because we sin; rather, it affirms that we sin because we are sinners. We have a fallen, corrupt nature, out of which flow the actual sins we commit. Original sin, then, describes the fallen condition of the human race.

The Scriptures are clear that there is something inherently wrong with our character, and everyday experience bears that out. Jonathan Edwards remarked in his treatise on original sin that even if the Bible did not state that there is a problem with our moral disposition, we would have to affirm it on the basis of rational observation. We cannot avoid the pervasive presence of evil in the world. The universality of sin screams for an explanation. Even among pagans, there is a tacit acknowledgment that no one is perfect.

If we were by nature good or even morally neutral, we would expect a certain percentage of people to maintain their natural goodness or their neutrality and to live without succumbing to sin. Some say we could indeed maintain goodness or neutrality were it not for the sinful climate in which we live, but the fact that society is made up of human beings negates that argument. We are fallen, and therefore society is fallen. We have met the enemy, and it is us. The Scriptures teach us that original sin is itself a judgment of a righteous God upon creatures that He created to be good. As a penalty upon Adam and Eve for their sin, God gave them over, along with all their progeny, to their wicked inclinations.

MORAL INABILITY

When Augustine analyzed the sinfulness of human beings, he noted that when Adam and Eve were first created, God made them *posse peccare*, which simply means they had the ability to sin. *Peccare* means "to sin." Something pure is called "impeccable" and an insignificant sin is sometimes referred to as a "peccadillo." Both of these words come from the Latin *peccare*. Augustine said that Adam and Eve were not created as sinners, but they had the power to sin. We know that was true because they *did* sin. They did not do the impossible; they did what they obviously had the power to do. However, Augustine said, Adam and Eve also were created *posse non peccare*, which means they had the ability *not* to sin. God gave them the command not to eat the fruit from the forbidden tree, and they had the moral ability to obey God. So they had both the ability to sin and the ability not to sin.

Augustine explained that at the fall, the human race lost *posse non peccare*, and our position became *non posse non peccare*, which means we no longer have the ability not to sin. In other words, the power of sin is so deeply rooted in the hearts and souls of mortal people that it is impossible for us not to sin. We are so sinful by nature that we will never encounter someone who does not sin. The only person who ever accomplished a sinless life was Jesus Christ. Our inability not to sin is called the "moral inability of human beings."

This does not mean that we cannot do anything that conforms outwardly to the law of God. We can accidentally keep the law. By way of illustration, picture a man who enjoys driving his car at fifty-five miles per hour. His car performs well at that speed, and he feels safe and comfortable, even though others on the highway speed past him going sixty-five or seventy miles per hour. One day a policeman pulls him over and gives him a commendation for being a safe driver. The man gets an award for his obedience. The trooper goes on his way and the man gets back on the highway. Eventually he drives into a school zone where the speed limit is fifteen miles per hour, but he keeps driving fifty-five miles per hour because that is the speed at which he likes to drive. His desire has never been to obey the law. The fact that he did so on the highway was merely a fortuitous circumstance. That is what theologians call "civic virtue."

Sometimes we obey the law of God because it serves our personal best interests. We might not steal because we have found that crime does not pay. We might do noble gestures for the applause of men, because we are running for office, or for some other motivation, but fallen man lacks the motivation to obey the law out of a pristine love for God. Jesus said, "You shall love the Lord your God with all your heart and with all your soul and with all your mind. This is the great and first commandment. And a second is like it: You shall love your neighbor as yourself" (Matt. 22:37–39). Martin Luther said that the great transgression is a violation of the great commandment, but we do not think in those terms. No one loves God perfectly, with all his heart, soul, and mind.

This is also why we make theological mistakes. We attribute our misinterpretations to the Bible itself, claiming that it is too difficult to understand or that it is ambiguous. Yet God is not the author of confusion. God actually has revealed Himself clearly, but we come to the text with biases that interfere with the light of God's Word. There are many things taught in Scripture that we simply do not want to hear, so we find ways to distort the Bible in order to escape the judgment it brings to our consciences.

Sometimes, in attempting to interpret Scripture, we make a so-called innocent mistake. This can happen when we use a defective translation or when we have not sufficiently mastered the structure of Greek or Hebrew grammar. Yet if we loved God with all our heart, soul, and mind, would not our mastery of His Word be different? We spend so much time filling our minds with things other than a knowledge of His Word. We are lazy; we are not diligent in our pursuit of His truth. Such things contribute to the distortions we create.

GOD'S STANDARD

Jesus said, "No one is good except God alone" (Mark 10:18), and Paul said, "None is righteous, no, not one" (Rom. 3:10). These statements seem extreme because we see people doing good things. As I noted above, theologians call such good deeds civic virtue. Mothers sacrifice for their children and people return the wallets of strangers without keeping the money they find inside. But for an act to be truly good, to really hit the mark of God's standard, it must correspond outwardly to what the law requires and it also must be motivated by love for God. Even redeemed people offer less-than-perfect obedience to God, a condition greatly aggravated in those estranged or alienated from Him.

When theologians speak about moral inability or original sin, they have in mind this state of *non posse non peccare*. We are not morally able to do the good that God requires. When Jesus described the condition of man, He said, "No one can come to me unless it is granted him by the Father" (John 6:65). Jesus started with a universal negative that describes human ability. He was not saying that no one is *allowed* to come to Him; He was saying that no one *can*, or is able to, come to Him unless God does something. Just before this, Jesus said, "It is the Spirit who gives life; the flesh is no help at all" (v. 63). In the New Testament, *flesh* generally refers to our fallen condition, our bondage to sin. Another phrase the Bible uses is "under sin." We are not on top of sin, but sin is on top of us. The Bible tells us that the desires of our hearts are only evil continually (Gen. 6:5).

So, to embrace Christ, to come to God and to do the things of God, requires that we somehow be liberated from the prison of original sin. This is accomplished for us by the sovereign, supernatural work of the Holy Spirit. That is why Jesus said that for a person to see, let alone enter, the kingdom of God, he must be born again (John 3:3). That which is born of the flesh is flesh, and in our flesh we can do nothing. Because of our fallenness, we are in a morally impotent position.

This conception of humans' moral inability is called the Augustinian view, and not everyone throughout Christian history has agreed with it. Many in the church today claim that although we are fallen, we have a modicum of righteousness left in our souls by which we can take the first step toward our reconciliation with God by reaching out to Him. Conversely, the Augustinian view says that we are so corrupt as to be dead—not just sick but *dead*. We are in such bondage to sin that we can do nothing apart from God's rescuing grace, which initiates the process of our redemption.

The Augustinian tradition, within which I stand, says that the fall extends to the whole person—mind, heart, and body. Our bodies fail us, our eyesight becomes dim, our hair becomes gray, and our strength dissipates. We become ill, and eventually we die. The Bible says all of this is a result of the influence of sin upon our bodies, but the power of sin also affects our hearts, our wills, and our minds. We can think, but our thinking is distorted; we make logical errors and allow bias to cloud our judgment. We have wills; we have not lost the ability to make choices, for we are still creatures made in the image of God. In the fall, we lost the image of God in the narrow sense. We lost the ability to be perfectly righteous. Yet we are still in the image of God in the wider sense; in other words, we are still human. As corrupt as we may be, our humanity has not been erased by the fall.

However, the power of our humanity was radically affected by the fall, and that is what leaves us in the state of which Paul speaks in Romans: "None is righteous, no, not one; no one understands; no one seeks for God. All have turned aside; together they have become worthless; no one does good, not even one" (Rom. 3:10–12).

When churches reach out to "seekers," I do not know whom they have in mind, because the Bible says that no one in his natural state seeks after God. If I said that publicly in the secular arena today, I would be laughed to scorn, but that is the assessment of God as He judges us according to His standard of goodness and righteousness.

——•——

Chapter 21

TRANSMISSION OF SIN

If sin is basic to our nature, such that we can do nothing but sin, how can God judge us for sinning? That is a legitimate question and an obvious one in light of the doctrine of original sin, so we need to consider how our sin nature was transferred from Adam to his posterity. The Bible makes abundantly clear that there is a connection:

> Just as sin came into the world through one man, and death through sin, and so death spread to all men because all sinned—for sin indeed was in the world before the law was given, but sin is not counted where there is no law. Yet death reigned from Adam to Moses, even over those whose sinning was not like the transgression of Adam, who was a type of the one who was to come.
>
> But the free gift is not like the trespass. For if many died through one man's trespass, much more have the grace of God and the free gift by the grace of that one man Jesus Christ abounded for many. And the free gift is not like the result of that one man's sin. For the judgment following one trespass brought condemnation, but the free gift following many trespasses brought justification. For if, because of one man's

trespass, death reigned through that one man, much more will those who receive the abundance of grace and the free gift of righteousness reign in life through the one man Jesus Christ.

Therefore, as one trespass led to condemnation for all men, so one act of righteousness leads to justification and life for all men. (Rom. 5:12–18)

The Apostle Paul here is establishing a contrast between the second Adam, Christ, and the first Adam, but he also is showing that they had a kind of parallel relationship. Through one man's righteousness—Christ's—we are redeemed, just as through another man's unrighteousness—Adam's—we were plunged into ruin and death. We do not complain about the vicarious transfer of righteousness from Christ to us; it is the transfer of unrighteousness from Adam to us that gives us so many problems. There are different theories about how this transfer takes place.

A MYTH?

Among liberal theologians, the popular view is that the story of Adam and Eve is a myth. There was no historical Adam and no historical fall, they say. Rather, Genesis 3 is merely a parable that points to the fact that every human being is born good and righteous, but then experiences temptation and a personal, individual fall. In other words, every individual duplicates in his or her life what the Scriptures say in parabolic form that Adam and Eve did.

There are several problems with this view, of course. First, it flatly denies what the Scriptures teach. Additionally, Paul is arguing in Romans 5 that the law has been in the world from the beginning, before Moses, the proof of which is the fact that sin was in the world. Sin reigned from Adam up until Moses. Paul makes the point that apart from law, there can be no sin, and if there is no sin, there can be no just punishment for sin. Death reigned, Paul says, from Adam to Moses. People died before Mount Sinai, including infants. If it is true, as the liberals suggest, that Adam and Eve were not real people but simply characters in a myth, then they have to explain infant mortality. Why would babies die? The explanation they give is that there really is no link between sin and death. However, this argument collides head-on with the teaching of Scripture.

REALISM

Among those who take biblical revelation seriously and hold to a historical fall, there is still serious debate as to how the transmission of original sin takes place. The two most common viewpoints regarding the transfer of guilt from Adam to other human beings are found in the school of realism and the school of federalism.

The school of realism has a less sophisticated version and a more sophisticated, philosophical version. The realists argue that God can justly punish sinners born with a sin nature only if the sin nature itself is a just punishment for something we did. In other words, Adam sinned and God gave him over to a sinful nature as part of the punishment for his actual sin. God's giving people over to what they want to do is a just punishment. Yet it is one thing to give *Adam* over to his sin nature as a result of his sin and quite another thing to give *Adam's children* over to a sin nature because of what Adam did.

We read in Ezekiel, "The fathers have eaten sour grapes, and the children's teeth are set on edge" (Ezek. 18:2), and one of Ezekiel's messages is that God will not punish one person for a sin that someone else commits. So if that principle is true, how does it apply to our inherited fallen nature? The realists say that God would be just to visit us with a fallen nature only if we had actually fallen there in the garden with Adam. The realist position in one sense teaches that we *were* there, which is partly why the movement is called "realism." However, for that to be true, our souls—which were united with our bodies (presumably at conception in our mothers' wombs)—must have been present in the garden, so that we participated in the fall of Adam and Eve.

The biblical argument used to support this claim is drawn from Abraham's encounter with Melchizedek, which is recorded in the Old Testament (Gen. 14; Ps. 110) and recounted in Hebrews (ch. 7). The

New Testament heralds Jesus not only as our Savior but also as our King and our Priest. For Jesus to be King, He had to come from the tribe of Judah, because the Davidic kingdom is promised to the descendants of that tribe. The New Testament, which establishes the lineage of Jesus, shows that Jesus did indeed come from the tribe of Judah, so He is qualified to be the king of Israel. However, since He was from the tribe of Judah, He could not also have been from the tribe of Levi. The Levitical or Aaronic priesthood (named for Aaron, the first high priest) was restricted in the old covenant to members of the tribe of Levi. So when the New Testament declares that Jesus is our Great High Priest, its writers are faced with the problem of His biological bloodline.

The author of Hebrews answers by means of several citations from the Old Testament, particularly from the messianic psalms, in which God declared that He was going to raise up a king and a priest forever. Hebrews argues that there is another priesthood mentioned in the Old Testament besides the Levitical priesthood, and it is found in the cryptic reference to the ministry of the mysterious figure Melchizedek, whose name means "king of righteousness" (Heb. 7:2). The author of Hebrews also says Melchizedek had no mother or father (v. 3). The statement of his lack of parentage could simply mean that there was no genealogical record of his background, or, as some commentators believe, it could mean he was not of normal human descent but was perhaps a preincarnational appearance of Christ. This is a very popular theory.

In the encounter between Melchizedek and Abraham, two things happened. Abraham paid a tithe to Melchizedek, and Melchizedek gave a blessing to Abraham. In Jewish fashion, the author of Hebrews says that the greater grants the blessing to the lesser (v. 7). Since Abraham paid a tithe to Melchizedek, and Melchizedek blessed Abraham, it is clear that Melchizedek was superior to Abraham. By extension, Abraham's position in the Hebrew lineage made him greater than his son Isaac, and Isaac was greater than his son Jacob, and Jacob was greater than his sons, which included Levi. So if Abraham was greater than Levi, and if Melchizedek was greater than Abraham, then obviously

Melchizedek was greater than Levi. Therefore, if Jesus is a priest after the order of Melchizedek, His priesthood is not inferior to the Levitical priesthood but superior to it. That is how the author of Hebrews argues:

> But this man who does not have his descent from them received tithes from Abraham and blessed him who had the promises. It is beyond dispute that the inferior is blessed by the superior. In the one case tithes are received by mortal men, but in the other case, by one of whom it is testified that he lives. One might even say that Levi himself, who receives tithes, paid tithes through Abraham, for he was still in the loins of his ancestor when Melchizedek met him. (Heb. 7:6–10)

One school of realists says that this text can only be understood as teaching that Levi was really there when Abraham paid the tithe, and that proves the preexistence of the human soul. That is a huge stretch. Even the text offers a qualification—"One might even say." We can say from a genetic standpoint that our great-grandchildren are already present in our bodies, but we do not mean that those actual children are present in us.

The more sophisticated version of realism does not depend upon a literal pre-existence. It is a philosophical kind of realism, such as we find in Plato, Augustine, and Jonathan Edwards. It holds that in God's mind we do pre-exist our birth because God from all eternity has had a perfect idea of each one of us. He has known us from eternity past, and God's ideas of people are real ideas that incorporate the full reality of who we are. That teaching carries within it several philosophical assumptions, but it is an option that many have embraced throughout church history, and one I find fascinating.

FEDERALISM

Another view is federalism, which emphasizes the representative character of Adam. In the garden, Adam operated as a substitute for us, as the federal head of the human race, just as officials in a federal republic represent the people. In the same way, Jesus entered into corporate solidarity with God's people. He represented us. In His work on the cross, He is our vicarious substitute, who stood in our place, and God counts us righteous because He transferred our guilt to Christ and Christ's righteousness to us.

According to this view, our salvation rests upon the validity of some kind of representation. If we object in principle to representation before God, we lose our salvation, because the only way we can be saved is through the representative work of another.

Adam, whose name means "mankind," was acting as the federal head of the human race, representing himself and all people subsequently born, so when he fell, all whom he represented fell with him. We can be held accountable for what he did because he represented us. This claim usually prompts people to complain that they did not choose Adam as their representative.

At the time of the American Revolution, the Colonists demanded representatives in the English Parliament. They cried, "No taxation without representation!" They demanded the right to choose their own representatives, a sacred right in the United States to this day. We want the right to ensure we are accurately represented. We do not want to trust someone to appoint our representatives for us.

Yet in the case of Adam, God selected our representative, and that was the only time, apart from the cross, in all of human history when we were perfectly represented. This is because God's choice of a representative was a righteous choice by a perfectly holy being, and it was made on the basis of His perfect knowledge. He knew us in advance, and He knew our representative. Therefore, we cannot say to God that Adam misrepresented us, which is the basic assumption we make when we try to escape the transfer of guilt. We think we would have acted differently than Adam if we had been in the garden. However, Adam represented us flawlessly because he was God's chosen representative.

We can be held accountable for deeds done by someone else if the other committed those deeds on our behalf. If I hire a man to kill someone, and I make sure he does the murder while I am out of town,

I can be held accountable for first-degree murder even though I did not pull the trigger. That analogy breaks down, however, because we did not select Adam. The point is that Adam was chosen perfectly by an omniscient, righteous God, and Adam did our work for us, according to God's judgment. That is why the sin of one man brought about our ruin, and our only hope to escape from it is the righteousness of another representative.

Chapter 22

———

THE COVENANTS

A major theme in the book of Hebrews is the superiority of Christ, particularly in His role as our Great High Priest. When the author speaks of the greatness of Jesus in this regard, he makes a contrast between the covenant that God made with His people through Moses and the new covenant that was mediated through His Son, Jesus Christ:

> For every high priest is appointed to offer gifts and sacrifices; thus it is necessary for this priest also to have something to offer. Now if he were on earth, he would not be a priest at all, since there are priests who offer gifts according to the law. They serve a copy and shadow of the heavenly things. For when Moses was about to erect the tent, he was instructed by God, saying, "See that you make everything according to the pattern that was shown you on the mountain." But as it is, Christ has obtained a ministry that is as much more excellent than the old as the covenant he mediates is better, since it is enacted on better promises. (Heb. 8:3–6)

The author goes on to explain how the new covenant is better than the old covenant and makes the old covenant obsolete. In Hebrews, the new covenant is shown to be better not only because we have a better mediator than Moses but also because we have a better promise. That is significant because it opens up some knowledge about the very nature of covenants.

The basic structure or framework for the unfolding of the plan of redemption in Scripture is expressed through covenant. Basically, a covenant is an agreement between two or more parties based principally on a promise. There are several covenants in biblical history. There is the covenant that God made with Adam and Eve—the Adamic covenant. There is the covenant that God made with Noah—the Noahic covenant; God set His rainbow in the sky as the sign of that covenant. Later, God entered a covenant with Abraham—the Abrahamic covenant—which was renewed with his descendants Isaac and Jacob. When we think of the old covenant, we have in mind the covenant God made with Israel through Moses at Mouth Sinai—the Mosaic covenant or the Sinaitic covenant.

We make covenant promises in virtually every arena of life. When we enter into an employment relationship, both the employer and the employee make certain promises. Additionally, the structure of marriage is based on the concept of covenant. In marriage, promises are made by two people, and they are sealed with sacred vows in the presence of God. Even our national government is based on the concept of a covenant, or an agreement, between those who govern and those who are governed. There are promises involved in every covenant. In the ancient world, covenants had stipulations or laws in addition to promises; that is, promises were made on the condition of certain stipulations being fulfilled.

The concept of covenant is vitally important to our understanding of biblical Christianity. In the final analysis, our Christian lives rest on trust or faith in a promise—the promise of God to redeem us through the person and work of Jesus. In a very real sense, in terms of covenant, God has given us His Word. John introduces Christ in his gospel as the incarnation of the Word. God did not just speak His word of promise; that promise was incarnated in the Word, who is Christ. For that reason, it is impossible to overemphasize the importance of the covenant structure.

COVENANTAL FRAMEWORK

Theologians speak in general terms of three major covenants in Scripture: the covenant of redemption, the covenant of works, and the covenant of grace.

We hear very little in the church today about the covenant of redemption, yet I find it to be one of the most thrilling aspects of systematic theology. God did not make the covenant of redemption with human beings; rather, He made it with Himself. It is a covenantal agreement that was made in eternity past among the three persons of the Godhead. In the drama of redemption, we see the activity of Father, Son, and Spirit, and creation itself was a Trinitarian work. God the Father called the world into being, yet when He brought order out of the darkness, it was because the Spirit of God was hovering over the waters and bringing things into being (Gen. 1:2). The New Testament is replete with references to Christ's being the agent through whom the Father created all things. For instance, "All things were made through him, and without him was not any thing made that was made" (John 1:3). Creation involved the Father, the Son, and the Holy Spirit.

Theologians make a functional distinction among the members of the Godhead. The Father *initiated* the plan of salvation; this means the Father is behind the eternal decrees of election, and He sent the Son into the world to accomplish our redemption. The Son *accomplished* redemption for us. Finally, redemption is *applied* to our personal lives by the Holy Spirit. How does Christ's work make us redeemed people? The Spirit regenerates us; that is, He quickens us, imparting spiritual life and creating faith in our hearts. The Spirit also sanctifies us, and He will glorify us in heaven. This is the work of redemption, and it involves all three members of the Trinity working in agreement.

Years ago, a controversy arose among German theologians that presupposed a struggle between the Father and the Son. Supposedly, in His earthly ministry, Christ persuaded the Father to back off from His wrath toward the human race. That, of course, was a serious departure from the biblical understanding of how redemption takes place. The covenant of redemption indicates that the Father, the Son, and the Holy Spirit were in complete agreement about human salvation. The Son did not come to this world reluctantly. Rather, the Son was pleased to fulfill the plan of the Father and to become incarnate. In the garden of Gethsemane on the eve of His atonement, He was praying and sweating drops of blood in His agony. He said, "Father, if you are willing, remove this cup from me. Nevertheless, not my will, but yours, be done" (Luke 22:42). In effect, He said, "I would prefer any other way, but I am in agreement with You, Father, whatever Your will is."

COVENANT OF WORKS AND COVENANT OF GRACE

The primary difference between the covenant of works and the covenant of grace is that the former concerns the relationship God had with Adam and Eve before the fall, while the latter concerns the relationship God has with the descendants of Adam after the fall. The covenant of works refers to the probationary state in which Adam and Eve were created. God gave them certain commands along with the promise of everlasting life, which was symbolized by the Tree of Life in the garden of Eden. The primary stipulation was that they were not to eat of the Tree of the Knowledge of Good and Evil. In the covenant of works, the destiny of the human race was decided on the basis of performance, specifically, on the basis of the obedience of Adam and Eve. If they remained obedient, they would enter into an eternal state of blessedness. However, if they failed to conform to that stipulation, then they would die, along with their descendants. Adam and Eve miserably failed that test. They violated the covenant, and as a result the world was plunged into ruin.

We tend to think of redemption as the regaining of the paradise that Adam and Eve lost, but that is a misunderstanding. Redemption is not merely a restoration to where Adam and Eve were before they fell, but a promotion to the state that they would have achieved had they been successful in obeying the covenant terms.

Another misunderstanding comes from how we identify the two covenants. Because the first is called "the covenant of works" and the other is called "the covenant of grace," we tend to think that the first covenant had no grace. Yet for God to enter into any covenant with a creature, to give any promise to us whatsoever under any conditions, is in itself a gracious act. God is not required to promise His creatures anything.

After the covenant of works was broken, God provided a new

opportunity for man to be redeemed. He spared Adam and Eve and redeemed them despite their fallenness, and He did this on the basis of a new promise—the promise of redemption in the work of Christ. The Scriptures tell us we are saved by grace, and grace comes through the person and work of Christ. Christ saved us by becoming our champion. He became our substitute. That is why the New Testament refers to Him as "the second Adam." He came into the world and placed Himself under the stipulations of the original covenant of works. As the new Adam, He went back to the original situation of Adam and Eve in paradise, which was dramatized in the wilderness when Jesus experienced forty days of temptation by Satan.

Throughout His earthly life, Jesus was exposed to temptation, which is why theologians emphasize that we are saved not only by the death of Christ but also by the life of Christ. In His life of perfect obedience, Christ fulfilled all the terms set forth in the original covenant of works, so that, in the final analysis, we are saved by works. That truth does not negate justification by faith alone; it validates it. Justification is through faith in Christ alone because Christ alone fulfilled the covenant of works. We are still saved by works, but not by *our* works. We are saved by the works of Christ. Again, the covenant of grace does not nullify the covenant of works; on the contrary, it fulfills the terms of the covenant of works.

Some think that the Old Testament is all about God's justice and wrath, while the New Testament is all about His mercy, grace, and love. Yet the clearest example in Scripture of God's wrath and justice is found not in the Old Testament but in the New Testament. It is found at the cross. Here the wrath of God was poured out on Christ, and God's justice was satisfied fully and completely in that act. Yet that act is also the clearest example in Scripture of the grace of God, because His wrath was received by another. It was received by our substitute, who submitted to the terms of the first covenant and fulfilled all the obligations for all who put their trust in Him. The covenant of works and the covenant of grace together fulfill the promises of God from all eternity.

Part Four

CHRISTOLOGY

———

Chapter 23

THE CHRIST OF THE BIBLE

This section of systematic theology, Christology, is perhaps the most intimidating, yet it is one of the richest sections of our study. Here we focus on the person and work of Christ Himself. It is significant that our faith is called "Christianity," for our attention is rightly focused on the One who has redeemed us. Any study of the person of Christ can only scratch the surface, because the portrait of Jesus in Scripture is so deep that it defies human ability to grasp it exhaustively.

> Then I saw in the right hand of him who was seated on the throne a scroll written within and on the back, sealed with seven seals. And I saw a mighty angel proclaiming with a loud voice, "Who is worthy to open the scroll and break its seals?" And no one in heaven or on earth or under the earth was able to open the scroll or to look into it. (Rev. 5:1–3)

In John's vision of heaven, the verdict is about to be pronounced, and a loud voice says, "Who is worthy to open the scroll?" John is filled with anticipation as he waits to see who will step up, who has been declared worthy. He continues:

> I began to weep loudly because no one was found worthy to open the scroll or to look into it. And one of the elders said to

me, "Weep no more; behold, the Lion of the tribe of Judah, the Root of David, has conquered, so that he can open the scroll and its seven seals."

And between the throne and the four living creatures and among the elders I saw a Lamb standing, as though it had been slain, with seven horns and with seven eyes, which are the seven spirits of God sent out into all the earth. And he went and took the scroll from the right hand of him who was seated on the throne. (vv. 4–7)

Then the four living creatures and the twenty-four elders prostrate themselves before the Lamb and sing His praises. Then we hear the praise of the angels:

Worthy is the Lamb who was slain, to receive power and wealth and wisdom and might and honor and glory and blessing! (v. 12)

We can see John's mood swing through this sequence of events. He is excited that someone is going to come and open the scroll, but then he is plunged into depression because no one is found worthy. Then the angel tells John not to weep because One has been found worthy, the Lion of Judah. He is expecting a massively powerful beast to come roaring in to rip open the scroll, but instead he sees a slain Lamb. This imagery is a vivid example of the profound contrast between Christ's humiliation and His exaltation, between His sufferings and His triumphs. It also gives us a hint into the complexity of His character and worth.

JESUS IN THE GOSPELS

Why did God see fit to provide the world with four Gospels? Why not just one definitive biography of Jesus? It pleased God for His own reasons to give us four biographical portraits of Jesus, all looking at His person and work from slightly different perspectives. In Matthew's gospel, we are given a Jewish perspective. The emphasis is on Jesus as the fulfillment of numerous Old Testament prophecies. Matthew shows clearly that Jesus was the Messiah who had been promised in centuries past. Mark's gospel is brief and almost abrupt in its clipped fashion. Mark follows the life of Jesus, showing a blaze of miracles across the landscape of Palestine. There is also the portrait provided by Luke the physician, who was part of the Gentile community and a companion of the Apostle Paul on his missionary journeys to the Gentile nations. Luke shows that Jesus did not come solely to save Jewish people, but also men and women from every tribe, tongue, and nation. Luke provides many insights into the teaching of Jesus through the parables, and Jesus' wisdom is expressed in Luke's gospel. Two-thirds of John's gospel is devoted to the last week of Jesus' life. John provides a highly theological portrait of Christ as he demonstrates that Jesus is the incarnation of truth, the light of the world, and the One in whom there is abundant life.

In the Gospel narratives, we also see how a variety of people responded to Christ. We see the response of the shepherds, who came from the fields outside of Bethlehem at the announcement of the newborn baby Jesus (Luke 2:8–20). We see the response of the aged Simeon, who came into the temple when Jesus was presented for His dedication. On that occasion, Simeon said, "Lord, now you are letting your servant depart in peace, according to your word; for my eyes have seen your salvation that you have prepared in the presence of all peoples" (vv. 29–31). We see Jesus confound the doctors in the temple as a young boy (vv. 41–52). We are introduced to His public ministry by John the Baptist, who sees Him coming to the Jordan River and sings the *Agnus Dei*: "Behold, the Lamb of God, who takes away the sin of the world!" (John 1:29). We see Jesus through the eyes of Nicodemus, who comes at night to inquire of Him, saying, "Rabbi, we know that you are a teacher come from God, for no one can do these signs that you do unless God is with him" (John 3:2). We see Jesus the Rabbi, who not only confounded the other rabbis when He was a child but also went on in adulthood to surpass in wisdom and insight the greatest teachers of His day. We see Jesus talk to an outcast woman by the ancient well of Jacob in Samaria at Sychar, which leads her to say, "Sir,

I perceive that you are a prophet" (John 4:19). As the conversation progresses, Jesus exposes the woman to herself, and she realizes that she is speaking to the promised and long-awaited Messiah. We see Him at the praetorium of Pilate, where Pilate announces, "I find no guilt in this man" (Luke 23:4). Later, we hear Pilate speak words to the crowd that have been immortalized in Christian history: "Behold the man!" (John 19:5). We see a portrait of Jesus from the centurion at the cross, who, after he witnesses the crucifixion, says, "Truly this was the Son of God!" (Matt. 27:54). We see it in doubting Thomas, who, when he sees the risen Christ, cries out, "My Lord and my God!" (John 20:28).

In short, we find the portrait of someone without parallel in human history. The record we see of Jesus in the Gospels is that of an absolutely pure man, a man without sin, a man who could say to His accusers, "Which one of you convicts me of sin?" (John 8:46). This portrait of Jesus is staggering.

We also have Jesus' testimony of His identity: "For I have not spoken on my own authority, but the Father who sent me has himself given me a commandment—what to say and what to speak" (John 12:49). Jesus, in His desire to conceal for a season His true identity because of misconceptions about who the Messiah would be, nevertheless made some bold and extravagant claims, such as the "I am" declarations in John's gospel: "I am the bread of life. Your fathers ate the manna in the wilderness, and they died. This is the bread that comes down from heaven, so that one may eat of it and not die" (6:48–50). Some were so enraged by those words that they walked no more with Him.

"I am the vine; you are the branches," He said. "Whoever abides in me and I in him, he it is that bears much fruit, for apart from me you can do nothing" (15:5). He also said, "I am the door" (10:9), contrasting Himself with the false prophets of the day, who were poor shepherds more concerned with their paychecks than with the care and nurture of the sheep. Jesus said, "I am the good shepherd. I know my own and my own know me" (v. 14). He also said, "I am the way, and the truth, and the life" (14:6).

Even more dramatic was this comment: "Your father Abraham

rejoiced that he would see my day. He saw it and was glad. . . . Truly, truly, I say to you, before Abraham was, I am" (John 8:56, 58). He did not say, "Before Abraham was, I was." He said, "I *am*." These "I am" statements come from two Greek words: *egō* ("I") and *eimi* ("am"). In Greek, either of these words would be sufficient on its own to say, "I am," yet Jesus did not merely say, "*Egō* the way, the truth, and the life," or "*Eimi* the door." Instead, he used both—"*Egō eimi*"—which made his point emphatically. The significance of that was not missed by the first-century community. Greek-speaking Jews wrote the sacred name of God as "Yahweh," which is translated, "I am who I am," so when Jesus used such language about Himself, He was clearly identifying Himself with the sacred name of God.

He claimed nothing less than the authority of God when He used the title "Son of Man," referring to the one who comes to the presence of the Ancient of Days, ascending with the clouds of heaven (Dan. 7:13). Using that phraseology, Jesus said, "The Son of Man is lord even of the Sabbath" (Mark 2:28). God instituted and regulates the Sabbath, so for Christ to say He was lord of the Sabbath was to identify Himself with deity. On another occasion, He healed a man so that the religious authorities "may know that the Son of Man has authority on earth to forgive sins" (Matt. 9:6; Mark 2:10; Luke 5:24). Once again the enemies of Jesus were outraged that Jesus was "making himself equal with God" (John 5:18).

THE APOSTOLIC TESTIMONY ABOUT JESUS

Beyond what we find in the Gospel portraits, we have the Apostolic testimony. The Apostle Paul unveils for us the ministry of Christ as Savior. He explains the atonement, and how Christ as our Mediator accomplished redemption for us. The portrait of Christ is filled out also in the letters of Peter and John, and in the epistle to the Hebrews, where Christ is shown to be "the radiance of the glory of God and the exact imprint of his nature" (Heb. 1:3), as well as superior to angels, to Moses, and to the Aaronic priesthood of the Old Testament. From Matthew to Revelation, the central motif of the New Testament is Christ.

JESUS IN THE OLD TESTAMENT

We find that He is the theme of the Old Testament, too. The tabernacle, which is described in great detail, is heavily symbolic of Jesus Himself. In His person and work, He is the tabernacle of the Old Testament. All the details of the Old Testament sacrificial system find their fulfillment in the ministry of Jesus, and the books of the prophets are filled with references to the One to come. We do not go only to the New Testament to learn of Jesus; He is proclaimed throughout the Old Testament, too. From Genesis to Revelation, we find the story of Jesus, the Christ.

We see in this magnificent portrait of Jesus the perfect man, but not just the perfect man—we see the One who indeed is God with us, God incarnate, and it is because of this rich and profound portrait of Jesus that the church, in setting forth her theological formulations in the early centuries, had to come to grips with the difficulty of being faithful both to the humanity of Jesus and to the deity of Christ. The difficulty was evidenced at the Council of Nicea and at the subsequent Council of Chalcedon.

———

Chapter 24

ONE PERSON, TWO NATURES

We live in a time when the person of Christ is a matter of great controversy among theologians. However, this is not a new problem. In the fourth century, the Arian controversy precipitated the Council of Nicea (AD 325). Another controversy brought about the ecumenical Council of Chalcedon (AD 451). The nineteenth century saw the advent of liberalism, and in the twentieth century there was the group called the Jesus Seminar, both of which sought to define Christ with no regard for biblical integrity. The church has had to define her understanding of the person of Christ repeatedly.

TWO HERESIES

The fifth century witnessed a two-pronged assault on Christian orthodoxy. First, there was the Monophysite heresy, brought about by a man named Eutyches. The name of this position comes from the prefix *mono*, meaning "one," and the word *physis*, which means "nature." The Monophysites believed that Christ had only one nature; they denied that He was one person with two natures, one divine and one human. Even before Eutyches, some had argued that Christ had only one nature. Of those, some said that Christ was merely human, with no deity. Others, such as the Docetists, argued that He was completely divine, with no humanity. Eutyches formulated the idea that Christ had a *theanthropic* nature. The term comes from the Greek word *theos*, which means "god," and the word *anthrōpos*, which means "man." Eutyches said that Christ's nature was neither truly divine nor truly human; rather, it was a mixture of the divine and human.

The other heresy of the fifth century was Nestorianism. Nestorius argued that since Christ has two distinct natures, one divine and the other human, He must therefore have two distinct personalities. If there are two natures, there must be two persons.

So the doctrine of Christ was attacked from both sides, one denying the dual nature of Christ by reducing it to a single, confused mixture of divine and human, and the other affirming two natures but denying their unity.

THE CHALCEDONIAN COUNCIL

These twin heresies prompted the Council of Chalcedon, and from that council came the classic formulation of the dual nature of Christ, namely, that Christ is one person with two natures—*vera homo vera Deus*. The word *vera* comes from the Latin *veritas*, meaning "truth." The idea here is that Christ is "truly man and truly God." Christ has a true human nature *and* a true divine nature. These two natures are perfectly united in one person.

Along with that affirmation, the Chalcedonian Council put forth four negatives.* As I noted earlier, throughout its history, the church has sought to describe certain concepts by way of negation. For example, in some ways we can define God by what He is not. He is infinite, meaning He is *not* finite. He is immutable, meaning He is *not* mutable. Likewise, the framers of the Chalcedonian Creed put forth four negatives, confessing that Christ is truly human and truly God, and that these two natures are perfectly united with *no* mixture, confusion, separation, or division.

The first two of these negatives, directed at the Monophysite heresy, states that the two natures, the divine and the human, are not blended so as to render a deified human nature or a humanized divine nature. The human nature is always human, subject to the normal limitations

---

* The Chalcedonian Creed is included in the appendix.

of humanity, and the divine nature is always divine. For instance, the divine mind did not lose its omniscience in the incarnation; the divine mind knew everything, even though the human mind did not.

SUI GENERIS

The church has had to grapple with the implications of that idea in considering some of Jesus' words. At one point, the disciples asked Jesus, "What will be the sign of your coming and of the end of the age?" Jesus replied, "But concerning that day and hour no one knows, not even the angels of heaven, nor the Son, but the Father only" (Matt. 24:3, 36). In other words, Jesus told His disciples that He did not know when the end of the age would come. Was that an indication of the human nature or the divine nature?

When we look at the life of Jesus as it is displayed on the pages of Scripture, certain actions are easy to assign to His human nature. When Jesus perspired in the garden of Gethsemane on the night before His crucifixion, was that a divine manifestation? Is sweat something we would expect from God? No, God does not sweat. Likewise, He does not get hungry, bleed, or cry. Most importantly, the divine nature did not die on the cross. If the divine nature had died on the cross, the universe would have ceased to exist. All these events evidenced Jesus' humanity.

In the same way, when Jesus said He did not know the timing of the end of the age, it obviously was a statement of His humanity. Some object that if God knows everything, and if in Christ there is a perfect union of the divine nature and the human nature, how could there be anything that Jesus did not know? That is similar to questioning how Jesus, with His divine nature, could have experienced hunger, which the Bible clearly says He did. The point is the importance of distinguishing between the divine nature and the human nature so that we do not confuse them or blend them in such a way as to obscure the reality of either.

The fact that Jesus did not know the day or the hour of the end of the age does not indicate a separation between His human nature and

His divine nature. There is no separation, but there is a distinction. His human mind was always in unity with His divine mind, and in the New Testament we see Jesus display supernatural knowledge frequently. He reveals things that no human could possibly know. Where did He get that information? He got it from the One who is omniscient. Yet it is one thing for the divine nature to communicate knowledge to the human nature; it is another thing for the divine nature to swallow the human nature and deify the human mind of Christ. The human mind had access to the divine mind, if you will, but they were not the same, so there were certain things that Jesus did not know, by His own testimony.

That perplexed even the brilliant thirteenth-century theologian Thomas Aquinas, who formulated what he called "the accommodation theory." Aquinas said that Jesus had to know the day and the hour because He is God incarnate. Given the perfect union of His two natures, how could the divine mind know something that the human mind did not know? Aquinas said that this could not be, so Jesus must have known and chosen not to tell the disciples because the answer to their question was too mysterious or theologically difficult for them to grasp. However, with all due respect to Thomas, if Jesus told His disciples that He did not know when He actually did know, He was lying, and even one lie would have disqualified Him from being our Savior. We have to take seriously what Jesus said about the limits, humanly speaking, of His knowledge.

So the first two negatives of the Chalcedonian Creed, *without mixture* and *without confusion*, were designed to address the Monophysite heresy. The other two, *without separation* and *without division*, were designed to confront the Nestorian heresy, affirming that the presence of two natures in Jesus did not mean He was not one person.

All four negatives set for us the boundaries in which we seek to understand the mystery of the incarnation. I stress the word *mystery*, because even with the formulations provided by the church, no one has ever penetrated the depths of how Christ can be truly God and truly man. We have One who is *sui generis*. He is in a class by Himself. Only one person in all of human history has ever been God incarnate, and the mystery of the incarnation is beyond our full understanding.

HUMAN AND DIVINE

The value of Chalcedon is twofold. First, there is the affirmation every Christian has to make—Christ is truly human and truly divine. Second, when the church tries to explain the nature of His unity, it falls back on negatives, thereby establishing borders past which we dare not travel. The only thing on the other side of those borders is some kind of heresy. One of my seminary professors said to his students, "If you try to think concretely about the union of the human nature and the divine nature, if you go beyond the negative categories established by Chalcedon, you must choose your heresy." The Chalcedonian Creed restricts us so that no matter how we conceive of the two natures, we must not think of them as an amalgamated blending or a stark separation from one another. They are united yet distinct.

An important phrase of the creed has been woefully neglected historically: "Each nature retaining its own attributes." Christ did not lay aside any of His divine attributes. The divine nature of Christ is eternal, infinite, immutable, omniscient, and omnipotent. The human nature also retains the attributes of humanity; it is finite and restricted by space and time. The Chalcedonian formula provides us some direction as we continue our study of the person of Christ.

———

Chapter 25

THE NAMES OF CHRIST

A fascinating element of the Bible is the significance that is often attached to names and titles. The names and titles for God the Father are many, and they reveal something of His character. The same is true for Jesus.

I recall an address given by a scholar at a seminary convocation. The attendees were expecting an academic discourse, but he surprised everyone by simply reciting the names and titles for Jesus found in Scripture: "Lord," "Son of God," "Son of Man," "Son of David," "Immanuel," "the Word," and so on. It took him forty-five minutes to exhaust all the names and titles. Each one of them reveals something to us about the character or work of Christ. In this chapter, I want to look at three of the more prominent titles ascribed to Jesus in the New Testament.

CHRIST

We know Him best as Jesus Christ, but that is not really His name. His name is Jesus, Jesus Bar-Joseph, or Jesus of Nazareth. However, "Christ" is a title. It is applied to Jesus more frequently than any other title in Scripture. Sometimes the Bible reverses the order and speaks of "Christ Jesus." The word *Christ* comes from the Greek word *christos*, which is the translation of the Old Testament word *Messiah*, and it means "one who is anointed."

When Jesus gave His first recorded sermon in the synagogue, He read from the prophet Isaiah: "The Spirit of the Lord is upon me, because he has anointed me to proclaim good news to the poor. He has sent me to proclaim liberty to the captives and recovering of sight to the blind, to set at liberty those who are oppressed, to proclaim the year of the Lord's favor" (Luke 4:18–19). After reading that text, Jesus said to those listening, "Today this Scripture has been fulfilled in your hearing" (v. 21). He was identifying Himself with Isaiah's words about the Messiah.

The concept of the Messiah is extremely complex, but there are several interwoven strands in progressive biblical revelation regarding the function, the character, and the nature of this Messiah who would come and deliver His people, Israel. In a sense, for Christ to be the Messiah, He had to be the Shepherd, the King, the Lamb, and the Suffering Servant, all of which were prophesied in Isaiah. The different strands come together in a marvelous way. In fact, one of the extraordinary evidences for the divine inspiration of the Bible is the way in which all the strands of messianic expectations set forth in the Old Testament converge and are fulfilled in one person in a dramatic way. In John's vision in Revelation 5, he was led to expect a lion (v. 5), but he saw a lamb (v. 6). Jesus fulfilled both. He is the Lion of Judah, the new King of Israel, and He is also the Lamb, who was slain on behalf of His people.

LORD

The second most frequently used title for Jesus in the New Testament is "Lord." This title formed the earliest creed of the Christian community: *Iēsous ho kyrios*, "Jesus is Lord." This confession was at the center of the conflict that the early church experienced with the Roman authorities. Roman citizens were required to recite publicly the words *Caesar kyrios*, "Caesar is lord." The early Christians were deeply committed to the mandate they had received from Christ and from the Apostles to be obedient to the civil magistrate; they were careful to pay their taxes and obey the laws of the state. But one thing they would not do was ascribe to Caesar the honor that went with the term *lord*.

The term *lord* is not always used in a majestic way in the New Testament. In fact, there are three distinct meanings of the Greek word *kyrios*.

First, the word *kyrios* functioned as a simple, polite form of address, similar to the English word *sir*. When we read the New Testament and observe people meeting Jesus for the first time and addressing Him as "Lord," we must not immediately conclude that they had a deep understanding of the full measure of the majesty of Christ. They might simply have been addressing Him in a polite way. Of course, the word *sir*, even in the English language, can have a more exalted meaning, such as in England, when a man is knighted and becomes, for instance, Sir Winston Churchill or Sir Laurence Olivier.

The second way in which the term *kyrios* is used in the New Testament is with specific reference to a slave owner, a wealthy individual who had enough money to purchase bondservants. The bondservant or slave was a *doulos*, and one could not be a *doulos* unless he or she belonged to a *kyrios*, a lord. Thus, the term *lord* was used to refer to one who owned slaves. The Apostle Paul made frequent use of the title in this manner, often describing himself as a *doulos* of Jesus Christ and directing believers to think of themselves in that light: "You were bought with a price" (1 Cor. 6:20; 7:23). When we confess that Jesus is Lord, we understand that Christ purchased us by the atonement and therefore owns us. We are His possession.

The third and highest use of the term *kyrios* in the New Testament is the imperial use, which Caesar had sought to arrogate to himself, thereby causing great trouble for the Christians. Of course, someone can verbalize the title in a false way, feigning the imperial use, which is why Jesus said, "This people honors me with their lips, but their heart is far from me" (Matt. 15:8). However, the New Testament tells us, "No one can say 'Jesus is Lord' except in the Holy Spirit" (1 Cor. 12:3). This almost seems to contradict what Jesus said at the end of the Sermon on the Mount:

> Not everyone who says to me, "Lord, Lord," will enter the kingdom of heaven, but the one who does the will of my Father who is in heaven. On that day many will say to me, "Lord, Lord, did we not prophesy in your name, and cast out demons

in your name, and do many mighty works in your name?" And then will I declare to them, "I never knew you; depart from me, you workers of lawlessness." (Matt. 7:21–23)

So why does Scripture say no man can call Jesus "Lord" except by the Holy Spirit? Some say the statement is elliptical; in other words, what is omitted and must be inserted is that no one can *sincerely* call Jesus "Lord" unless he has been given the ability to do so by the Holy Spirit. Others believe it might have reference to the persecution some experienced for declaring publicly their faith in the lordship of Christ.

In any case, the real significance of the title "Lord" is found in what it translates from the Old Testament. Just as Christ has many titles in the New Testament, so God has many titles in the Old Testament. His name in the Old Testament is *Yahweh*, which is translated as "Lord" and indicated in Scripture by small capital letters—"LORD." When we see "Lord" without those small capital letters, it is translating a different Hebrew word, *Adonai*, which was the highest title used by the Hebrew people for God in the Old Testament. The term *Adonai* has to do with God's absolute sovereignty over all of His creation. An example of these two terms can be found in Psalm 8: "O LORD [*Yahweh*], our Lord [*Adonai*], how majestic is your name in all the earth! You have set your glory above the heavens" (Ps. 8:1). In the New Testament, we read Paul's hymn:

Have this mind among yourselves, which is yours in Christ Jesus, who, though he was in the form of God, did not count equality with God a thing to be grasped, but emptied himself, by taking the form of a servant, being born in the likeness of men. And being found in human form, he humbled himself by becoming obedient to the point of death, even death on a cross. Therefore God has highly exalted him and bestowed on him the name that is above every name, so that at the name of Jesus every knee should bow, in heaven and on earth and under the earth, and every tongue confess that Jesus Christ is Lord, to the glory of God the Father. (Phil. 2:5–11)

The name above every name is actually the title that God gives to Jesus, the title above every title—*Lord*. He is Lord, *Kyrios*; He is *Adonai* to the glory of God the Father.*

SON OF MAN

The third most frequently used title for Jesus in the New Testament is "Son of Man." Though it ranks third in the frequency of usage in the New Testament as a whole, it is far and away the primary title that Jesus used for Himself. That is significant. Of the more than eighty instances of this title in the New Testament, all but three are used by Jesus Himself. This fact refutes the higher critics, who say that much of the New Testament picture of Jesus was manufactured by His companions. If Jesus' companions had done that, we would expect them to have ascribed to Jesus their own favorite designations rather than Jesus'. By calling Himself "Son of Man" so frequently, Jesus was saying, "Here is how I identify Myself."

Some see in the designation an expression of Jesus' humility, but that is not accurate. In Daniel's vision of the inner chambers of heaven, God appears on the throne of judgment as the Ancient of Days, and He welcomes into His presence the one who is like "a son of man," who comes to Him on clouds of glory and is given the authority to judge the world (Dan. 7:13–14). In the New Testament usage of this title, the Son of Man is a heavenly person who descends to earth, and He represents nothing less than the authority of God. He comes to bring judgment to the world because He embodies the divine visitation, the day of the Lord. Therefore, this is an exalted title given uniquely to Jesus in the New Testament. As you read through the Scriptures and come upon this title, look at its context, and you will begin to see that it is a majestic and exalted designation for Jesus.

Every name and title given to Jesus in the New Testament has significance. Each one reveals something to us about who He is and what He has done.

---

* For a fuller treatment of the New Testament view of Jesus, see R.C. Sproul, *The Majesty of Christ*, audio teaching series (Sanford, Fla.: Ligonier Ministries, 1985, 1991).

Chapter 26

———

THE STATES OF CHRIST

Throughout the Bible, Christ is seen in various states, that is, various roles in which He acts at various times. However, discussions of the states of Christ do not begin with His birth at Bethlehem; instead, we must start with His preincarnate state. John writes:

> In the beginning was the Word, and the Word was with God, and the Word was God. . . . And the Word became flesh and dwelt among us, and we have seen his glory, glory as of the only Son from the Father, full of grace and truth. (John 1:1, 14)

The affirmation made here is that this Christ, who has appeared on the plane of history in space and time, existed before His conception and birth, and that His divine nature is eternal with the Father. We have in Jesus not simply the birth of a baby but the incarnation of God, the second person of the Trinity.

On many occasions during His earthly ministry, Jesus made reference to His previous state. For example:

> Truly, truly, I say to you, before Abraham was, I am. (John 8:58)

> And now, Father, glorify me in your own presence with the glory that I had with you before the world existed. (John 17:5)

Jesus was not incarnate before His birth in Bethlehem. Many wonder, therefore, whether Christ is found in the Old Testament. Some look at the commander of the Lord's army whom Joshua encountered during his military campaign (Josh. 5:13–15) or at the mysterious figure of Melchizedek to whom Abraham paid tithes and from whom he received a blessing (Gen. 14:18–20) and speculate that these mysterious figures were really Christ in disguise, as it were. However, even if they were, they were not prior incarnations. Those who believe that these Old Testament figures were the preincarnate Christ call those appearances "christophanies." A "theophany" is a visible manifestation of the invisible God; a christophany, therefore, is a manifestation of the second person of the Trinity prior to His birth.

JESUS INCARNATE

We move from the preincarnational state of Jesus to the state of His life on earth. The Apostles' Creed highlights the earthly manifestation of Christ:

> He was conceived by the Holy Ghost, born of the Virgin Mary, suffered under Pontius Pilate, was crucified, dead, and buried. He descended into hell. The third day He rose again from the dead. He ascended into heaven and sits on the right hand of God the Father Almighty, from whence He shall come to judge the quick and the dead.

The references in the Apostles' Creed are to the birth of Jesus, the death of Jesus, the resurrection of Jesus, the ascension of Jesus, the session of Jesus, and the return of Jesus. These describe different aspects or states of Jesus' existence during and after the incarnation.

Theologians typically speak of the life of Jesus as following a progression from humiliation to exaltation. He was born to a peasant woman, with the cloak of His humanity concealing His deity, thereby entering into His humiliation. Throughout His life, there was a progressive deepening of this humiliation as He moved toward the cross.

People rejected Him, and He was mocked, scourged, beaten, and finally crucified. After the humiliation reached its depths, there was an explosion of exaltation whereby God vindicated Him with the resurrection and surrounded Him with glory at His ascension.

I agree with this general framework, but it is important to note that in the midst of His humiliation, glory attended key moments of His earthly life.* For example, despite the humble circumstances of His birth, the event was not without the manifestation of glory. Just outside the village of Bethlehem, in the fields, the glory of God shone, and there was the greatest sound-and-light show that the world had known up until that point, the appearance of the angel choir (Luke 2:8–14). Even in the visitation of the magi, there was an element of glory ascribed to this babe in the manger, for the magi left magnificent treasures for Him (Matt. 2:1–11).

Jesus' baptism also was an act of humiliation. He willingly submitted to a cleansing rite that God had commanded for sinners, yet Jesus was not a sinner. He humbled Himself to become one with His people, to assume their obligation to obey every aspect of the law. At the same time, at His baptism the heavens opened and the Holy Spirit descended like a dove upon Him (Matt. 3:16).

Then, toward the end of His earthly ministry, after He had told His disciples about His forthcoming torture and execution, we are told:

> He was transfigured before them, and his face shone like the sun, and his clothes became white as light. And behold, there appeared to them Moses and Elijah, talking with him. And Peter said to Jesus, "Lord, it is good that we are here. If you wish, I will make three tents here, one for you and one for Moses and one for Elijah." He was still speaking when, behold, a bright cloud overshadowed them, and a voice from the cloud said, "This is my beloved Son, with whom I am well pleased; listen to him." When the disciples heard this, they fell on their

---

* For more on the key moments during the life of Christ, see R.C. Sproul, *The Glory of Christ* (Phillipsburg, N.J.: P&R, 2003).

145

faces and were terrified. But Jesus came and touched them, saying, "Rise, and have no fear." And when they lifted up their
eyes, they saw no one but Jesus only. (Matt. 17:2–8)

Later, John wrote in the prologue to his gospel, "We have seen his
glory" (John 1:14). Peter also made reference to the transfiguration in
his writings: "We . . . were eyewitnesses of his majesty. For when he
received honor and glory from God the Father, and the voice was borne
to him by the Majestic Glory, 'This is my beloved Son, with whom I am
well pleased,' we ourselves heard this very voice borne from heaven,
for we were with him on the holy mountain" (2 Peter 1:16–18). In the
midst of Jesus' progression from humiliation to exaltation, there was a
sudden intervention, an abbreviated intrusion, where the hidden, concealed, cloaked glory of Christ burst through for the eyes of His close
friends Peter, James, and John. They never forgot it.

We tend to think that no glory was evident at the cross, where Jesus
reached the depths of His humiliation. The common conception is that
the end of His humiliation, the line between humiliation and exaltation, took place at the resurrection, but I do not think that is correct.
If we look, for example, at the prophecy in Isaiah 53 of the Suffering
Servant of Israel, we note: "He was cut off out of the land of the living,
stricken for the transgression of my people. And they made his grave
with the wicked and with a rich man in his death, although he had
done no violence, and there was no deceit in his mouth" (vv. 8–9).

Normally, the Romans tossed the bodies of the victims of crucifixion into the refuse dump outside of Jerusalem. The name of that
garbage dump was Gehenna, which later became a metaphor for hell
itself. City refuse was taken daily to Gehenna, where it was added to a
fire that burned perpetually. Such imagery is used to describe hell, where
the flames are never extinguished. However, Joseph of Arimathea made
a special plea to Pilate to give Jesus a proper burial according to Old
Testament custom. The Word of God was thereby fulfilled. Instead of
being thrown into the garbage heap, Jesus' body was to be anointed
with precious spices and buried in a rich man's grave, fulfilling the

prophecy of Isaiah 53. Therefore, His exaltation began not at the resurrection but at the moment of His death. The pall of humiliation was lifted as His body was treated with great care.

Then there was the major burst of glory when God shook the whole earth and brought His Son back from the dead in order to indicate that He was completely satisfied with His Son's work. In His resurrected state, Jesus came out of the grave with the same body that had been put into the grave, but that body was changed. It was glorified. The resurrected Christ was in a glorified state, which was a foreshadowing of the new physical bodies that we will enjoy in the final resurrection, as Paul explains:

So is it with the resurrection of the dead. What is sown is perishable; what is raised is imperishable. It is sown in dishonor; it is raised in glory. It is sown in weakness; it is raised in power. It is sown a natural body; it is raised a spiritual body. If there is a natural body, there is also a spiritual body. Thus it is written, "The first man Adam became a living being"; the last Adam became a life-giving spirit. (1 Cor. 15:42–45)

So we shall ever be with the Lord in heaven.

KING OF KINGS

The final goal of Jesus' earthly ministry was not the cross or even the resurrection. The ultimate goal is His final return and the consummation of His kingdom. The penultimate goal, that which already has taken place, was His ascension.

This is one of the most misunderstood concepts in all the Bible. We tend to think of the ascension as Jesus merely going up from earth into heaven. He did ascend in the sense of going up, but there was a uniqueness to it. Concerning Jesus' ascension, Paul wrote: "In saying, 'He ascended,' what does it mean but that he had also descended into the lower regions, the earth? He who descended is the one who also ascended far above all the heavens, that he might fill all things"

147

(Eph. 4:9–10). The ascension was Jesus' elevation to His coronation. The Son of Man was received into heaven and crowned as the King of kings and the Lord of lords, and right now He rules in the highest political office of the universe. Christ has the position of cosmic authority right now because of the ascension. This is why the Apostles' Creed says, "He ascended into heaven and sits on the right hand of God the Father Almighty, from where He shall come to judge the quick and the dead."

We also have to add that He ascended not only to sit at the right hand of the Father in power but also to enter the heavenly sanctuary, where He functions as our Great High Priest forever. In the Old Testament, the high priest was allowed into the Holy of Holies only once a year, and when he died, someone else became high priest and took on that duty. But our High Priest never dies, and He is there interceding for His people perpetually in the heavenly Holy of Holies. He stays there at God's right hand, ruling as our King and ministering as our Priest. We are told:

For David did not ascend into the heavens, but he himself says, "The Lord said to my Lord, 'Sit at my right hand, until I make your enemies your footstool.'" Let all the house of Israel therefore know for certain that God has made him both Lord and Christ, this Jesus whom you crucified. (Acts 2:34–36)

And the author of Hebrews writes:

So also Christ did not exalt himself to be made a high priest, but was appointed by him who said to him, "You are my Son, today I have begotten you"; as he says also in another place, "You are a priest forever, after the order of Melchizedek." (Heb. 5:5–6)

It is from that place of exaltation that He will return in glory to consummate His kingdom.

———

Chapter 27

THE OFFICES OF CHRIST

As Moses was the mediator of the old covenant, Christ is the Mediator of the new covenant. A mediator is a go-between, an intermediary, someone who stands between two or more parties, oftentimes mediating a dispute.

From a theological standpoint, there is one Mediator between God and man (1 Tim. 2:5). However, there were three types of mediators in the Old Testament. Each was selected by God for a specific task and then enabled to perform the task by the Holy Spirit's anointing. These three mediatorial offices were prophet, priest, and king.

When we look at the offices held by Christ in the drama of redemption, we see that He has a *munus triplex*, a threefold office, for He fulfills all three of these Old Testament offices in one person. Christ is our Prophet, our Priest, and our King.

JESUS OUR PROPHET

In the Old Testament, the prophet, for the most part, was a spokesman, an agent of revelation by which God, instead of speaking directly from heaven to the congregation of Israel, put His words into the mouths of men. As the prophet stood facing the people, God stood behind him, a posture that indicated the prophet was speaking on God's behalf. The prophets' messages were often prefaced by "Thus says the Lord . . ."

In the Old Testament, we see an enormous struggle between true prophets of God and false prophets. Many people followed the false prophets; they were far more popular. The true prophets were often hated. Jeremiah and others endured much affliction because the people did not want to hear the true Word of God. When Jeremiah complained to God about the popularity of the false prophets, God said to him, "Let the prophet who has a dream tell the dream, but let him who has my word speak my word faithfully. What has straw in common with wheat? declares the LORD" (Jer. 23:28). God, in so many words, was saying, "Jeremiah, stop worrying about what the false prophets do. Your task is to be My spokesman, and you are called to be faithful in speaking whatever I tell you to say." So through the prophets, God gave His Word.

In the New Testament, we see that Christ is the Prophet *par excellence*. We tend to emphasize Christ's offices of Priest and King but neglect His role as Prophet. There is a progressive understanding about Jesus seen in those who met Him. The woman at the well said to him, "Sir, I perceive that you are a prophet" (John 4:19). That was quite an accolade, but she had not yet reached the zenith of her confession, which happened when she recognized Him as the Messiah (v. 29). Jesus not only proclaims the Word of God; He *is* the Word of God (John 1:1). The author of Hebrews writes, "Long ago, at many times and in many ways, God spoke to our fathers by the prophets, but in these last days he has spoken to us by his Son, whom he appointed the heir of all things, through whom also he created the world" (1:1–2). Elsewhere, Jesus said, "For I have not spoken on my own authority, but the Father who sent me has himself given me a commandment—what to say and what to speak" (John 12:49). Jesus is the faithful Prophet of the New Testament.

Jesus is not just the subject of prophecy; He is the chief object of prophecy. He did not just teach about the future or declare the Word of God; He *is* the Word of God, and He is the focal point of all the prophetic teaching of the Old Testament.

JESUS OUR PRIEST

Unlike the Old Testament prophets, who faced the people when speaking for God, the Old Testament priests faced God and had their backs to the people. Like the prophet, the priest was a spokesman, but he spoke *for* the people rather than *to* them. He made intercession on behalf of the people and prayed for them. Additionally, the priest offered sacrifices to God for the people. The chief sacrifices were offered on the Day of Atonement by the high priest. But before the high priest could make sacrifices for the people, he had to make sacrifices for his own sin. His sacrifice, just like that of the people, had to be repeated annually.

Jesus is our Priest. The Old Testament text most frequently quoted in the New Testament is Psalm 110. It contains an extraordinary statement about the character of the Messiah:

The LORD says to my Lord: "Sit at my right hand, until I make your enemies your footstool."

The LORD sends forth from Zion your mighty scepter. Rule in the midst of your enemies! Your people will offer themselves freely on the day of your power, in holy garments; from the womb of the morning, the dew of your youth will be yours. The LORD has sworn and will not change his mind, "You are a priest forever after the order of Melchizedek." (vv. 1–4)

In the New Testament, the author of Hebrews gives much attention to the perfect priesthood of Christ. One key evidence of the higher nature of Jesus' priesthood is the fact that He did not have to make any sacrifices for His own sin before entering the temple. The sacrifice He offered was once for all, and it was not an animal sacrifice. Christ offered Himself, because "it is impossible for the blood of bulls and goats to take away sins" (Heb. 10:4). He is a Priest forever after the order of Melchizedek, continuing His mediatorial work even to this moment—not by continually offering sacrifices to satisfy the justice of God but by interceding for His people in the heavenly Holy of Holies within the heavenly temple. Just as Christ is both the subject and the object of prophecy, He is the subject and the object of the priesthood. He is the perfect Priest and perfect intermediary, now and forever.

CHRIST OUR KING

The third office of Christ is also indicated in Psalm 110: "The LORD says to my Lord: 'Sit at my right hand'" (v. 1). This is a reference to the office of king. Many have a difficult time reconciling the office of king with that of a mediator, but if we go back to the roots of the Old Testament, we will see it. The king of Israel was not autonomous; he did not have absolute authority in himself. He received his office from God. His calling was that of vice-regent, by which he was to manifest the justice and rule of God Himself. The king was a mediator in that he was under the law of God, yet he helped to establish and maintain the law of God to the people. Sadly, the history of the kings in the Old Testament is filled with corruption and the failure of those monarchs to carry out their responsibility.

We find the same principle in the New Testament with respect to civil magistrates. The Bible allows for two spheres of operation—the church and the state—which have different duties, but never does Scripture uphold the separation of the state from God, because all rulers are appointed by God. They are ordained to uphold righteousness and establish justice, and they are accountable to God for how they exercise their reign.

A few years ago, I was invited to speak at the governor's inaugural breakfast in Tallahassee, Florida. On that occasion, I solemnly reminded the governor that to be a governor is to be a minister of God, and that since only God can make one a governor, God would hold him accountable for how he governs. That is true of any ruler in any nation and in any situation. However, God sees a world ruled by corrupt kings, those who deviate from righteousness and justice.

The closest model in the Old Testament to the ideal king—David— was himself corrupt. Yet David introduced the royal golden age in Israel, and after he died, the people longed to see the restoration of the Davidic kingdom. God said through the prophet Amos: "In that day I will raise up the booth of David that is fallen and repair its breaches, and raise up its ruins and rebuild it as in the days of old" (Amos 9:11).

At the heart of messianic expectancy in the Old Testament was the longing of the people to have a king like David once again. In Psalm 110, God promised that His Son would be that King, and that He would reign forever and ever. So when Christ came, He was heralded as the newborn King. In fact, He was crucified because of His claims to kingship. He said to Pilate: "My kingdom is not of this world. If my kingdom were of this world, my servants would have been fighting, that I might not be delivered over to the Jews. But my kingdom is not from the world" (John 18:36). God took Christ to His coronation and installed Him at His right hand as the ruler of the whole universe, as the Shepherd-King whose reign will go on eternally.

The only difference between the kingdom today and the kingdom that we will know in the future is its visibility. Jesus is King right now. He holds the highest political office in the universe because He has been installed into that position by God, which is at the heart of the Apostles' Creed: "[He] suffered under Pontius Pilate, was crucified, dead and buried. . . . The third day He rose again from the dead. He ascended into heaven and sits on the right hand of God the Father Almighty." To be at the right hand of God is to be in the position of authority, by which He rules not just the church but also the world. That is why the church cries, "Hallelujah!" Our Messiah is not only our Prophet and Priest but also our King.

Chapter 28

———◆———

WHY DID CHRIST DIE?

In this chapter and the two following chapters, we will turn our attention to the atonement, but three short chapters cannot possibly do
justice to the importance of this glorious doctrine.*

In the early Middle Ages, Anselm of Canterbury wrote three
monographs for which he became famous. Two were in the realm of
apologetics—the *Monologion* and the *Proslogion*—but perhaps his
most famous book, *Cur Deus Homo* ("Why the God-Man?"), probed
the mystery of the atonement. He searched the New Testament to see
why it was necessary for Christ to become man and what actually took
place in the drama of the atonement. Anselm was concerned with its
purpose and its significance. His teaching has had an enormous influence on the church's understanding of the cross of Christ.

The New Testament uses a variety of metaphors for the atonement
and offers more than one point of consideration. The atonement is
like a tapestry with several strands woven together, and below we will
consider those strands.

UNDERSTANDING THE ATONEMENT

In some contexts, the New Testament speaks of the cross of Christ as
an act of redemption. In its most basic sense, redemption has to do with

---

* For a deeper study of the atonement, see R.C. Sproul, *The Cross of Christ*, audio teaching
series (Sanford, Fla: Ligonier Ministries, n.d.).

some kind of purchase, a commercial transaction in which something is bought from someone else. Christ Himself makes reference to the redemption of His people carrying a high cost, namely, His own blood. On the cross at the end of His suffering, He cried out, "It is finished" (John 19:30), and the word translated as "finished" was a commercial term. It was used when someone made a final installment on a series of payments, just as we might stamp "Paid in full" on a final invoice.

Closely related are various types of so-called ransom theories. One of the most popular is that Christ paid a ransom to Satan in order to release His people from the devil's captivity. Just as somebody today may be inclined to pay a ransom to a kidnapper, so Christ is said to have paid a ransom to the prince of this world, who had taken Christ's people hostage. However, I think this theory gives more authority to Satan than he actually possesses. Others talk about Christ paying a ransom to the Father by virtue of completing a debt owed to God, which I think is the correct view.

Closely connected to the commercial transaction aspect is the Old Testament idea of the bride price. The book of Exodus sets forth the rules and regulations for those entering into marriage and for indentured servants. For a man to gain approval to marry, he had to pay the bride's father a dowry, mainly to show the father that he had the means to provide for a wife and the offspring who would issue from that union. Likewise, when someone sold himself as a slave in order to work off a debt, if he brought a wife and children into that indentured slavery, at the time of his release he was free to take his wife and children with him. However, if he entered slavery as a single man, only to marry another slave and have children during his enslavement, he was not allowed to take the wife and children at the time of his liberation. The law was not meant to be cruel; it was meant to ensure that the bride price would be paid.

The theological significance is that Christ has a bride—the church—and the New Testament, in its teaching on the atonement, affirms that Christ purchased His bride. He paid the bride price. Likewise, He paid a price to redeem slaves. The Apostle Paul writes, "You are not your own, for you were bought with a price" (1 Cor. 6:19–20). The concept of purchase is central to the biblical understanding of the atonement.

Another view that has been stressed, particularly in the twentieth century by Lutheran theologians, is known as *Christus victor*. In this view, the cross was a cosmic victory wherein Christ set captives free by dealing a mortal blow to the forces of wickedness in a titanic struggle between good and evil. In that regard, it was the fulfillment of the ancient curse that God had pronounced on the Serpent in Eden: "I will put enmity between you and the woman, and between your offspring and her offspring; he shall bruise your head, and you shall bruise his heel" (Gen. 3:15).

According to this view, Christ experienced pain and injury while obtaining this victory, but His pain was nothing compared to that inflicted upon the prince of evil.

There are many strands to consider when looking at the atonement, and some people make the mistake of focusing exclusively on one strand, trying to find in it the entire significance of the atonement. We must see that all of the strands are aspects of a complex work of redemption.

Unorthodox theories of the atonement have also been raised. One of the most popular is the governmental theory, which suggests that Christ did not pay the actual price for mankind's sin on the cross, but that His death was a meaningful substitute for the punishment of humans. Christ's suffering allowed God to extend forgiveness while still demonstrating His displeasure with sin and maintaining divine justice.

THE SATISFACTION THEORY

The view of the atonement that has captured the most attention since the teaching of Anselm is the satisfaction theory. This theory goes back to Anselm's elaboration of the need for an atonement. The principle underlying the satisfaction theory is the justice of God.

Some time ago, I spoke with a man who told me that he believes in God but not in the Christian God, because it is ridiculous to believe in a God who would require a blood sacrifice for reconciliation with human beings. He asked, "What kind of God would be so vengeful as

WHY DID CHRIST DIE?

to require this sort of thing?" I answered, "A just God." The man could not swallow that. He thought that a truly just God would unilaterally forgive people for their sins and not impose a requirement.

Many people prefer to think strictly in terms of God's love, grace, or mercy, and they dislike the idea that God is a God of justice. However, if we look at the biblical understanding of justice, we see that justice is related closely to both righteousness and goodness. Justice and righteousness are distinguished in the Bible but never separated. Justice is a necessary element of true righteousness, and by extension it is a necessary element of goodness. My discussion with the skeptic was really about whether God is good. He did not like the Christian faith because He thought that Christianity teaches a bad God. A good God, in his view, would not exact punishment for sin. But on the contrary, the atonement dramatically illustrates the goodness of God.

When God announced that He was going to pour out His judgment on Sodom and Gomorrah, Abraham interceded on behalf of the people. Abraham was worried that God in His wrath would bring injury to innocent people along with the wicked. Abraham raised a question, the answer to which could only be yes: "Shall not the Judge of all the earth do what is just?" (Gen. 18:25). Abraham's thinking was right on the mark. He understood that the supreme Judge of all human affairs does only what is right. We can take comfort in knowing that the Judge of heaven and earth is always and everywhere righteous. He is omniscient in His judgments and perfect in His evaluation. He has all the mitigating circumstances in mind when He renders a decision. In addition to His perfect knowledge, this Judge is good. A judge who never punishes evil is not good because he is not just.

When Paul explored the mystery of the cross, he said that God is both just and the Justifier (Rom. 3:26). We can grasp the meaning of this by making a distinction between kinds of indebtedness. When we sin against God, we incur a moral debt. God's law imposes an obligation, and we are called to meet that obligation, which is perfection. If we sin even once, we become debtors who cannot possibly pay our debt.

It is helpful to distinguish between pecuniary debt and moral debt.

A pecuniary debt is one in which a sum of money is owed in a transaction. Picture a small boy entering an ice cream store. He orders an ice cream cone, and when the waitress gives him the cone, she tells him he owes her two dollars. His face sinks as he reaches in his pocket and pulls out only a dollar bill. He says, "My mommy gave me only one dollar." What would you do if you were watching this unfold? Very likely, you would reach in your pocket, extract a dollar bill, and hand it to the waitress, saying, "Here, I'll pay for the other half of the cone." The boy looks up at you and says, "Gee, thanks," and goes on his way. But does the waitress have to accept your payment? The answer is yes, because the debt has been incurred financially. As long as you put money on the counter on behalf of that little boy, it is legal tender, and the waitress has to accept the payment.

The result would be different if we change the story a bit. Picture that small boy entering the shop again, but instead of ordering a cone, he waits until the waitress goes to the back of the shop, at which time he runs behind the counter, scoops ice cream into a cone, and attempts to dash out of the store. You watch as the store proprietor catches him and then calls the police. You feel bad for the boy, so you address the policeman, saying: "Wait a minute, officer. Let's forget about this. I'll pay for the boy's cone." Then you hand the proprietor two dollars. The policeman looks at the proprietor and asks, "Do you want to press charges?" The policeman understands that the shop owner is not obligated to accept your payment for the ice cream cone because, in this case, more than a financial transaction is involved. A law has been broken; a moral debt has been incurred. The proprietor is therefore free to accept or to refuse your payment.

We can look at the atonement in light of that second illustration. It was not a bystander's idea that the price should be paid by a substitute; rather, it was the owner's idea. It was God the Father who sent His Son into the world to pay the price of our moral guilt. The Father said to the Son, "I will accept Your payment on behalf of these guilty people who cannot pay their debt."

God does not negotiate His justice. He does not sacrifice His righteousness or discard His integrity. He said, in essence, "I am going to make sure that sin is punished." That is the justness of the cross. The mercy of the cross is seen in that God accepted the payment by a substitute. Paul's words become clear: God is both just and the Justifier of the ungodly.

Chapter 29

SUBSTITUTIONARY ATONEMENT

I studied at a rather liberal seminary. In my class on homiletics, which teaches one how to preach, the professor was more of a speech instructor than a theologian, so at the end of each student's sermon, he would give a critique of the delivery and the organization, but he typically refrained from any criticism of the theological content. One day, however, a student gave what I thought was a stirring message on the substitutionary satisfaction view of the atonement, but when he was finished, the homiletics professor was beside himself with anger. He said to the student, "How dare you preach the substitutionary satisfaction theory of the atonement in this day and age!" I raised my hand and asked, "Excuse me, but what is it about this day and age that has made the classic biblical doctrine of the atonement suddenly obsolete?"

That is one example of the fierce resistance abounding against the classical view of the atonement. There are those who believe it is simply barbaric and prescientific to assert that a substitute had to shed his blood to satisfy the demands of God's justice. However, the idea of substitution is so deeply rooted in the biblical concept of redemption that to eliminate it from our theology and our Christology is simply to discard the Scriptures altogether.

Karl Barth once made the observation that, in his judgment, the single most important Greek word in the New Testament is *huper*, which means "on behalf of." Among the titles given to Jesus in the New

Testament is "the last Adam," or "the second Adam," which communicate that Christ became a representative for us in a way analogous to Adam, who was our first representative. At the fall of one man, Adam, ruin and death came on the world, and through the other Man's obedience, redemption and eternal life came. Jesus was the successful Adam, who did *on behalf of* His people what the first Adam failed to do.

REMOVAL OF SIN

In the Old Testament, we see the concept of atonement worked out in Israel through an elaborate sacrificial system. On the annual Day of Atonement, several animals were involved, as detailed in Leviticus 16. After the high priest sacrificed a bull to atone for his own sin, two goats were brought, and lots cast over them. The procedure for one of the goats gives us the concept of the word *scapegoat*; the high priest laid his hands on the head of the goat, symbolizing the transfer or imputation of the sins of the people to the goat. Then the goat was driven out into the wilderness, outside of the presence of God's blessing; it bore the people's sins and carried them away. Yet that was only part of the atonement; the other part was the slaying of the second goat. The blood of the second goat was sprinkled upon the mercy seat, the lid of the ark of the covenant. The mercy seat was called "the atonement cover," because the blood spilled on it indicated the means by which the people's sins were atoned for, and the people reconciled to God.

In the New Testament, we are reminded that those substitute animals used on the Day of Atonement were but shadows of a reality that would come later. The author of Hebrews writes:

> For since the law has but a shadow of the good things to come instead of the true form of these realities, it can never, by the same sacrifices that are continually offered every year, make perfect those who draw near. Otherwise, would they not have ceased to be offered, since the worshipers, having once been cleansed, would no longer have any consciousness of sins? But in these sacrifices there is a reminder of sins every year. For

it is impossible for the blood of bulls and goats to take away sins. (10:1–4)

The value of those atoning sacrifices in the Old Testament was in the way they dramatized the authentic atonement yet to come. In other words, people were justified by believing in the promise of God, by seeing those rites as shadows of a future reality. They received real atonement only from Christ. In the Old Testament ceremony, the concept of substitution was central.

My friend John Guest, an Anglican evangelist, once preached on the cross of Christ and asked this question: "Had Jesus come to this earth and scratched His finger on a nail so that a drop or two of blood was spilled, would that have been sufficient to redeem us? If we are saved by the blood of Christ, wouldn't that have been enough?" Guest was making the point that it is not the blood of Christ that saves us as such. For the Israelites, the shedding of blood meant the giving of life, because the punishment for sin originally was death. What was required as payment for transgression against God was the life of the perpetrator. In the Old Testament sacrificial system, God was saying to the people of Israel, "You have committed capital offenses against Me, and the law requires your death, but I will accept in the place of your death the death of a substitute, symbolized by the death of animals."

EXPIATION AND PROPITIATION

The Scriptures speak of two distinct aspects of this substitutionary action: *expiation* and *propitiation*. Expiation, which contains the prefix *ex-*, meaning "from" or "out of," is the removal of guilt from someone. This is the horizontal dimension of atonement. This aspect is seen in the drama of the scapegoat. The sin of the people was transferred to the goat, and then the goat carried away the sins as it was removed from the presence of God into the outer wilderness. The psalmist uses the language of expiation: "As far as the east is from the west, so far does he remove our transgressions from us" (Ps. 103:12).

In reality, of course, our sins are transferred not to a scapegoat but to

Christ, who as the Lamb of God took our guilt upon Himself. He became the sin-bearer, thereby fulfilling the prophecies related to the Servant of the Lord, found chiefly in Isaiah 53: "He was pierced for our transgressions; he was crushed for our iniquities; upon him was the chastisement that brought us peace, and with his wounds we are healed" (v. 5).

Propitiation involves the vertical dimension of atonement. In the act of propitiation, God's righteous wrath is appeased, and His justice is satisfied. The moral obligation that we owe for our sins is paid to God, who is thereby placated. He is fully satisfied with the price that is paid by our substitute. If we do not have a substitute, then there can be no expiation and no propitiation, because we are not capable of satisfying the demands of God's justice. If we were, there would be no need for an atonement, but since we cannot pay our moral debt, there is an absolute need for a substitute.

I frequently find myself in discussions with skeptics who raise questions about the truth claims of Christianity. If I answer one question to their satisfaction, they are always ready with another one. Finally, I stop that endless cycle by asking them, "What do you do with your guilt?" This is usually a conversation stopper because they have no answer apart from some form of denial. It is tragic to hear people say they have no guilt. Everyone is guilty before God. We need both the vertical and the horizontal aspects of atonement, and both involve a substitute.

COVENANTAL STRUCTURE

The Bible's explanation of atonement is found in its covenantal structure. The covenant stipulations God set forth—His commandments—were to be obeyed. The covenants had dual sanctions: rewards for keeping the law and punishments for violating it. The language used in Scripture to express those dual sanctions is blessing and curse. In Deuteronomy, for example, God said to the people:

> Blessed shall you be in the city, and blessed shall you be in the field. Blessed shall be the fruit of your womb and the fruit of your ground and the fruit of your cattle, the increase of your

herds and the young of your flock. Blessed shall be your basket and your kneading bowl. Blessed shall you be when you come in, and blessed shall you be when you go out. (28:3–6)

Conversely:

But if you will not obey the voice of the LORD your God or be careful to do all his commandments and his statutes that I command you today, then all these curses shall come upon you and overtake you. Cursed shall you be in the city, and cursed shall you be in the field. Cursed shall be your basket and your kneading bowl. Cursed shall be the fruit of your womb and the fruit of your ground, the increase of your herds and the young of your flock. Cursed shall you be when you come in, and cursed shall you be when you go out. (28:15–19)

The motif of the curse is central to the concept of covenant. We read in the Old Testament that the Israelites broke the covenant both corporately and individually. All of us are covenant breakers, which means all of us stand under the curse. The world is cursed; our labor is cursed; the Serpent is cursed; the man is cursed; the woman is cursed. We are all under the curse of God. The covenant curse was not some sort of voodoo witchcraft. To be cursed of God is to be cut off from His presence and blessing.

Conversely, to be blessed of God in the Old Testament was to be drawn close to Him, to have the light of His countenance. Christ fulfilled this in a substitutionary way, which is dramatically taught by the Apostle Paul: "And the Scripture, foreseeing that God would justify the Gentiles by faith, preached the gospel beforehand to Abraham, saying, 'In you shall all the nations be blessed'" (Gal. 3:8). That is the old gospel, the promise of divine blessing:

So then, those who are of faith are blessed along with Abraham, the man of faith.

SUBSTITUTIONARY ATONEMENT

> For all who rely on works of the law are under a curse; for it is written, "Cursed be everyone who does not abide by all things written in the Book of the Law, and do them." Now it is evident that no one is justified before God by the law, for "The righteous shall live by faith." But the law is not of faith, rather "The one who does them shall live by them." Christ redeemed us from the curse of the law by becoming a curse for us—for it is written, "Cursed is everyone who is hanged on a tree." (vv. 9–13)

That is the crux of the matter—Christ has redeemed us from the curse of the law by becoming a curse for us.

When Paul probes the depths of the atonement, he goes to the concept of the curse. The price for sin is to experience the curse of God. Christ became a curse. He was delivered into the hands of the Gentiles. It is significant that He was not killed by His own people but by Gentiles, who were considered to be "unclean people" who dwelt "outside the camp." Jesus died outside the city of Jerusalem (Golgotha was outside the city limits). He had to be taken outside the camp, numbered among the Gentiles, and considered unclean, and God plunged the world into darkness while Christ was being crucified, indicating that the light of God's countenance had turned away. Christ cried out from the cross, "My God, my God, why have you forsaken me?" (Matt. 27:46). He had to be forsaken because the penalty for sin is divine forsakenness. Jesus was cut off from the land of the living on our behalf, so that we would not be cut off.

Chapter 30

———•———

THE EXTENT OF THE ATONEMENT

The distinctives of Reformed theology are often summarized using the acrostic *TULIP*, the *L* of which represents the concept of limited atonement. Those who hold to TULIP are called "five-point Calvinists." Four-point Calvinists object to the *L*, to the concept of limited atonement. So the area of dispute between five- and four-point Calvinists has to do with the extent of the atonement. In other words, for whom did Christ die?

There is a lot of confusion about what is meant by "limited atonement." Historically, Reformed theologians have not used that term. They have had a preference for "definite atonement," as distinguished from "indefinite atonement," because the issue is not the value of the atonement. The sacrifice that Christ offered the Father was perfect. He could not have done more than He did to effect the redemption of mankind.

The atonement is often summarized with the phrase "sufficient for all and efficient for some," meaning that it was limited in its efficacy to a certain group of people but was sufficient to cover the sins of the whole world. There is very little disagreement over the fact that the atonement is not applied efficaciously to all people, so this phrase merely defines the difference between universalism and particularism. It deals with the sufficiency of Christ's death and not specifically with God's intent in the atonement.

Universalism is the theory that Jesus died effectually for the sins of all people, so everyone in the universe is saved. Universalists claim, therefore, that all people are saved through the efficacy of Christ's atonement. Universalism is, at least in evangelical circles, an extremely minute viewpoint. In fact, someone claiming to be a universalist cannot rightly claim also to be an evangelical, because evangelicals believe in an actual hell where there are unrepentant people.

Particularism says that only some are saved. There is strong agreement within evangelicalism about particularism, the view that the effect of the cross is applied only to some. This does not mean that a limit is placed on the value or merit of the atonement of Jesus Christ. Its meritorious value is sufficient to cover the sins of all people, and anyone who puts his or her trust in Jesus Christ will receive the full measure of the benefits of that atonement.

It is also important to understand that the gospel is to be preached universally. This is another controversial point, because although the gospel is offered universally to all who are within earshot of the preaching of it, it is not offered without any conditions. It is offered to anyone who repents and believes. Obviously, the merit of the atonement of Christ is given to all who repent of their sins and believe. So the issue is not about the *sufficiency* of the cross; it is about its *design*.

THE DESIGN OF THE ATONEMENT

In order to consider the design of the atonement, we must first identify the designer. Who designed the atonement in the first place? From all eternity, the Father, the Son, and the Holy Spirit were in perfect agreement about creation and redemption. God is the designer. He is the One who sent Christ into the world. Did He do so merely hoping that people would take advantage of the opportunity? Some say so. Some say that God has no idea what people are going to do because His knowledge is limited by the choices of human beings. Such thinking negates Scripture, however, which tells us: "Jesus knew from the beginning who those were who did not believe, and who it was who would betray him" (John 6:64). Also, Jesus said, "All that the Father gives me will come to me, and whoever comes to me I will never cast out" (John 6:37). Christ was acutely conscious as He prepared to do the work of redemption that He was doing it for the ones whom the Father had given Him, so it was not going to be an exercise in futility.

The problem with a hypothetical redemption concept is that Christ could die theoretically for *everyone* but actually for *no one*—that is, if no one accepts the offer of the gospel. It would then be theoretically possible for the cross to be futile.

This is where we are forced to think about the cross in terms of our understanding of the character of God. If God designed the atonement, if the cross was God's plan of redemption, then that is what we should expect to occur. The efficacy of the cross is fulfilled to the exact degree that God originally intended.

Many believe that the salvation of people rests ultimately on man. However, no one is lost outside of the providence of God. Nothing in the ultimate design and plan of redemption depends on us for its efficacy. It depends on God alone. That is the issue. In the final analysis, salvation is not of man but of the Lord.

THE DOCTRINE OF ELECTION

Reformed theologians say that one must believe to receive the benefits of the cross, but even that faith is a gift from God. Christ fulfills the eternal design of salvation so that every person for whom He died is saved. Jesus died only for the elect; He did not die for everyone. Many object to this, pointing out the Bible's teaching that Christ died for the sins of the whole world (1 John 2:2). Yes, Christ did die for people from all *parts* of the world, which is the way the Scriptures speak of "the world." In other words, from a biblical standpoint, Jesus did not die merely for Jews. He died for Jews and Gentiles of every kind. He died for people from every tribe, tongue, and nation. He died for the whole of the elect, which includes people from every part of the world. However, He did not die for the nonelect. He did not die for Satan. He did not die for those who, in God's eternal decree, are not the special objects of His favor of election.

Holding to the *L* in TULIP is the litmus test of whether one really believes what the other letters represent. People say they believe in total depravity—the *T*—but they do not believe in limited atonement. They say they believe in unconditional election—the *U*—meaning that God has sovereignly chosen from all eternity those whom He will save merely out of his own good pleasure, but they do not hold to limited atonement. However, we cannot believe one and not believe the other. If we believe that election is unconditional and that it is grounded in God's sovereign mercy and grace from all eternity, then we must also see the purpose of the cross. The *value* of the cross extends universally, but God's *design* and *purpose* for the cross were to save only some of fallen humanity by satisfying the demands of His justice. He determined to apply the work of His Son to the benefit of those whom He chose from the foundation of the world.

The cross has always been part of the eternal plan of God's redemption, and its design is intended for the elect. It is comforting to know that Christ did not die in vain, and that His accomplished redemption will certainly be applied to those whom He purposed to save.

Part Five

PNEUMATOLOGY

Chapter 31

THE HOLY SPIRIT IN THE OLD TESTAMENT

The most significant event of my life was my conversion. At the time, I was engaged to be married, and I attempted to explain to my fiancée in great detail the circumstances of my conversion to Christ and what it would mean for our relationship. We communicated mainly by letter and telephone because we attended different colleges, and we carried on this discussion for many months. I felt I was getting nowhere. Finally, she came to visit my campus, and I decided to take her to a prayer meeting. I spent the entire morning beforehand on my knees praying for her and for that occasion, and to my great delight, she was converted to Christ at that meeting, and I went on to marry her. On the day of her conversion, she said to me, "Now I know who the Holy Spirit is." I thought that was a fascinating response to her awakening to Christ, and over the years I have reflected on it quite a bit. It is significant that she said, "I know *who* the Holy Spirit is" rather than "I know *what* the Holy Spirit is."

A common misconception in the world's perception of Christianity is that the Holy Spirit is a kind of impersonal force or simply an active power of God rather than a true person, a member of the divine Trinity. But Jesus and the Apostles referred to the Holy Spirit as "He." Scripture shows us that the Holy Spirit has a will, knowledge, and affections—all the things that make up personhood are attributed to Him.

A major point of confusion about the Holy Spirit concerns the differences between His activity in the Old Testament and His work in the New Testament and in the lives of Christians today. The activity of the Holy Spirit goes all the way back to creation: "In the beginning, God created the heavens and the earth. The earth was without form and void, and darkness was over the face of the deep" (Gen. 1:1–2a). The unformed world is described as dark, empty, and formless. Carl Sagan, in his work *Cosmos*, makes the dogmatic assertion that the universe is cosmos, not chaos, which is the difference between order and confusion.* In biblical categories, it is the difference between pure darkness and light, between a vacuous universe ultimately empty of anything significant and that which is filled and teeming with the fruit of the Creator. In the beginning verses of the book of Genesis we find a dramatic proclamation of cosmos, yet the world was without form, and darkness was over the face of the deep.

However, in the next clause of Genesis 1:2, we meet the Holy Spirit for the first time: "And the Spirit of God was hovering over the face of the waters." Another word for *hovering* is *brooding*. This is the idea that was communicated when God sent the angel Gabriel to visit the peasant girl Mary in Nazareth to tell her that she was about to become a mother. Mary asked the angel, "How will this be, since I am a virgin?" (Luke 1:34). The angel replied, "The Holy Spirit will come upon you, and the power of the Most High will overshadow you" (v. 35). The verb used to describe the Holy Spirit's coming upon Mary carries the same connotation as the term used in Genesis 1 to describe the creative power of the Spirit of God. The Holy Spirit came into the formlessness and hovered or brooded. As a hen broods over her eggs in order to bring forth life, so the Spirit produced order and substance and light. God, as the New Testament says, is not the author of confusion (1 Cor. 14:33). He does not generate chaos. The Spirit of God

---

* Carl Sagan, *Cosmos* (New York: Ballantine, 1985).

brings order out of disorder; He brings something out of nothing; He brings light out of darkness.*

THE SPIRIT OF POWER

As we read the Old Testament, we cannot help but be struck by both God's majesty and His power. When an earthquake occurs or a tornado sweeps through the Plains states, we see pictures of the devastation and feel overwhelmed by the power of nature. But those things are nothing compared to the transcendent power of the Lord of all nature. His power exceeds that of anything that happens on this planet. We see this power manifested in the Old Testament primarily by the Holy Spirit, who in the Greek language is called the *dynamis* of God. The word *dynamis* is translated as "power." It is the word from which we get the English word *dynamite*. The Holy Spirit is shown to be the Spirit of power.

Earlier, we studied the threefold office of Christ—Prophet, Priest, and King. All those were offices of mediators, and they were *charismatic* offices. They were not the only charismatic offices; the judges, who preceded the kings in Israelite history, were also charismatic leaders. The term *charismatic* comes from the Greek *charisma*, which has to do with giftedness. Those who were uniquely gifted were anointed by the Holy Spirit. The Spirit of God came upon Samson, for example, and he was empowered to do mighty feats. The same was true of Gideon and the prophets; the Holy Spirit came upon them and empowered them for ministry. The Holy Spirit also anointed the priests and the kings so that they could perform their work.

The most gifted person in the Old Testament was Moses, who received empowerment to lead God's people out of Egypt. But Moses foresaw a better day, when all of God's people would be anointed by His Spirit. At one point in the Old Testament, after God had miraculously delivered the Israelites from Egypt, the people began to complain that they had nothing to eat except manna, the bread from heaven that God had provided for them in the desert. They began to pine for

---

* For more on the activity of the Holy Spirit, see R.C. Sproul, *The Mystery of the Holy Spirit* (repr., Fearn, Ross-shire, England: Christian Focus, 2009).

the "the cucumbers, the melons, the leeks, the onions, and the garlic" (Num. 11:5) they had enjoyed when they were slaves in Egypt. Their complaints displeased Moses, and he, too, began to complain: "I am not able to carry all this people alone; the burden is too heavy for me. If you will treat me like this, kill me at once, if I find favor in your sight, that I may not see my wretchedness" (vv. 14–15). God chose not to kill Moses; rather, He provided help for him:

> Then the LORD said to Moses, "Gather for me seventy men of the elders of Israel, whom you know to be the elders of the people and officers over them, and bring them to the tent of meeting, and let them take their stand there with you. And I will come down and talk with you there. And I will take some of the Spirit that is on you and put it on them, and they shall bear the burden of the people with you, so that you may not bear it yourself alone." (vv. 16–17)

So God gave the same Spirit anointing to seventy elders that He had previously given only to Moses. But in that context, Moses said, "Would that all the LORD's people were prophets, that the LORD would put his Spirit on them!" (Num. 11:29).

Just because people in the Old Testament were anointed by the Holy Spirit and empowered to do certain tasks did not mean that they had been born of the Holy Spirit. They were not necessarily believers. We see the Holy Spirit come upon King Saul and later *depart* from him. We see the anointing of Balaam and of others who inadvertently gave prophecies under the power and inspiration of the Holy Spirit, but those individuals were not necessarily believers. In the Old Testament, the anointing of the Holy Spirit was a special gift given mostly to believers, but not only to believers. And the anointing of the Spirit was not the same as the gift of rebirth.

We do see some parallels in this regard between the Old Testament and the New Testament. In the Old Testament, the Spirit's empowering was given only to isolated individuals—the prophets, the priests, the kings, the judges, and the artists and craftsmen who were called by God to fashion the furnishings and decorations for the tabernacle. The first time we read of the Holy Spirit filling people, it was the craftsmen, the artists who were uniquely gifted by the Spirit for their work (Ex. 28:3). The critical point is that not everyone in the camp, not every believer, had this gift. It was limited. But Moses hoped that would change. That is exactly what happened at Pentecost in the New Testament (Acts 2).

Chapter 32

THE HOLY SPIRIT
IN THE NEW TESTAMENT

When God created human beings, He did not simply create inert statues, as an artist does when he rearranges stones or clay. When God finished forming the figure He made from the dust, He condescended to breathe into it so that man became a living *ruah*, a living spirit (Gen. 2:7; 1 Cor. 15:45). God breathed His own life into the man. That is one of the great mysteries—life itself.

From the Bible, we know that the source of life is the Holy Spirit. Paul said that in God we live, move, and have our being (Act 17:28). Even a pagan cannot breathe without the power of the Holy Spirit. Although the Bible speaks of Christ being conceived in the womb of Mary through the power of the Holy Spirit, in a more *general* sense no one is conceived in the womb except by the Holy Spirit.

THE SPIRIT OF LIFE

In both Hebrew and Greek, we find a play on words with regard to *spirit*. The Greek word *pneuma*, which is translated as "spirit," is also translated as "wind" or "breath." There is a close link between the Spirit of God and the breath of life. However, the chief concern in the New Testament with the relationship of the Holy Spirit to life is not the original creation of life but the creative energy necessary for spiritual life. Christ said, "I came that they may have life and have it abundantly" (John 10:10). There Christ was not speaking about *bios*, a Greek word for "life" or "living things." Christ used a different word, *zōē*, because He was referring to a particular quality or kind of life, the living spiritual life that only God can bring to those who are spiritually dead. Jesus addressed those words to people who were biologically alive but spiritually dead, to those whose vital signs were functioning but who were dead to the things of God.

Christ as the Redeemer came to give us life, and the person of the Trinity who applies the redemptive work of Christ to our lives is the Holy Spirit. So as we look at the work of the Trinity, we note that God the Father initiated the plan of redemption; Christ performed all that was necessary to effect our redemption; and the Holy Spirit applies Christ's work to us and makes it ours by imparting new life to dead souls, which theologians call "regeneration." The New Testament emphasizes that regeneration is the function of the Holy Spirit.

What is regeneration? The prefix *re-* means "again." So, regeneration is a repetition of something original. We can repaint a house, but doing so implies that it has already been painted at least once before. Just so, regeneration can occur only if there has been a prior generation.

In biblical terms, the prior generation is man's physical birth, but although man is born physically alive, he is born spiritually dead. We are born in a state of corruption. Paul wrote:

> And you were dead in the trespasses and sins in which you once walked, following the course of this world, following the prince of the power of the air, the spirit that is now at work in the sons of disobedience—among whom we all once lived in the passions of our flesh, carrying out the desires of the body and the mind, and were by nature children of wrath, like the rest of mankind. (Eph. 2:1–3)

Paul is not speaking of physical death here. The death to which he refers is spiritual death. What Paul teaches here is antithetical to the popular view of the relationship between God and people that per-meates our society and even our churches—the idea that we all are children of God by nature. Many believe that all people are part of God's family; but no one is born a Christian. One can be born into a godly family, but he is not born a Christian. Everyone is born as a child of wrath. By nature we are alienated from God, at enmity with Him, and dead in our sin.

Since we are naturally dead to the things of God, the only way to become a Christian is through the work of the Holy Spirit, who makes us spiritually alive. In Ephesians 2, Paul is writing about regeneration, the resurrection of the human spirit from spiritual death. When Nico-demus, a ruler of the Jews, came to Jesus, he said, "Rabbi, we know that you are a teacher come from God, for no one can do these signs that you do unless God is with him" (John 3:2). Nicodemus demonstrated sound judgment there, but he still did not understand who Jesus was. So Jesus told him, "Truly, truly, I say to you, unless one is born again he cannot see the kingdom of God" (v. 3). Nicodemus continued to ques-tion Jesus' teaching, so Jesus said to him, "Are you the teacher of Israel and yet you do not understand these things?" (v. 10). As a member of the Sanhedrin, a Pharisee, Nicodemus was a theologian, and he should have known these things, for they were taught in the Old Testament Scriptures. In other words, Jesus was not introducing a new idea here. It is not as though people in the Old Testament era were saved apart from regeneration. Abraham had to be born of the Holy Spirit, as did David and everyone who has ever been redeemed. Regeneration is an absolute requirement for salvation.

This is why it is redundant to use the phrase "born-again Chris-tian." What other kind of Christian is there? According to Jesus, there are no non-born-again Christians. The reason people use the expres-sion today is to distinguish true believers from those who claim one can be redeemed without being regenerated. Regeneration is a central role of the Spirit of God in both the Old Testament and the New Tes-tament. The Spirit is the One who creates new genesis, who gives us spiritual birth.

HOLY NURTURER

Not only does the Holy Spirit regenerate us, but He also is the principal nurturer of Christians. The New Testament emphasizes the role of the Holy Spirit in sanctification. He is the One who shapes us into conformity with the image of Christ and nurtures us to spiritual maturity. So not only does the Spirit quicken us, imparting to us faith and spiritual life so that we become justified, but He also nurtures those whom He has raised from spiritual death throughout their lives—leading, influencing, and working within them to bring about the actual transformation of their character from sinners to saints.

Notice that it is the Spirit to whom the title "Holy" is attached. In Scripture, it is clear that holiness is an attribute that belongs equally to each member of the Trinity, but it is specifically attributed to the Spirit because of His ministry, His concentrated function in the plan of redemption. He is the One whom God sends to make us holy.

In stages—beginning with our regeneration and continuing throughout our lives in the process of sanctification, until it culminates in our glorification—the Holy Spirit accomplishes His work. The Holy Spirit initiates the crucial change in our character, then He nurtures it during our lives and finishes it at the end. His ministry is multifaceted. He was there in the original creation, and He is the power of re-creation. He was there in the original giving of life, and He is there in the imparting of spiritual life. He is there in sanctification, and He will be there in glorification.

HOLY TEACHER

Additionally, the Holy Spirit empowered people in the Old Testament. He is the One who inspired sacred Scripture, the writing of the Bible. And not only did He inspire the original record of Scripture, He also illumines it: "No one comprehends the thoughts of God except the Spirit of God," Paul tells us (1 Cor. 2:11), so the Holy Spirit helps us understand Scripture by shedding light into our dark minds. He is our supreme teacher of the truth of God. He is the One who convicts us of sin and of righteousness. He is our Paraclete, the helper whom Christ promised to give to His church.

———•———

Chapter 33

THE PARACLETE

A central point in one of Jesus' discourses is hate. We are accustomed to the centrality of love in the teaching of Jesus, but in His Upper Room Discourse, Jesus talked about the hatred the world has for Him. Because of that hatred, Jesus was zealous to alert His disciples to what they should expect from the world: "If the world hates you, know that it has hated me before it hated you. If you were of the world, the world would love you as its own; but because you are not of the world, but I chose you out of the world, therefore the world hates you" (John 15:18–19). Jesus then went on to speak about persecution.

But earlier in that discourse, Jesus had provided His disciples with a promise of divine assistance in the midst of persecution and all the trials of the Christian life—the Comforter, or Paraclete, whom He would send to be with His people in the midst of a hostile world.

ANOTHER

Christ introduced the Paraclete this way: "I will ask the Father, and he will give you *another* Helper [Paraclete], to be with you forever" (John 14:16; emphasis mine). Notice that the Holy Spirit is introduced as "another" Paraclete. Obviously, for there to be another Paraclete, there had to have been at least one previous Paraclete. So the Greek word *paraklētos*, or Paraclete, belongs in the first instance not to the Holy Spirit but to Jesus Himself. In the New Testament, Jesus is revealed as the Paraclete, and the Holy Spirit is the second Paraclete, another Paraclete alongside of Jesus. There is great significance to this, not only as it relates to Jesus, but also as it relates to the person and the work of the Holy Spirit.

In His discourse, Jesus said:

> If I had not done among them the works that no one else did, they would not be guilty of sin, but now they have seen and hated both me and my Father. But the word that is written in their Law must be fulfilled: "They hated me without a cause."
>
> But when the Helper comes, whom I will send to you from the Father, the Spirit of truth, who proceeds from the Father, he will bear witness about me. And you also will bear witness, because you have been with me from the beginning.
>
> I have said all these things to you to keep you from falling away. They will put you out of the synagogues. Indeed, the hour is coming when whoever kills you will think he is offering service to God. And they will do these things because they have not known the Father, nor me. But I have said these things to you, that when their hour comes you may remember that I told them to you. (John 15:24–16:4)

Another Comforter

The context for Jesus' discussion about the sending of the Comforter, the Holy Spirit, is hatred and anticipated persecution. Historically, the ministry of the Holy Spirit has been associated with comfort, and we give Him the title "Comforter." This is an aspect in which we miss something significant about the Spirit's ministry.

The nineteenth-century philosopher Friedrich Nietzsche was quite critical of the impact of Christianity on Western civilization. He declared that God was dead, having died of pity. Nietzsche abhorred what he considered to be the ethic of weakness propagated by the Christian church in Western Europe, with its emphasis on humility, patience, and kindness. He said that authentic humanity is found only in "the superman" who expresses "the will to power." An authentic person, according to Nietzsche, is one who, in the final analysis, is a conqueror. He called for an ethic of strength and machismo. Adolf Hitler passed out copies of Nietzsche's books as Christmas presents to his henchmen before his rise to power in Germany.

Just as Nietzsche misunderstood the Christian ethic, our culture has greatly misunderstood Jesus' reference to the Holy Spirit as another Paraclete, another Comforter. When we think of someone who brings comfort, we have in mind one who ministers to us in the midst of pain, one who dries the tears from our eyes and gives consolation when we are downcast. But that is not what Jesus had in mind. Of course, the New Testament does teach that God brings consolation to His people. In fact, the birth of Christ was heralded as the appearance of "the consolation of Israel" (Luke 2:25), so I do not mean to suggest that the Holy Spirit does not minister to us in our pain and affliction. He is indeed the One who gives us the peace that surpasses all understanding (Phil. 4:7), but that is not the idea that Jesus is addressing here.

The word *paraklētos* comes from Greek culture. The prefix *para-* means "alongside of," which we find in English words such as *parachurch*, *paralegal*, and *paramedic*. You'll recall that we noted earlier how someone or something that is *para* is alongside something else. The root of the word *paraklētos* comes from the verb *kaleō*, which means "to call." So *paraklētos* literally means someone who is called to come alongside of someone else. In the Greek culture, a paraclete was a family attorney who came to defend family members accused of wrongdoing. The paraclete was the defender, the strengthener, to assist people in times of trouble.

Another Advocate

John used the same Greek word, *paraklētos*, in his first epistle, but most translations do not render it as "comforter" or "helper"; they translate it as "advocate": "But if anyone does sin, we have an advocate

184

[*paraklētos*] with the Father, Jesus Christ the righteous" (1 John 2:1). That is why we say that Christ was the original Paraclete. We do not think of Him as our Advocate, but we should. An "advocate" had specific reference to an attorney, someone who would plead for another, and that is the imagery we find in the New Testament with respect to Jesus. The wonder is that Jesus is both our Judge and our Advocate. When we go on trial before almighty God, Christ will be sitting on the bench as Judge, and as we enter that courtroom, we will discover that the Judge is also our Attorney. Jesus Christ is our Advocate, our Paraclete, who will defend us before the Father.

We also need a defender in the midst of this hostile world. That is why, in the midst of His discourse about hatred, persecution, and affliction, Jesus promised to send another Advocate. He promised the Holy Spirit, who will be our family attorney, there for us on permanent retainer. He will be there to encourage us, to defend us, and to strengthen us in the heat of the battle. The image of the Comforter is not of One who comes to dry our tears *after* the battle but of One who comes to give us strength and courage *for* the battle.

That is precisely where the term *Comforter* is misunderstood today. Language undergoes small changes as time passes. During the Elizabethan era, the word *comforter* was closely tied to its Latin roots: *cum*, which means "with," and *forte*, which means "strength." Originally the word *comfort* meant "with strength," not "consolation." So Jesus was telling those who would face adversity and hatred not to be discouraged because He was going to send another Comforter to strengthen them in the midst of it.

SANCTIFIER

Paul wrote that in Christ we are more than conquerors (Rom. 8:37). The word he used was *hypernikōmen*, which in Latin is *supervincemus*—"superconquerors." We cannot help but think of Nietzsche when we read that. He wanted conquerors. Well, true conquerors are those developed by the Holy Spirit.

One of the key ways He strengthens us for confrontation with the world is with truth. Later in the Upper Room Discourse, Jesus said:

I still have many things to say to you, but you cannot bear them now. When the Spirit of truth comes, he will guide you into all the truth, for he will not speak on his own authority, but whatever he hears he will speak, and he will declare to you the things that are to come. He will glorify me, for he will take what is mine and declare it to you. All that the Father has is mine; therefore I said that he will take what is mine and declare it to you. (John 16:12–15)

We see here again that the ministry of the Holy Spirit is to apply the work of Christ to His people, and He does this by sanctifying us, by revealing the truth of God to us, and by coming to us in strength. Jesus' Upper Room Discourse (John 14–17) is an extremely important portion of the New Testament. It is the final teaching session Jesus had with His disciples on the night in which He was betrayed, the eve of His execution. In these four chapters of John's gospel, we are given more information about the person and work of the Holy Spirit than we get in all the rest of the New Testament.

Jesus was preparing His disciples for His imminent departure and ministering to them in their fear:

These things I have spoken to you while I am still with you. But the Helper, the Holy Spirit, whom the Father will send in my name, he will teach you all things and bring to your remembrance all that I have said to you. Peace I leave with you; my peace I give to you. Not as the world gives do I give to you. Let not your hearts be troubled, neither let them be afraid. (John 14:25–27)

They had been strengthened and encouraged by His presence, but He was going away. Yet they were not left to fend for themselves. The

Holy Spirit would be with them to speak truth, to encourage them, and to cause them to be faithful in the midst of trouble. Christ kept this promise on the Day of Pentecost, when He sent the Holy Spirit to His people, the church. Therefore, when the persecution came, the church of Christ blossomed. His people were consciously aware of the strength that Christ had given them to stand against a hostile world.

Chapter 34

THE BAPTISM
OF THE HOLY SPIRIT

More books have been written on the person and work of the Holy Spirit in the last fifty years than in all of the previous Christian history combined. This tremendous outpouring of literature is due in large part to the so-called charismatic movement, which began in the nineteenth century and then crossed over into mainline denominations in the middle of the twentieth century.

PENTECOSTALISM

The roots of the charismatic movement are found in Pentecostalism and its doctrine and teaching concerning the baptism of the Holy Spirit. In original Pentecostal theology, the baptism of the Holy Spirit and the phenomenon of speaking in tongues were linked to a unique doctrine of sanctification, a kind of perfectionism expressed as "the second blessing" or "the second work of grace." These Pentecostals believed that the first work of grace was conversion, but that there was an equally dramatic second work of the Spirit by which one could have complete sanctification in this life. The thinking was that someone who experienced this second blessing was rendered perfect with respect to spiritual obedience, which is how the movement came to be called "perfectionism." Over the years, Pentecostals have espoused different degrees and types of perfectionism.

Over time, Pentecostal doctrine has crossed denominational boundaries and made an impact on virtually every denomination. There has been an attempt to integrate the theology of the baptism of the Holy Spirit with historic Christianity, which has resulted in neo-Pentecostal theology. The chief difference between older Pentecostalism and neo-Pentecostalism involves the baptism of the Holy Spirit. Neo-Pentecostals do not consider the Spirit's baptism to be a second work of grace for purposes of sanctification. Rather, it is a divine operation of the Spirit designed to gift and empower people for ministry. In that regard, it fits more closely with the New Testament concept of the function of the Spirit.

Yet there is disagreement among the various parties of neo-Pentecostal theology. Many today still believe that the indispensable sign that one has received the baptism of the Holy Spirit is speaking in tongues. They claim that those who do not speak in tongues have not received the baptism. Others believe that tongues-speaking may or may not accompany the experience of the Spirit's baptism. However, all neo-Pentecostals believe that there is a time gap between conversion to Christ and the reception of the baptism of the Holy Spirit. In other words, one can be a Christian and yet not have the baptism of the Holy Spirit. They believe that every Christian has the possibility of being baptized in the Spirit, but not all have received it.

The biblical justification for this idea of a temporal gap between conversion and baptism in the Spirit is found in the book of Acts, chiefly the account of the day of Pentecost. In Acts 2 we read:

When the day of Pentecost arrived, they were all together in one place. And suddenly there came from heaven a sound like a mighty rushing wind, and it filled the entire house where they were sitting. And divided tongues as of fire appeared to them and rested on each one of them. And they were all filled with the Holy Spirit and began to speak in other tongues as the Spirit gave them utterance. . . . And all were amazed and perplexed, saying to one another, "What does this mean?" (vv. 1–4, 12)

Luke includes in his narrative not only a description of what happened but also an explanation of this strange phenomenon. The narrative continues:

> But others mocking said, "They are filled with new wine."
> But Peter, standing with the eleven, lifted up his voice and addressed them: "Men of Judea and all who dwell in Jerusalem, let this be known to you, and give ear to my words. For these people are not drunk, as you suppose, since it is only the third hour of the day. But this is what was uttered through the prophet Joel:
> "'And in the last days it shall be, God declares, that I will pour out my Spirit on all flesh, and your sons and your daughters shall prophesy, and your young men shall see visions, and your old men shall dream dreams; even on my male servants and female servants in those days I will pour out my Spirit, and they shall prophesy.'" (vv. 13–18)

When Peter interpreted the meaning of these events on the Day of Pentecost, he pointed the people to the Old Testament prophecy of Joel, where Joel preached about the future coming of the kingdom of God, at which time God would pour out His Holy Spirit on all flesh.

POURED OUT ON ALL FLESH

We noted in an earlier chapter that the anointing of the Spirit was restricted in the Old Testament to certain individuals such as Moses, yet God distributed the Spirit to seventy elders in the community, who then began to prophesy (Num. 11:24–25). When Joshua heard the elders prophesying, he told Moses to forbid it, but Moses replied, "Are you jealous for my sake? Would that all the LORD's people were prophets, that the LORD would put his Spirit on them!" (v. 29). Moses wished that God would give His Spirit to all the people of the community, and he prayed for that.

When we get to Joel, the prayer of Moses has become a prophecy.

Joel says that the time will come when God will pour out His Spirit on the whole of God's people. There will be no more haves and have-nots. We see in the book of Acts that Peter viewed the events of Pentecost as the fulfillment of Joel's prophecy, which is completely contrary to the idea that God gives His Spirit to some believers but not to all, as Pentecostals have taught.

The people who were gathered on Pentecost were Jewish believers from many provinces. They had assembled to celebrate the Old Testament feast of Pentecost, and when the Spirit fell upon the Jewish believers, He fell on *all of them*. Every one of those Jewish believers received the outpouring of the Holy Spirit. Pentecost marked a new epoch in God's plan of redemption.

We see three additional episodes in the book of Acts that we can think of as "mini-Pentecosts." In Acts 8, we read of the giving of the Holy Spirit to the Samaritan believers:

> Now when the apostles at Jerusalem heard that Samaria had received the word of God, they sent to them Peter and John, who came down and prayed for them that they might receive the Holy Spirit, for he had not yet fallen on any of them, but they had only been baptized in the name of the Lord Jesus. Then they laid their hands on them and they received the Holy Spirit. (vv. 14–17)

That passage is used to support the idea of a time gap between conversion and receiving the Spirit, and it certainly was the case for the Samaritan believers. They had believed in Jesus, but they had not yet received the Holy Spirit.

Then, in Acts 10, we see what happened in Cornelius' household:

> While Peter was still saying these things, the Holy Spirit fell on all who heard the word. And the believers from among the circumcised who had come with Peter were amazed, because the gift of the Holy Spirit was poured out even on the Gentiles.

For they were hearing them speaking in tongues and extolling God. (vv. 44–46)

Peter was visiting Cornelius, who is identified in Acts as a God-fearer, a Gentile believer who had converted to Judaism but had remained uncircumcised. Peter was at Cornelius' house when the Holy Spirit fell upon these God-fearing Gentiles. Peter then directed that the Gentiles be baptized: "Then Peter declared, 'Can anyone withhold water for baptizing these people, who have received the Holy Spirit just as we have?' And he commanded them to be baptized in the name of Jesus Christ" (vv. 46–48). These God-fearers were to be grafted into the New Testament church; they were to be full members of the new covenant community because God had given them the Spirit. Later, in Acts 19, we see something similar take place with the Ephesian Christians. They also receive the Holy Spirit.

So there are four accounts of outpourings of the Holy Spirit in the book of Acts. There are two important things to note about these outpourings. First, all who were present as believers in these episodes received the Holy Spirit. Second, Luke describes four distinct groups of people: the Jews, the Samaritans, the God-fearers, and the Gentiles. From the book of Acts and the epistles of the Apostle Paul, we learn that one of the biggest controversies in the opening years of the Christian church was the place of Gentiles the body of Christ. Gentiles were aliens to the commonwealth of Israel and strangers to the Old Testament covenant, and because of that, partial membership had been given to God-fearers, absolutely no membership had been given to Samaritans, and the Gentiles were considered outside the camp. So as the gospel was preached to these groups, the issue arose as to what should be done with those among them who became believers. Were they to have full membership in the body of Christ?

If we look at the literary structure and progress of the book of Acts, we see that Luke traces the expansion of the Apostolic church, beginning with the Jews and radiating out to all nations, just as Christ traced it out in His parting words to the disciples: "But you will receive power when the Holy Spirit has come upon you, and you will be my witnesses in Jerusalem and in all Judea and Samaria, and to the end of the earth" (Acts 1:8).

That is how the book of Acts unfolds. As each segment is touched—Samaritans, God-fearers, and Gentiles—God verifies their inclusion with full privileges and membership in the New Testament church by giving them the Holy Spirit.

My problem with Pentecostal theology is that it has a low view of Pentecost. The significance that the New Testament gives to Pentecost is that the outpouring of the Holy Spirit is to the whole church and therefore to every believer. As Paul writes, "For in one Spirit we were all baptized into one body—Jews or Greeks, slaves or free—and all were made to drink of one Spirit" (1 Cor. 12:13). The biblical doctrine has no room, in my judgment, for a concept of Christians who have the baptism of the Holy Spirit and Christians who do not have it. The baptism comes with conversion. It is not the same thing as conversion, but the principle is that all Christians receive the baptism of the Holy Spirit.

Chapter 35

THE GIFTS OF THE SPIRIT

Much debate ensues when the topic of the gifts of the Holy Spirit is introduced, especially the gift of speaking in tongues. Certain questions about the gifts make a dogmatic position difficult to reach.

For example, was the *glossolalia*, or speaking in tongues, that occurred in the Corinthian church (described in 1 Cor. 12–14) identical to what happened at Pentecost? The tacit assumption is that they are one and the same, but some scholars have indicated that perhaps, at least at Pentecost, the miracle was not so much in the *speaking* as it was in the *hearing*; that is, it was a miracle of translation. At Pentecost, those gathered from different backgrounds and regions were able to understand the utterances of the Jews in the assembly. The Bible is not explicit about it, so it remains a matter of speculation. A related question is whether what occurred in the Corinthian community was miraculous, and, if so, whether the speaking in tongues that is reported today is equally miraculous, or whether people have a natural ability to speak unintelligibly under the influence of the Holy Spirit. The debate continues.

Another question associated with the gifts, particularly tongues, is whether God intended them to continue through Christian history. There is exceedingly sparse evidence for that. The annals of church history rarely mention the occurrence of tongues. Some argue that this relative silence has eschatological significance. The idea comes from "the early rain" and "the latter rain" prophesied in Joel 2:23. According to this view, "the early rain" was the outpouring of the Spirit on the first-century church, and today's revival of tongues speaking is "the latter rain," a harbinger of the final moments of redemptive history before Christ's return.

There is also the question of whether speaking in tongues is a necessary indicator that one has been baptized in the Holy Spirit.

PAUL'S TEACHING TO THE CORINTHIANS

The most lengthy discussion of the gifts of the Spirit is found in 1 Corinthians 12–14. One of the most popular chapters in all of the Bible is 1 Corinthians 13, which we call "the love chapter," but it is popular mainly because it is so often taken out of context. The Apostle Paul's discourse on the supremacy of love in 1 Corinthians 13 begins this way: "If I speak in the tongues of men and of angels, but have not love, I am a noisy gong or a clanging cymbal" (1 Cor. 13:1). However, this chapter is part of a broader discourse that begins in chapter 12: "Now concerning spiritual gifts, brothers, I do not want you to be uninformed" (v. 1). Paul desires that God's people be knowledgeable about spiritual gifts and use them accordingly. The Corinthian church was one of the most troubled churches that Paul dealt with in his ministry. There were internal disputes and forms of misbehavior that occasioned at least two Apostolic letters filled with rebuke and admonition. At the end of the first century, Clement, the bishop of Rome, wrote a letter to the Corinthian church to address these same problems, which apparently had not been resolved. In his letter, he reminded the Corinthians of Paul's Apostolic instruction:

> You know that when you were pagans you were led astray to mute idols, however you were led. Therefore I want you to understand that no one speaking in the Spirit of God ever says "Jesus is accursed!" and no one can say "Jesus is Lord" except in the Holy Spirit. (1 Cor. 12:2–3)

Paul then launches into instruction about the gifts:

Now there are varieties of gifts, but the same Spirit; and there are varieties of service, but the same Lord; and there are varieties of activities, but it is the same God who empowers them all in everyone. To each is given the manifestation of the Spirit for the common good. For to one is given through the Spirit the utterance of wisdom, and to another the utterance of knowledge according to the same Spirit, to another faith by the same Spirit, to another gifts of healing by the one Spirit, to another the working of miracles, to another prophecy, to another the ability to distinguish between spirits, to another various kinds of tongues, to another the interpretation of tongues. All these are empowered by one and the same Spirit, who apportions to each one individually as he wills. (vv. 4–11)

A DIVERSITY OF GIFTS

There is no reason to believe that Paul's list of spiritual gifts is exhaustive. He was making the point that the Spirit gives numerous and diverse gifts to the people of God. So the first thing we learn about the gifts of the Holy Spirit is that they are diverse. Paul also teaches that the purpose of the gifts is the edification of the whole body. In the context of this discussion of spiritual gifts, Paul gives us rich insight into the very nature of the church. Christ had created a church and given her these gifts of the Holy Spirit to edify and strengthen the whole body.

Paul continues: "For just as the body is one and has many members, and all the members of the body, though many, are one body, so it is with Christ. For in one Spirit we were all baptized into one body—Jews or Greeks, slaves or free—and all were made to drink of one Spirit" (vv. 12–13). This is didactic information on the baptism of the Holy Spirit. Paul's theme here is that all the members of the church of God, both Jew and Gentile, have been empowered by the Holy Spirit for ministry.

This text formed the root of a Reformation principle—the priesthood

THE GIFTS OF THE SPIRIT

of all believers. This principle was important to Martin Luther, and because of his emphasis on it, many believed he was seeking to get rid of the clergy. That was not the case. Luther's point was that even though certain individuals hold the office of pastor, elder, or deacon, the ministry of the church is not restricted to a handful of professionals. The whole body has been equipped by the Holy Spirit to participate in the mission of the church.

ONE BODY

It is significant that when Paul discusses the gifts of the Spirit, he does it in the context of the church and follows the metaphor of the church as the body of Christ. The church is organized and has diverse parts, just like the human body has diverse parts. Paul labors the point that each portion of the body of Christ has a specific task to perform and has been given the ability to do that task in order to help meet the full mission of the church, just as the individual parts of the human body have specific functions to fulfill for the well-being of the whole body:

> For the body does not consist of one member but of many. If the foot should say, "Because I am not a hand, I do not belong to the body," that would not make it any less a part of the body. And if the ear should say, "Because I am not an eye, I do not belong to the body," that would not make it any less a part of the body. If the whole body were an eye, where would be the sense of hearing? If the whole body were an ear, where would be the sense of smell? But as it is, God arranged the members in the body, each one of them, as he chose. If all were a single member, where would the body be? As it is, there are many parts, yet one body. (vv. 14–19)

Paul here is using an old form of argument, the *reductio ad absurdum* argument, which takes human reasoning to its logical conclusion and shows that the results are absurd. He is addressing those who wanted to make the gift of tongues the supreme test of spirituality in the life of the church. Paul is saying, "If you want to make tongues the only significant gift, that is no different than saying that the whole body should be an eye. That would give us acute vision, but we would be deaf and dumb."

Paul continues: "Now you are the body of Christ and individually members of it. And God has appointed in the church first apostles, second prophets, third teachers, then miracles, then gifts of healing, helping, administrating, and various kinds of tongues" (vv. 27–28). It is significant that the gift of tongues is mentioned last in a list that begins with Apostles, because the Apostolic office was the chief office of authority in the New Testament.

Paul then asks rhetorically, "Are all apostles?" (v. 29). According to the structure of the Greek here, the only answer that can be given is no. "Are all prophets?" The answer again must be no. "Are all teachers?" The answer must be no. "Do all work miracles?" Again, the answer grammatically must be no. "Do all possess gifts of healing? Do all speak with tongues?" (vv. 29–30). According to the structure of the Greek here, the answer is obvious. So it is clear that not everyone in the body of Christ has been gifted with tongues. Later Paul expresses an Apostolic desire that all would speak in tongues (14:5), but not everyone does.

THE GIFT OF PROPHECY

He goes on: "But earnestly desire the higher gifts. And I will show you a still more excellent way" (12:31). Those are the words that immediately precede the beginning of chapter 13: "If I speak in the tongues of men and of angels, but have not love, I am a noisy gong or a clanging cymbal" (13:1). The Apostle makes clear that the gift of love is far more important to the people of God than these more spectacular gifts: "Love never ends. As for prophecies, they will pass away; as for tongues, they will cease; as for knowledge, it will pass away. For we know in part and we prophesy in part, but when the perfect comes, the partial will pass away" (vv. 8–10).

We get the crux of his instruction at the beginning of chapter 14:

"Pursue love, and earnestly desire the spiritual gifts, especially that you may prophesy" (v. 1). What does the Apostle mean by "prophesy"? Is he using this term in the specific sense of being an agent of revelation, as was the case with Old Testament prophets and the New Testament Apostles? I do not think so, and the vast majority of New Testament commentaries argue that when Paul encourages people to prophesy, he has in mind the ability to articulate the truth of God. The preacher preaching and the individual Christian bearing witness to his faith are prophetic actions, but not in the sense of giving new revelation to the community of God, as the Old Testament prophets did. Even in the Old Testament, a distinction was made between *fore*-telling and *forth*-telling. The primary accent is not on future prediction but on speaking forth the truth of God, and I believe this is what Paul is encouraging people to do.

THE GIFT OF TONGUES

One argument that Paul's teaching about tongues here in 1 Corinthians is different from what occurred at Pentecost is that he seems to suggest that tongues-speaking is a kind of prayer language:

> For one who speaks in a tongue speaks not to men but to God; for no one understands him, but he utters mysteries in the Spirit. On the other hand, the one who prophesies speaks to people for their upbuilding and encouragement and consolation. The one who speaks in a tongue builds up himself, but the one who prophesies builds up the church. Now I want you all to speak in tongues, but even more to prophesy. The one who prophesies is greater than the one who speaks in tongues, unless someone interprets, so that the church may be built up.
>
> Now, brothers, if I come to you speaking in tongues, how will I benefit you unless I bring you some revelation or knowledge or prophecy or teaching? (14:2–6)

In other words, Paul is saying that there is no profit to the people of God without the intelligible content of the truth of God being communicated to the people. The problem with tongues, then and now, is that they are unintelligible, which makes many scholars of the New Testament believe that the contemporary phenomenon of tongues is simply the human ability to experience ecstatic utterance under the influence of the Holy Spirit. This is not to deny that people are communicating with the Holy Spirit when they engage in this activity; it is simply that it does not require a miraculous enabling in order to do it.

A problem we face with the phenomenon of tongues is that there are manifold records of the practice among pagan religions and cults such as Mormonism. There are many who deny the deity of Christ and yet claim to have this ability, and there is no discernible difference between what they are doing and what Christians are doing in their prayer life under the influence of the Holy Spirit.

Paul continues by giving strict instructions for how the gift of tongues was to be used in the early church. He places the accent on order rather than on disorder, and he instructs that gatherings are not to be interrupted by tongues unless there is an interpreter present, someone who can make it intelligible. Great sensitivity is to be exercised when an unbeliever comes into the meeting and has no idea what is going on.

In sum, Paul does not say that tongues are bad and prophecy is good. His distinction is not between the good and the bad but between the good and the better. Tongues are fine, but prophecy is better. He is saying, "It is fine if you want to pray in tongues, but desire the higher gifts of the Spirit for the edification of the church." The great warning for us today is to not exalt this particular gift—even if what occurs now is the same thing that happened in the Corinthian community—to the level of a sign of super-spirituality or of special empowerment by God.

Chapter 36

———•———

THE FRUIT OF THE SPIRIT

Our interest is piqued when something unusual, extraordinary, or spectacular takes place in our midst. Christians are particularly drawn to extraordinary manifestations of the presence of God. Because of this tendency within us to gravitate toward the exciting, we tend to focus more on the gifts of the Holy Spirit than on the fruit of the Spirit. Yet it is the chief goal of the Holy Spirit to apply the fruits of the gospel in order to fulfill God's mandate: "This is the will of God, your sanctification" (1 Thess. 4:3).

The greatest sign of a believer's progress in the things of God is not a spectacular manifestation of his gifts, whatever those gifts may be. Someone can be a gifted preacher or teacher, yet show little evidence of growth in spiritual maturity. We are going to be evaluated at the end of our lives not by the number of gifts we display or by the talents God has given to us, but by how much fruit we have borne as Christians.

WALK BY THE SPIRIT

Paul discusses the fruit of the Spirit in his letter to the Galatians, and he begins his discussion this way: "But I say, walk by the Spirit" (Gal. 5:16). This is an Apostolic mandate. As Christians, we are called to walk by the Spirit. That does not mean our primary task is to pursue mysticism or shortcuts to spirituality. Over the years, countless students have asked me, "Dr. Sproul, how can I become more spiritual?" or "How can I become more gifted?" I have heard only one student ask, "How can I become more righteous?" Yet Jesus Himself said, "Seek first the kingdom of God and his righteousness, and all these things will be added to you" (Matt. 6:33). We are called to demonstrate spiritual growth, to walk in the Spirit of God, and this demonstration is not seen in the manifestation of the gifts but in the fruit of the Holy Spirit.

SARX

Paul continues: "Walk by the Spirit, and you will not gratify the desires of the flesh. For the desires of the flesh are against the Spirit, and the desires of the Spirit are against the flesh, for these are opposed to each other, to keep you from doing the things you want to do. But if you are led by the Spirit, you are not under the law" (Gal. 5:16–18). Paul here gives a contrast between flesh and spirit. The Greek word translated here as "flesh" is *sarx*, and the word rendered as "spirit" is *pneuma*. The word *sōma*, which is usually translated "body," sometimes functions as a synonym for *sarx*; in other words, sometimes the term *sarx* simply refers to the physical character or nature of our body.

However, the New Testament often speaks of our corrupt nature, our fallenness, as *sarx*. Paul, on one occasion, said, "Even though we once regarded Christ according to the flesh, we regard him thus no longer" (2 Cor. 5:16). The phrase used here, *kata sarka*, means "after the flesh" or "according to the flesh." He was saying that he had previously viewed Christ from an ungodly, worldly perspective. Earlier, Jesus said, "That which is born of the flesh is flesh, and that which is born of the Spirit is spirit" (John 3:6). He was not talking about our physical bodies but about our fallen nature, which includes not only our bodies but also our minds, our wills, and our hearts.

So when we encounter the word *sarx* in the New Testament, how do we know whether it is referring to our fallen human nature or to our physical capacities? In general, any time we see *sarx*, or "flesh," discussed in direct contrast to *pneuma*, or "spirit," what is being discussed is not the difference between the physical body and the spirit, but the difference between the corrupt, fallen nature and the new, regenerate man. That is clearly the case in Galatians 5.

ROTTEN FRUIT

Before Paul explains what it means to be led by the Spirit and details for us the fruit of the Spirit, he shows us what the fruit of the Spirit is *not*:

> Now the works of the flesh are evident: sexual immorality, impurity, sensuality, idolatry, sorcery, enmity, strife, jealousy, fits of anger, rivalries, dissensions, divisions, envy, drunkenness, orgies, and things like these. I warn you, as I warned you before, that those who do such things will not inherit the kingdom of God. (Gal. 5:19–21)

This is one of the scariest passages in the Bible, for it tells us in no uncertain terms that those who practice such things will not inherit the kingdom of God. We know people who made profound professions of faith in Christ but who then fell into adultery, struggled with alcohol abuse, or battled pride and contentiousness throughout their lives. We might conclude that anyone who falls into one of these sins has no hope of salvation, but Paul is not saying that if someone gets drunk once, he will not go to heaven. He is saying that if such things *define* us, if they constitute a lifestyle, that is an indication that we are in the flesh and not in the Spirit. In other words, we are still unregenerate and will not be included in the kingdom of God. This flies in the face of antinomianism, which claims that people can be regenerate and never evidence any progress in the Christian life. Antinomians need to read this portion of Galatians to see Paul's sober warning. If these or similar sins are your regular and impenitent practice, you will not inherit the kingdom of God.

SPIRITUAL FRUIT

In contrast to the works of the flesh, Paul lists the fruit of the Spirit:

> But the fruit of the Spirit is love, joy, peace, patience, kindness, goodness, faithfulness, gentleness, self-control; against such

things there is no law. And those who belong to Christ Jesus have crucified the flesh with its passions and desires.

If we live by the Spirit, let us also keep in step with the Spirit. Let us not become conceited, provoking one another, envying one another. (vv. 22–26)

Paul is admonishing believers not to fall into the works of the flesh but to manifest the fruit of the Spirit. That tells us that even Christians have to battle with the old nature. There is an element of flesh that remains in the Christian that has to come under the constant scrutiny of the Word of God and the discipline of the Holy Spirit, so that we may be convicted of sin and flee from it and seek to cultivate the opposite kind of practice. That which is cultivated is that which bears fruit, and Jesus Himself said, "You will recognize them by their fruits" (Matt. 7:20).

How do we want to be remembered? Do we want it said that we earned much money, that we won many battles, or were prodigious in extraordinary feats? Or do we want to be remembered as those who manifested love, joy, peace, patience, kindness, goodness, faithfulness, gentleness, and self-control? These are the things God wants from us. These are the things God delights in, yet we do not make them a priority. For instance, we all are aware that we should be more loving. Even though much has been written about that particular fruit, we tend to have a superficial understanding of what love is. Love in its spiritual dimension is inseparably related to the other fruit.

There is a difference between the fruit of the Spirit and the gifts of the Spirit. Concerning the gifts of the Spirit, Paul's focus is unity and diversity, but that is not the case with the fruit of the Spirit. When he teaches about the gifts of the Spirit, he emphasizes that the Spirit distributes individual gifts to particular people for the edification of the whole church. One may have the gift of administration while another may have the gift of giving, teaching, or helps. Conversely, the fruit of the Spirit, in all its fullness, is to be manifest in every Christian's life.

Consider what a few aspects of the fruit of the Spirit should look like in the lives of believers:

Gentleness

Often today, the idea of being gentle or meek is associated with a lack of strength, but actually a gentle person is one who has strength but restrains the use of it.

I once had a discussion with a young man who had been elevated into a position of authority in an organization. His subordinates had complained that he was tyrannical in his management. He told me, "They don't respect my authority because they think I'm too young, so I have to show them who's boss."

I told him: "You have authority, and with that authority you have power, and with that power comes a high degree of responsibility. One of the secrets of leadership is that when you have the power, you can afford to be gracious. You don't need to be tyrannical. When someone is insecure in his position of power, he fails to be gentle."

Gentleness is akin to sensitivity. To be gentle is to use less force than possible in a given situation. We can take a cue from Jesus at this point, for He was exceedingly tender with the weak and the powerless of this world. He was gentle with a woman caught in adultery, while others were ready to rip her to shreds (John 8:3–11). Yet when the powerful of His day, the Pharisees, came to Jesus trying to exercise their strength, He responded with great strength. In other words, He was strong against the strong, firm against the powerful, but tender with the weak. We have a tendency to think we must treat everyone in the same manner, but this is not the case. We must learn how to monitor and moderate our strength. That is how we manifest the spiritual fruit of gentleness.

Joy

Joy is to be a mark of the Christian life. As Christians who are walking in the Spirit of God, we are not to be grumblers. However, the joy of the Spirit does not preclude grief or the experience of pain and affliction. The point is, as Paul explains elsewhere, that in all things we should learn to rejoice (e.g., Phil. 4:4). The basic reason for our joy is our relationship with God, for we know that the redemption we have in Christ is never threatened by the loss of a loved one, the loss of possessions, the loss of a job, or the loss of anything else. We might suffer all kinds of painful setbacks and afflictions, but those things should not rob us of the foundational joy we have in Christ. We can rejoice in all things because everything else is insignificant compared to the wonderful relationship we enjoy with our heavenly Father through the work of Christ on our behalf. But this joy has to be cultivated. The more we understand our relationship with God, the more we will understand His promises in our lives, and the greater the joy we will experience.

Patience

All the fruit we are called to bear imitates the very character of God. God is the author of joy, He is kind and gentle, and if anyone can be said to be patient, it is God. He is not quick to anger. He is not hasty to judge. He is forbearing, and He gives people time to turn to Him. We are to emulate Him in His patience.

Kindness

Kindness is a difficult virtue to define, yet there is a sense in which it does not need to be defined, because everyone knows what it is. To be kind is simply to be caring and considerate of others. This fruit, too, should mark every believer.

From this brief look at the fruit of the Spirit, we can see the priority of the Holy Spirit. This is what God desires from us. It is not so much what we do but who we are that pleases or grieves the Spirit.

Chapter 37

ARE MIRACLES FOR TODAY?

B efore we leave our brief overview of the person and work of the
Holy Spirit, there is one more subject to address, a much-debated
issue in the church today: should Christians today expect miracles, or
did miracles cease at the end of the Apostolic age? A related question
is this: can Satan and his minions perform miracles? These questions
are raised in the context of the so-called miraculous gifts of the Spirit.

Most people in the evangelical church today believe that miracles
still occur and that Satan and his demons have the power to perform
miracles. Those who hold the opposite view, including me, are often
vastly misunderstood on this point. We will consider in this chapter
some of the problems surrounding these matters and why historic ces-
sationism is the view of the orthodox Reformed.

MIRACLES DEFINED

When people talk about miracles, they do not always mean the same
thing. Some say that any answer to prayer is a miracle. Others argue
that any supernatural work, such as the regeneration of the human
soul, is a miracle, and some even go so far as to say that anything
amazing or fascinating, such as the birth of a baby, is a miracle. However, babies are born every day; there is nothing extraordinary about
it. If ordinary things are actually miracles, then miracles should not be

thought of as extraordinary. The significance of miracles in Scripture lies in their extraordinary character.

There were periods in biblical history when flurries of miracles occurred in short periods of time. The most notable of these periods, of course, was during the life of Jesus. Jesus' life was attended by an abundance of miracles. However, we also see periods of miracles during the life of Moses, and later in the life of Elijah. Still, during most periods of the Old Testament, miracles were absent. They did not occur on a consistent basis.

While the word *miracle* occurs frequently in English translations, it does not correspond exactly to any one word in the original languages. Theologians extrapolate the concept of miracles from three words in the biblical record (particularly the New Testament): *powers*, *wonders*, and *signs*. Miracles are manifestations of divine power; they inspire wonder and awe; and they are significant. When describing a miracle, John frequently used the word *sēmeion*, which is translated as "sign." When Jesus turned water into wine at the wedding feast in Cana, John wrote, "This, the first of his signs, Jesus did at Cana in Galilee, and manifested his glory. And his disciples believed in him" (John 2:11).

THE PURPOSE OF MIRACLES

Signs point to something beyond themselves. They have significance; they signify something. What were the so-called miracles or signs of the New Testament designed to signify? What did they point to?

Obviously, they had important value in what they accomplished. Jesus satisfied the needs of the wedding host when He made wine out of water, and He certainly met the needs of sick people when He healed them and of grieving parents when He raised their children from the dead. But what was the significance of those things?

In order to answer that question, we can look first at Nicodemus. When Nicodemus came to Jesus at night, he said to Him, "Rabbi, we know that you are a teacher come from God, for no one can do these signs that you do unless God is with him" (John 3:2). Nicodemus was saying that Jesus must have been from God because of the signs

He performed. Later, Jesus Himself said, "Believe me that I am in the Father and the Father is in me, or else believe on account of the works themselves" (John 14:11).

To see this idea in its full measure, we can look at a warning in Hebrews:

> Therefore we must pay much closer attention to what we have heard, lest we drift away from it. For since the message declared by angels proved to be reliable, and every transgression or disobedience received a just retribution, how shall we escape if we neglect such a great salvation? It was declared at first by the Lord, and it was attested to us by those who heard, while God also bore witness by signs and wonders and various miracles and by gifts of the Holy Spirit distributed according to his will. (2:1–4)

The author of Hebrews is saying that God confirms the truth of His Word through miracles. That point is often woefully neglected, but it has important implications. If the Scriptures say we know God's Word is true because its authors have been authenticated by miracles, how then can one who is not an agent of revelation also perform miracles? If all kinds of people can do these things, their "signs" prove nothing about their authority or whether they have been sent as spokesmen for God. At stake in this issue is the authority of Christ, the authority of the Apostles, and the authority of the Bible itself.

Moses was called by God from a burning bush to stand up to Pharaoh and lead the Israelites out of Egypt. Moses staggered at this command and said, "But behold, they will not believe me or listen to my voice, for they will say, 'The LORD did not appear to you'" (Ex. 4:1). So God instructed Moses to throw his staff on the ground. Moses did, and the stick became a serpent. Then God told Moses to place his hand in his shirt, which he did, and Moses' hand became leprous. God was planning to confirm His Word by miracles; these "signs" would be the means by which Moses would demonstrate that he was God's spokesman and appointed leader.

The Roman Catholic Church claimed miracles to argue against the Reformers in the sixteenth century. Rome said: "We have miracles in our history, and those miracles prove the truth of the Catholic Church. Where are your miracles? How can you authenticate the truth of your claims if you have no miracles?" The Reformers replied, "We do have miracles that prove our teaching, and they are recorded in the New Testament." Anyone can claim a miracle, but only a spokesman appointed by God has the actual power to perform one.

MIRACLES TODAY?

Today, many people claim to perform miracles. However, if they actually do perform miracles in the biblical sense, we have to conclude either that their teachings are endorsed by God or that such works do not authenticate true Apostolic teaching. For that reason, we must make a distinction between the word *miracle* in the narrow sense and *miracle* in the broad sense. Theologians are careful to define *miracle* narrowly. *Miracle* in the broad sense refers to God's ongoing supernatural activity in the life of His people—His answers to our prayers, the outpouring of His Spirit, and the changing of our souls. Certainly these activities continue down to this day. However, according to the narrow definition used by theologians, a miracle is an extraordinary work performed by the immediate power of God in the perceivable world, an act against nature that only God can do, such as bringing life out of death.

Most of those who hold to the continuation of miracles today stop short of claiming the kind of miracles we find in the Bible, such as raising people from the dead, but there are some who go even that far. Do we see resurrections happening today? I do not think so. The question is not whether God can or did perform miracles; it is whether He is doing so today. We have to make a distinction between the quality of miracles some today are claiming to do and the miracles we find in Scripture. So-called miracles today are not of the sort that only God can do.

SATAN AND MIRACLES

Because we are warned in Scripture against the crafty ploys of Satan, who performs lying signs and wonders, the majority of evangelicals believes that Satan can perform *bona fide* miracles. For instance, the magicians of Egypt performed extraordinary acts in their contest with Moses, and those acts are usually attributed to demonic power and influence. However, if Satan can perform a *bona fide* miracle, how do we know that the Bible is the Word of God and how do we know that Jesus is the Son of God? In the Bible, miracles do not prove the existence of God; they authenticate His work. When Paul spoke to the Greek philosophers at Athens, he said that Christ had been confirmed as the Son of God by His resurrection (Acts 17:31). Yet how do we know that the resurrection was not brought about by Satan, and how do we know that Satan did not enable Jesus to do all the works that He did? That was the accusation the Pharisees made against Jesus.

I do not believe Satan did those things because I do not believe Satan is God or that he can do things that only God can do. Jesus warned that Satan can perform lying signs and wonders that are able to deceive even the elect (Mark 13:22). Yet what is a lying sign or wonder? Satan does not have the power that only God has, but he is more sophisticated than any human being.

The famous magicians of our day do not claim to do miracles. They make clear that their tricks are mere sleight of hand. That was not the case in the ancient world. The magicians of antiquity claimed to have supernatural powers. They claimed to do magic, but it was all trickery. The magicians of Pharaoh's court pulled all they could from their bag of tricks, but they exhausted their feats in a short time. Moses kept going, however, because Moses was no magician. He had been anointed with the power of God to do what no magician could do. In like manner, Satan can be clever and deceive people, but he cannot do things that only God can do. He cannot do a real miracle in the narrow sense of the word.

Part Six

SOTERIOLOGY

Chapter 38

———

COMMON GRACE

The word *soteriology* is not commonly used in the church, but it is an important word because it pertains to our salvation. The word *soteriology* comes from the Greek verb *sōzō*, which means "to save." The noun form, *sōtēr*, means "savior."

The Scriptures speak of salvation in more than one way. We are accustomed to using the term *salvation* or speaking of "being saved" in the sense of being redeemed by God for eternity. In a sense, the great calamity from which we are saved is God Himself; that is, we are saved from having to face Him in His wrath on the day of judgment. God is, at the same time, the Savior and the One from whom we are saved.

However, the Greek verb *sōzō* refers to any act of rescue from a dire circumstance. Someone restored from a life-threatening disease is saved. Someone rescued from capture in battle is saved. Any rescue from calamity is a kind of salvation.

The central concern among Reformed theologians who study salvation is the concept of grace. G.C. Berkhouwer once observed that the very essence of theology is grace. From beginning to end, salvation is of the Lord, and it is not something we earn or deserve. It is given freely from the mercy and love of God.

GRACE DEFINED

At the outset, we must distinguish between grace and justice. Justice is something that is earned or merited by our works. When Paul writes about salvation, he makes clear that if salvation is by works, then it cannot be of grace, but since it is of grace, it is not of works. So justice is related to a standard of merit. In contrast, grace is undeserved; that is, it is not earned or merited. Rather, grace is given freely by God. He is not obligated or required to give it. The Apostle Paul quotes what God said to Moses: "I will have mercy on whom I have mercy, and I will have compassion on whom I have compassion" (Rom. 9:15). Grace is always a divine prerogative, never a requirement.

It is critical that we understand this, because we are prone to thinking that God owes us something. We often believe that if God were really good, He would give us a better life in some way, but if we think that God owes us something, we are actually thinking about justice, because grace is never owed. God is not obligated to give grace to anyone. The classic definition of grace is "unmerited favor." When God behaves in a favorable manner toward us even though we have no claim to it by our merit, that is always grace.

COMMON GRACE

Another important distinction is between common grace and special grace. Special grace involves the redemption that God gives to the saved. By contrast, common grace is called "common" because it is virtually universal. It is the grace that God gives to all people indiscriminately. Common grace is the mercy and kindness that God extends to the human race. The Bible says that God in His providence sends rain on the just and on the unjust (Matt. 5:45), and this is an example of common grace. There may be two farmers in the same town, one devout and committed to the things of God, and the other as pagan as he can possibly be. Both need the rain for their crops, and God in His goodness waters the earth, so both profit from the showers. Neither farmer deserves the rain to nurture his crops, but God's rain falls upon both, not just the devout man.

God's common grace extends far beyond rain. People who are not in fellowship with God enjoy many favors from Him. Changes in the human standard of living over time—quality of life, improved health, and better safety—trace the progress of God's grace through history. Of course, not everyone enjoys an equal standard of living, and certainly the basic standard of living in America is much greater than that in other parts of the world. Nevertheless, even in those areas, life expectancy and quality of life tend to be significantly better than in centuries past. Life has become easier.

Many simply attribute these improvements to science or education, but we must also factor in the influence of the Christian church over the past two thousand years. Orphanages were begun by the Christian community, as were hospitals and schools. Christians even drove the development of science in many ways. Believers have taken seriously their God-given responsibility to be good stewards of the planet. If we chart the history of the influence of the church on many different spheres, we see that, contrary to those who decry the impact of religion on the world, the general quality of life on earth has been vastly improved by the influence of Christianity.

We are called to be imitators of God, which is what it means to be made in the image of God. So if God is concerned about the general welfare of the human race, Christians also are called to be concerned about the general welfare of the human race. In fact, Jesus says that if our neighbor (or even our enemy) is naked, we are to clothe him; if he is hungry, we are to feed him; if he is thirsty, we are to give him drink; if he is in prison, we are to visit him; if he is sick, we are to minister to him (Matt. 25:34–36). The parable of the good Samaritan (Luke 10:25–37) indicates Jesus' priority that the church be concerned not only with the special-grace realm of evangelism but also with the general welfare of the human race. Elsewhere, James tells us that the essence of true religion is the care of orphans and widows (James 1:27).

Nineteenth-century liberalism rejected the supernatural aspects of the Christian faith, including the virgin birth, the resurrection, the atonement, and the deity of Christ. The liberals tried to remain viable from a social perspective by creating a new agenda for the church—humanitarian outreach. They began to emphasize the social agenda at the expense of evangelism. Orthodox Christians had to double their efforts at evangelism to make up for the repudiation of supernaturalism by the liberal wing. As a result, evangelicals began to see social concern as solely a liberal matter and to focus exclusively on personal salvation.

Both sides were wrong. The church is called not only to the ministry of special grace but also to the ministry of common grace. As Christians, we are to be concerned about poverty and hunger, about supplying people with the basic necessities of life, in addition to evangelism.

When the AIDS epidemic began, many Christians refused to involve themselves in any sort of support for its victims because they saw the disease as the consequence of sin—drug addiction and homosexual activity. However, if we find someone sick and dying in a ditch, we do not ask him how he got in that ditch. The love of Christ constrains us to pull him out of that ditch and do everything we can to help him, which is the point of the parable of the good Samaritan. No one is qualified to receive the ministry or the mercy of God. If someone with AIDS is not qualified to be helped by the mercy of the church, then neither am I, and neither are you. All of us receive the benefits of mercy on the basis of grace, and those of us who have received uncommon grace—special grace—should be first in line to demonstrate mercy.

When can a Christian join hands or stand shoulder to shoulder with pagans, with contrary religions, or even with apostate religions? Francis Schaeffer once said that when it comes to matters of common grace, the Christian must work together with all kinds of people who are not Christians. When I march for the rights of the unborn, I will stand next to anyone, if they share the same concern. That is just one arena in which we are to reach out and be supportive of people. However, I will not stand shoulder to shoulder in a worship service with members of a Satanic cult or sit at a prayer breakfast with Muslims, because such events fall in the realm of special grace. We need to understand the difference between the two.

SPECIAL GRACE

In Romans 9 we read these words from God: "Jacob I loved, but Esau I hated" (v. 13). So what does this do with our popular concept that God loves everyone unconditionally? God does not love everyone unconditionally; we must make a distinction between God's *love of benevolence* and His *love of complacency*, where *of* defines that out of which the love arises.

God's love of benevolence has to do with His general concern for the welfare of human beings. In that sense, it can rightly be said that God loves everyone, in that he is benevolent toward everyone. God's love of complacency is different. When people today call someone "complacent," they usually mean he is smug or arrogant, but that is not what theologians mean when they speak of God's love of complacency. Theologians speak of complacency in the sense of satisfaction or delight. God's love of complacency has to do with His redemptive love that is focused chiefly on His beloved Son, yet spills out to those who are in Christ. God has a special love for the redeemed that He does not have for the rest of the world.

Chapter 39

ELECTION AND REPROBATION

" In those days a decree went out from Caesar Augustus that all the world should be registered" (Luke 2:1). This sentence from Luke's narrative of the birth of Jesus calls attention to the authority of Caesar Augustus, who was one of the most powerful rulers of the ancient world. When a ruler such as Caesar issued a decree, the command was imposed upon all those under his dominion. Caesar's decree was the reason Jesus was born in Bethlehem. However, long before Augustus thought about issuing a decree that would lead Mary and Joseph to Bethlehem, God had issued a decree that the Messiah would be born there. Above and beyond the decrees of kings and emperors always stands the decree of almighty God.

Theologians are concerned about divine decrees because we know that God is sovereign. His sovereignty involves His authority and government over all that He has made. God rules the universe, so when He issues a decree according to His counsel and eternal plan, that decree comes to pass.

PREDESTINATION

The Scriptures reveal many aspects of God's eternal decrees, but those that have provoked the most controversy concern His plan of salvation, chiefly, the decree of election. In this chapter, we come face-to-face with the very difficult doctrine of predestination. The word *predestination* provokes more theological discussion than perhaps any other word in the Bible.

When we set out on a trip, we have an intended destination, a place we hope to reach safely. Sometimes we speak of our "destiny," by which we mean our ultimate destination. When Scripture attaches to that word the prefix *pre-*, which means "beforehand" or "in advance of," it is indicating that God has decreed a destination for His people. Paul wrote:

> Blessed be the God and Father of our Lord Jesus Christ, who has blessed us in Christ with every spiritual blessing in the heavenly places, even as he chose us in him before the foundation of the world, that we should be holy and blameless before him. In love he predestined us for adoption as sons through Jesus Christ, according to the purpose of his will, to the praise of his glorious grace, with which he has blessed us in the Beloved. (Eph. 1:3–6)

When Paul introduces the ideas of predestination and election in this passage, he speaks of our being blessed. Paul did not see divine predestination in a negative light; rather, it evoked within him a sense of exultation and gratitude, and it moved him to glorify God. In other words, the Apostle saw the doctrine of predestination as a blessing. It is indeed a blessing that should evoke in us also a sense of profound gratitude and praise.

When Reformed theologians talk about the doctrine of predestination, the discussion includes what we call "the doctrines of grace." With the doctrine of predestination, perhaps more than any other doctrine, we are confronted with the depths and riches of the mercy and grace of almighty God. If we separate our thinking about predestination from the context of that blessedness, we will struggle endlessly with this doctrine.

John Calvin, who is often considered the chief of the predestinarians, said that the doctrine of predestination is so mysterious that it must be treated with great care and humility because it can easily be distorted so as to cast a shadow on the integrity of God. If handled wrongly, the doctrine can make God look like a tyrant who plays with His creatures, who rolls the dice, as it were, with respect to our salvation. Distortions of this sort are many, and if you struggle with the doctrine, you are not alone.* On the other hand, I believe the struggle is worthwhile, because the more we probe this doctrine, the more we come to see the magnificence of God and the sweetness of His grace and mercy.

If we are going to be biblical in our theology, we must have some doctrine of predestination, because the Bible—not Augustine, Luther, or Calvin—clearly introduces the concept. There is nothing in Calvin's doctrine of predestination that was not first in Luther's, and there is nothing in Luther's doctrine of predestination that was not first in Augustine's, and I think it is safe to say that there is nothing in Augustine's doctrine of predestination that was not first in Paul's. This doctrine has its roots not in the theologians of church history but in the Bible, which sets it forth explicitly.

In Ephesians 1, Paul says that we have been blessed with "every spiritual blessing in the heavenly places, even as he chose us in him before the foundation of the world, that we should be holy and blameless before him. In love he predestined us for adoption as sons." The predestination Paul is referring to here has to do with election. *Predestination* and *election* are not synonyms, although they are closely related. Predestination has to do with God's decrees concerning anything. A specific type of predestination is election, which has to do with God's choosing certain people in Christ to be adopted into the family of God, or, in simple terms, to be saved. From a biblical standpoint, God has a plan of salvation in which, from all eternity, He has chosen people to be adopted into His family.

Most who deal with the doctrine of predestination and the eternal decrees of God agree that election is unto salvation and in Christ,

---

* For more of the nuances involved in the doctrine of election, see R.C. Sproul, *Chosen by God*, rev. ed. (Carol Stream, Ill.: Tyndale, 1994).

yet there are two controversial issues that arise at this point. The first involves what theologians call "reprobation," which has to do with the negative side of God's decrees. The question is simply this: if God decrees that some are chosen or elected by God for salvation, does that not mean that some are *not* chosen and therefore in the class of the nonelect, or reprobate? This is where the issue of double predestination comes in. The other controversial issue involves the grounds upon which God makes His choice to elect people to salvation.

THE VIEW OF PRESCIENCE

A popular version of predestination is called "the view of prescience." The word *prescience* contains the word *science*, which comes from the Latin word for knowledge, along with the prefix *pre-*, which means "beforehand" or "in advance of." The prescience view holds that God's election is based ultimately on His prior knowledge of what people will do or not do. According to this view, God, in eternity past, looked down the corridors of time and saw who would embrace Christ and who would reject Him, and on the basis of that prior knowledge, He chose to adopt those who He knew would make the proper choice. So, in the final analysis, God chose us on the basis of His knowledge that we would choose Him. In my view, however, that does not explain the biblical doctrine of predestination. Frankly, I think it denies it, because, as I understand the Scriptures, the Bible is saying that we choose Him because He first chose us. Additionally, Scripture teaches that predestination is based solely on the good pleasure of God's will.

Paul says in Ephesians, "He predestined us for adoption as sons through Jesus Christ, according to the purpose of his will, to the praise of his glorious grace" (1:5). Here we learn why God does what He does—for His own glory. The ultimate goal of God's decrees is the glory of God, and the decisions and choices He makes in His plan of salvation are based upon the good pleasure of His will.

The typical objection at that point is this: "If God chooses one rather than another independently of what people do, then isn't He capricious and tyrannical?" Paul says that the choice comes from God's good pleasure; there is no such thing as the bad pleasure of God's will. Whatever God chooses is based on His internal righteousness and goodness. God does not make a bad choice or do anything evil, which is why Paul praises God for His plan of salvation.

GOD'S MERCY

What Paul hints at here in Ephesians 1, he develops more fully in his epistle to the Romans, particularly in Romans 8–9:

> When Rebekah had conceived children by one man, our forefather Isaac, though they were not yet born and had done nothing either good or bad—in order that God's purpose of election might continue, not because of works but because of him who calls—she was told, "The older will serve the younger." As it is written, "Jacob I loved, but Esau I hated." (9:10–13)

Paul is saying here that God made a decision to redeem Jacob but not Esau. Both were children of the same family; indeed, they were twins. God, before they were born, before they had done any good or evil, declared that He would give His benevolent and complacent love to one and withhold it from the other.

Paul continues: "What shall we say then? Is there injustice on God's part?" (v. 14a). Paul is making a critical point. When people learn that predestination is rooted in God's sovereign good pleasure, they often raise a question about the righteousness of God. Paul anticipates this objection; he raises the question rhetorically himself. Then he gives his unambiguous answer: "By no means!" (v. 14b). Other translations render his words as "Certainly not!" or "God forbid!" Then Paul reminds us of the Old Testament teaching: "For he says to Moses, 'I will have mercy on whom I have mercy, and I will have compassion on whom I have compassion'" (v. 15). Paul points out that it is God's sovereign prerogative to dispense His grace and mercy however He chooses to do it.

When we looked at the justice of God in an earlier chapter, we noted that everything outside the category of justice is nonjustice. Both injustice and mercy fall outside the category of justice, yet injustice is evil whereas mercy is not. When God considered a race of depraved, fallen human beings living in rebellion against Him, He decreed that He would give mercy to some and justice to others. Esau received justice; Jacob received grace; neither received injustice. God never punishes innocent people, but He does redeem guilty people. He does not redeem them all, and He is under no obligation to redeem any. The amazing thing is that He redeems some.

Paul then gives a conclusion: "So then it depends not on human will or exertion, but on God, who has mercy. . . . So then he has mercy on whomever he wills, and he hardens whomever he wills" (vv. 16, 18). Paul could be no clearer that our election is not based on our running, our doing, our choosing, or our willing; it rests ultimately on the sovereign will of God.

Chapter 40

EFFECTUAL CALLING

When we discuss predestination or election and the sovereignty of divine grace, we must face the question of what God actually does when He intervenes in a life in order to bring that person to faith. Historically, the Calvinist or Augustinian school says that election is purely the sovereign activity of God, whereas the Arminian or semi-Pelagian school sees a cooperative venture between man and God. Both sides—Calvinism and Arminianism—agree that grace is an absolute necessity for salvation. However, they differ over the degree to which grace is necessary. When a sinner turns from spiritual death to spiritual life, is that step accomplished through *monergism* or through *synergism*? The controversy between Calvinism and Arminianism, or between Augustinianism and semi-Pelagianism, comes down to these two words and their meanings.

MONERGISM, NOT SYNERGISM

The word *monergism* contains the prefix *mon-*, which means "one," and the word *ergon*, which means "work," so *monergism* indicates that only one does the work. *Synergism* contains the prefix *syn-*, which means "with," so synergism has to do with cooperation, with two or more people working together. Thomas Aquinas framed the question this way: is the grace of regeneration operative grace or cooperative grace? In other words, when the Holy Spirit regenerates a sinner, does

He contribute only some power, such that the sinner must add some of his own energy or power in order to bring about the desired effect, or is regeneration a unilateral work of God? To put it yet another way, does God alone change the heart of the sinner, or does the change of heart rest on the willingness of the sinner to be changed?

Paul writes:

And you were dead in the trespasses and sins in which you once walked, following the course of this world, following the prince of the power of the air, the spirit that is now at work in the sons of disobedience—among whom we all once lived in the passions of our flesh, carrying out the desires of the body and the mind, and were by nature children of wrath, like the rest of mankind. (Eph. 2:1–3)

In this passage, Paul was reminding the believers at Ephesus of their state before Christ. They were dead—spiritually dead. Dead people do not cooperate. We read in John's gospel that Lazarus had been dead for four days before Jesus arrived. The only power in the universe that could bring that corpse out of the tomb was the power of God. Christ did not invite Lazarus out of the tomb; He did not wait for Lazarus to cooperate. He said, "Lazarus, come out," and by the sheer power of that imperative, that which was dead became alive (John 11:43). Lazarus cooperated by walking out of the tomb, but there was no cooperation involved in his transition from death to life.

In similar fashion, Paul says in Ephesians that we are in a state of spiritual death. We are by nature children of wrath, and according to Jesus, no one can come to Him unless the Father draws him (John 6:44).

Paul continues:

But God, being rich in mercy, because of the great love with which he loved us, even when we were dead in our trespasses, made us alive together with Christ—by grace you have been saved—and raised us up with him and seated us with him in the heavenly places in Christ Jesus, so that in the coming ages he might show the immeasurable riches of his grace in kindness toward us in Christ Jesus. (Eph. 2:4–7)

In our flesh, we can do nothing; left to ourselves, we would never choose the things of God. While we are in that state of spiritual death, walking according to the course of this world and obeying the lusts of our flesh, God makes us alive. After God makes us alive, we reach out in faith, but that first step is something that God alone does. He does not whisper in our ear, "Will you please cooperate with Me?" Rather, He intervenes to change the disposition of the hearts of spiritually dead people by His Holy Spirit.

From the opening paragraph of his letter to the Ephesians, where he describes the sweetness of predestination, to this point, where he shows the exceeding riches of God's grace in His kindness toward us in Christ Jesus, Paul extols the marvelous wonders of divine grace. Then he says it again: "For by grace you have been saved through faith. And this is not your own doing; it is the gift of God, not a result of works, so that no one may boast. For we are his workmanship, created in Christ Jesus for good works, which God prepared beforehand, that we should walk in them" (2:8–10).

DOUBLE PREDESTINATION

He writes that by grace we are saved through faith, "and this is not your own doing." Grammatically, the antecedent of "this" includes the word "faith." We are justified through faith, but even the faith we have is not something we generate. It does not come from a fallen nature; it is the result of the creative activity of God, which is what Reformed theologians mean when they speak of monergistic regeneration. God intervenes in the hearts of the elect and changes the disposition of their soul. He creates faith in faithless hearts.

The idea of monergistic regeneration is repugnant to semi-Pelagians, who say that the Holy Spirit would not unilaterally come in and change people's hearts against their will. Yet the fallen human will is always and everywhere opposed to God, so the only way anyone will ever choose Christ willingly is if God intervenes to make him willing by re-creating his soul. He raises people from spiritual death and gives them spiritual life so that they not only can and will choose Christ, but also do it willingly. Underlying regeneration is the change of heart whereby the unwilling are made willing by the Spirit of God. In regeneration, those who have hated the things of God are given a whole new disposition, a new heart. That is exactly what Jesus said—unless one is born again, he cannot see the kingdom of God, let alone enter it (John 3:1–5).

The basic difference between Reformed theology and non-Reformed theology is the order of salvation with respect to faith and regeneration. The vast majority of professing evangelical Christians believe that faith comes before regeneration. In other words, in order to be born again, one has to believe. One has to choose Christ before rebirth can occur. If that were the case, we would have absolutely no hope of salvation, because a spiritually dead person at enmity with God cannot choose Christ. We cannot change others' hearts through evangelism, either. We can present the gospel; we can argue for it and try to be convincing. Yet only God can change the heart. Since only God has the power to change the nature of a human soul, we must say that regeneration precedes faith. That is the essence of Reformed theology. The Holy Spirit changes the disposition of the soul before someone comes to faith.

Does that mean, when we come to believe, that God believes through us? No, we are the ones doing the believing. Do we choose Christ? Yes, we choose Christ. We respond. Our wills are changed so that what we once hated, we now love, and we rush to the Son. God gives us the desire for Him in our souls. It is a distortion of the biblical view to say that natural man is running around desperately trying to find God, but God will not let some in because they are not on His list. No one tries to come to Christ apart from the special grace of God.

Both sides in the dispute agree that grace is a necessary condition. They simply disagree over monergism and synergism, over whether the grace of regeneration is effectual or, to use more popular language, irresistible. Those who say we have the power to refuse it are tangled in a hopeless theology. It does not take seriously the biblical view of the radical character of human fallenness. We are simply unable to convert ourselves or even to cooperate with God in the matter. Any cooperation presupposes that a change has already taken place, for until that change takes place, no one cooperates. Those who believe that man cooperates in regeneration hold to a form of works righteousness. How could it be otherwise, if some can enter in by making the "right" response? This is a denial of the gospel. There is no human righteousness in man's regeneration.

THE GOLDEN CHAIN

Theologians refer to "the golden chain" of salvation:

> And we know that for those who love God all things work together for good, for those who are called according to his purpose. For those whom he foreknew he also predestined to be conformed to the image of his Son, in order that he might be the firstborn among many brothers. And those whom he predestined he also called, and those whom he called he also justified, and those whom he justified he also glorified. (Rom. 8:28–30)

There is a chain there, a sequence, that begins with foreknowledge. Then follows predestination, calling, justification, and glorification. This is an elliptical statement—something is assumed but not spelled out. It is the word *all*. All whom God has foreknown He has predestined, all whom He has predestined He has also called, all whom He has called He has also justified, and all whom He has justified are glorified.

Some point out that foreknowledge precedes the other steps in this golden chain, which is why they hold to a prescience view of election. Yet predestination, regardless of what view you hold, has to begin with foreknowledge because God cannot predestine anyone whom He does not know about in advance. This necessitates that the chain begin with foreknowledge. Yet all who are foreknown are predestined, and all the predestined are called. Paul here does not have in mind everyone in the world, but only the predestined, who are foreknown and also called.

The point is that everyone who is called is justified, which means that everyone who is called gets faith, which means this text cannot be about what theologians refer to as "the external call of the gospel," which goes out to everyone. This text is about the internal call, the operative call, that work of the Holy Spirit that effectually changes the heart. The effectual call of the Holy Spirit brings to pass in our hearts what God purposed to do from the foundation of the world. *All* who have been predestined are called effectually by the Holy Spirit; *all* who are called by the Holy Spirit are justified; and *all* who are justified are glorified. If we applied Arminian categories to this golden chain, we would have to say that *some* who are foreknown are predestined; *some* who are predestined are called; *some* who are called are justified; and *some* who are justified are glorified. In that case, the whole text would mean nothing.

Chapter 41

———

JUSTIFICATION BY FAITH ALONE

The doctrine of justification has caused tremendous controversy in the history of Christianity. It provoked the Protestant Reformation of the sixteenth century, as the Reformers took their stand for *sola fide*, or justification by faith alone. Martin Luther maintained that the doctrine of justification by faith alone is the article on which the church stands or falls, and John Calvin agreed with him. They felt so strongly about this doctrine because they saw from Scripture that nothing less than the gospel itself is at stake when justification is debated.

The doctrine of justification addresses the most serious plight of fallen human beings—their exposure to the justice of God. God is just, but we are not. As David prayed, "If you, O Lord, should mark iniquities, O Lord, who could stand?" (Ps. 130:3). Obviously that is a rhetorical question; no one can stand up to divine scrutiny. If God were to extend the measuring rod of His justice and use it to evaluate our lives, we would perish because we are not righteous. Most of us think that if we work hard to be good people, that will suffice when we come to the judgment seat of God. The great myth of popular culture, which has penetrated the church, is that people can *earn* the favor of God, even though Scripture states clearly that by the works of the law no one shall be justified (Gal. 2:16). We are debtors who cannot pay our debt.

That is why the gospel is called "good news." As Paul wrote about the gospel: "For I am not ashamed of the gospel, for it is the power of God for salvation to everyone who believes, to the Jew first and also to the Greek. For in it the righteousness of God is revealed from faith for faith, as it is written, 'The righteous shall live by faith'" (Rom 1:16–17). In the final analysis, justification is a legal pronouncement made by God. In other words, justification can occur only when God, who is Himself just, becomes the Justifier by decreeing someone to be just in His sight.

SIMUL IUSTIS ET PECCATOR

The sixteenth-century debate concerned whether God waits for people to become righteous before He declares them just or whether He declares them just in His sight while they are still sinners. Luther propounded a formula that has survived since the time of that debate. He said that we are *simul iustis et peccator*, which means "at the same time just and sinner." Luther was saying that a justified person is simultaneously just and sinful. We are just by virtue of the work of Christ, yet we have not yet been perfected, so we still sin.

The Roman Catholic Church argues that Luther's doctrine was a legal fiction. How, the Roman theologians ask, can God declare people just when they are still sinful? That would be unworthy of God. Rome argues instead for what is called "analytical justification." They agree that justification occurs when God declares someone just; however, for Rome, God will not declare a person just until that person is, in fact, just. Protestants respond that when God declares a person just, there is nothing fictional about it. That person is just in God's sight by virtue of the real work of Jesus Christ, which is anything but fictional.

THE INSTRUMENTAL CAUSE

We say that justification is by faith alone, and the word *by* in that slogan was part of the sixteenth-century controversy. *By* refers to the means by which something is brought to pass. The controversy, therefore, concerned the instrumental cause of justification. Today we do not speak much about instrumental causes. In fact, that language goes back to ancient Greece, when the philosopher Aristotle distinguished between various types of causes: material, formal, final, efficient, and instrumental. By way of illustration, Aristotle used the creation of a statue by a sculptor. The sculptor fashions his block of stone. The material cause for the statue is the matter out of which the artwork is produced, the stone itself. The instrumental cause, the means by which the raw block of stone is transformed into a magnificent statue, is the hammer and chisel. This was the language used in the sixteenth-century debate.

INFUSION OR IMPUTATION?

The Roman Catholic Church said that the instrumental cause of justification is the sacrament of baptism. Baptism sacramentally confers upon the recipient the grace of justification; in other words, the righteousness of Christ is poured into the soul of the one receiving baptism. That pouring of grace into the soul is called "infusion." So Rome does not believe that people are justified apart from grace or faith, but that justification comes about as a result of an infusion of grace by which human righteousness is made possible.

Then, Rome said, in order for people to become righteous, they have to cooperate with the infused grace. People must assent to it to such a degree that righteousness is achieved. As long as people keep themselves from committing mortal sin, they remain in a justified state. However, according to Rome, mortal sin is bad enough to kill the justifying grace that a soul possesses, so those who commit a mortal sin lose the grace of justification. Yet all is not lost. A sinner can be restored to a state of justification through the sacrament of penance, which the Roman church defines as the second plank of justification for those who have made "shipwreck" of their faith. That is why people go to confession, which is part of the sacrament of penance. When one confesses his sins, he receives absolution, after which he must perform works of satisfaction that earn what Rome calls "congruous merit." Works of congruous merit are integral to the sacrament of penance, because these works of satisfaction make it fitting, or congruous, for God to restore the sinner to a state of grace. So

Rome actually has two instrumental causes of justification: baptism and penance.

Over against that view, the Protestant Reformers argued that the only instrumental cause of justification is faith. As soon as people take hold of Christ by faith, the merit of Christ is transferred to them. Whereas Rome holds to justification by infusion, Protestants hold to justification by imputation. The Roman Catholic Church says that God declares someone just only by virtue of his cooperation with the infused grace of Christ. For Protestants, the ground of justification remains exclusively the righteousness of Christ—not the righteousness of Christ *in* us but the righteousness of Christ *for* us, the righteousness that Christ achieved in His perfect obedience to the law of God. This righteousness, the first part of the ground of justification, is applied to all who put their trust in Christ. The other part of the ground of justification is Christ's perfect satisfaction of the negative sanctions of the law in His sacrificial death on the cross.

This means we are saved not only by the death of Jesus but also by His life. A double transfer takes place, a double imputation. As the Lamb of God, Christ went to the cross and suffered the wrath of God, but not for any sin God found in Him. He voluntarily took upon Himself our sins. He became the sin bearer when God the Father transferred or reckoned our sins to Him. That is what imputation is—a legal transfer. Christ assumed our guilt in His own person; our guilt was imputed to Him. The other transfer occurs when God imputes Christ's righteousness to us.

So when Luther said that justification is by faith alone, he meant that justification is by *Christ alone*, by what He accomplished to satisfy the demands of God's righteousness. Imputation involves a transfer of someone else's righteousness. Infusion involves an implantation of righteousness that inheres or exists within.

So the instrumental causes of justification, according to Rome, are the sacraments of baptism and penance, and for Protestants the instrumental cause of justification is faith alone. Additionally, the Roman Catholic view of justification rests upon infusion, but the Protestant view rests upon imputation.

ANALYTICAL OR SYNTHETIC?

Another difference is that the Roman Catholic view of justification is analytical, whereas the Reformation view is synthetic. An analytical statement is one that is true by definition; for example, "A bachelor is an unmarried man." The predicate, "unmarried man," adds no new information to the subject of the sentence, "a bachelor," so the statement is true by definition. However, if we say, "The bachelor is a wealthy man," we have said, or predicated, something about the bachelor not found in the subject, because not all bachelors are wealthy. In that case, we have a synthetic statement.

The Roman Catholic Church says that God does not declare people just until, under analysis, they *are* just. Protestants say that people are just synthetically, because they have something added to them, the righteousness of Jesus. So, for Catholics, righteousness must *inhere*, whereas for Protestants, righteousness is *extra nos*, or "outside of us." It is, properly speaking, not our own. It counts for us only when we lay hold of Christ by faith.

The wonderful good news of the gospel is that we do not have to wait until we have been purged in purgatory from all abiding impurities; the moment we put our trust in Jesus Christ, all that He is and all that He has become ours, and we are translated immediately into a state of reconciliation with God.

Chapter 42

———

SAVING FAITH

We saw in the previous chapter that the instrumental causes of justification, according to the Roman Catholic Church, are the sacraments of baptism and penance, but for Protestants the instrumental cause is faith alone. Additionally, the Roman Catholic view of justification rests upon an infusion of righteousness, whereas the Protestant view rests upon the imputation of Christ's righteousness. Many believe that Roman Catholics downplay the importance of faith, but that is not true. The Roman Catholic Church insists upon the necessity of faith for justification; however, it holds that faith is not sufficient by itself to justify anyone. There must also be works. The real difference, therefore, is that Rome believes in faith plus works and in grace plus merit, whereas the Reformed declare that justification is by faith alone and grace alone.

Faith is central to Christianity. The New Testament repeatedly calls people to believe on the Lord Jesus Christ. There is a definite body of content to be believed, which is part and parcel of our religious activity. At the time of the Reformation, the debate involved the *nature* of saving faith. What is saving faith? The idea of justification by faith alone suggests to many people a thinly veiled antinomianism that claims people can live any way they like so long as they believe the right things. Yet James wrote in his epistle: "What good is it, my brothers, if someone says he has faith but does not have works? Can that faith save him? . . . Faith by itself, if it does not have works, is dead" (2:14, 17).

Luther said that the sort of faith that justifies is *fides viva*, a "living faith," one that inevitably, necessarily, and immediately yields the fruit of righteousness. Justification is by faith alone, but not by a faith that is alone. A faith without any yield of righteousness is not true faith.

For the Roman Catholic Church, faith plus works equals justification; for antinomians, faith minus works equals justification; for the Protestant Reformers, faith equals justification plus works. In other words, works are the necessary fruit of true faith. Works are not factored into God's declaration that we are just in His sight; they are not part of the grounds for God's decision to declare us righteous.

ESSENTIAL ELEMENTS OF SAVING FAITH

What are the constituent elements of saving faith? The Protestant Reformers recognized that biblical faith has three essential aspects: *notitia*, *assensus*, and *fiducia*.

Notitia refers to the content of faith, the things we believe. There are certain things we are required to believe about Christ, namely, that He is the Son of God, that He is our Savior, that He has provided an atonement, and so on.

Assensus is the conviction that the content of our faith is true. One can know about the Christian faith and yet believe that it is not true. We might have a doubt or two mixed with our faith, but there has to be a certain level of intellectual affirmation and conviction if we are to be saved. Before anyone can really trust in Jesus Christ, he has to believe that Christ indeed is the Savior, that He is who He claimed to be. Genuine faith says that the content, the *notitia*, is true.

Fiducia refers to personal trust and reliance. Knowing and believing the content of the Christian faith is not enough, for even demons can do that (James 2:19). Faith is effectual only if one personally trusts in Christ alone for salvation. It is one thing to give an intellectual assent to a proposition but quite another to place personal trust in it. We can say that we believe in justification by faith alone and yet still think that we are going to get to heaven by our achievements, our works, or our striving. It is easy to get the doctrine of justification by faith into our

238

heads, but it is hard to get it into the bloodstream such that we cling to Christ *alone* for salvation.

There is another element to *fiducia* besides trust, and that is affection. An unregenerate person will never come to Jesus, because he does not want Jesus. In his mind and heart, he is fundamentally at enmity with the things of God. As long as someone is hostile to Christ, he has no affection for Him. Satan is a case in point. Satan knows the truth, but he hates the truth. He is utterly disinclined to worship God because he has no love for God. We are like that by nature. We are dead in our sin. We walk according to the powers of this world and indulge the lusts of the flesh. Until the Holy Spirit changes us, we have hearts of stone. An unregenerate heart is without affection for Christ; it is both lifeless and loveless. The Holy Spirit changes the disposition of our hearts so that we see the sweetness of Christ and embrace Him. None of us loves Christ perfectly, but we cannot love Him at all unless the Holy Spirit changes the heart of stone and makes it a heart of flesh.

FRUITS OF CONVERSION

Theologians have traditionally recognized several elements that accompany or follow saving faith. These are called "fruits of conversion." We will look at a few of them here.

Repentance

When someone is brought to faith by the Holy Spirit, he undergoes a conversion. His life turns around. This turning around is called "repentance," and it is an immediate fruit of genuine faith. Some include repentance as part of genuine faith. However, the Bible distinguishes between repentance and belief. We cannot have affection for Christ until we recognize and acknowledge that we are sinners and that we desperately need His work on our behalf. Repentance includes a hatred for our sin, which comes with the new affection we are given for God.

I am disturbed when ministers say, "Come to Jesus and all your troubles will be solved." My life did not get complicated until I became a Christian. Before I was a Christian, I followed a one-way street. I still am tempted by the course of this world, yet God has planted in my heart an affection and a trust for Christ. In other words, we repent because we hate our sin. Yes, part of us still loves our sin, but true repentance involves a godly sorrow for having offended God and a resolve to be rid of our sin. Repentance does not mean total victory over sin. If total victory were required, no one would be saved. Repentance is a turning away, having a different view of sin. The Greek word for "repentance," *metanoia*, literally means "a change of mind." Previously, we rationalized our sin, but now we realize that sin is an evil thing; we have a different mind-set about it.

Adoption

When God declares us just in Jesus Christ, He adopts us into His household. His only true son is Christ, but Christ becomes our elder brother by way of adoption. No one is born into the family of God. By nature, we are children of wrath, not children of God; therefore, God is not our Father by nature. We can have God as our Father only if He adopts us, and He will adopt us only through the work of His Son. But when we put our faith and trust in Christ, God not only declares us just, He also declares us His sons and daughters by way of adoption.

Peace

Paul writes to the Romans, "Therefore, since we have been justified by faith, we have peace with God through our Lord Jesus Christ" (5:1). The first fruit of justification is peace with God. We were enemies, but the war is over. God declares a peace treaty with all those who put their faith in Christ. When He does this, we do not enter an unstable truce, such that the first time we do something wrong, God starts rattling the sword. This peace is an unbreakable, eternal peace because it has been won by the perfect righteousness of Christ.

Access to God

Paul also writes, "Through [Christ] we have also obtained access by faith into this grace in which we stand, and we rejoice in hope of the glory of God" (Rom. 5:2). Another fruit is access to God. God does not allow His enemies into an intimate relationship with Him, but once we have been reconciled to God through Christ, we have access into His presence, and we have joy in the glory of who He is.

Chapter 43

————

ADOPTION AND
UNION WITH CHRIST

In his first epistle, the Apostle John makes a statement of Apostolic astonishment: "See what kind of love the Father has given to us, that we should be called children of God; and so we are. The reason why the world does not know us is that it did not know him. Beloved, we are God's children now" (1 John 3:1–2). We cannot help but notice a sense of amazement in John's writing. The fact that we are the children of God is something we tend to take for granted, but the Apostolic church never did.

CHILDREN OF GOD

We live in a culture that has been heavily influenced by the nineteenth-century interest in the study of world religions. As a result of increased travel capabilities, people at that time became knowledgeable of other religions of which they previously had been ignorant. There was a frenzy of interest, particularly in Germany, in the study of comparative religion. In fact, comparative religion became a new academic discipline. During this period, anthropologists, sociologists, and theologians examined the world's religions and sought to penetrate to the core of each one to distill its essence and discover similarities among Hindus, Muslims, Jews, Christians, Buddhists, and others.

Among those scholars was Adolf von Harnack, who wrote a book titled *Das Wesen des Christentums*, translated into English as *What Is Christianity?* In this book, he sought to reduce Christianity to the most basic common denominator it shares with other religions. He said the essence of the Christian faith is found in two premises: the universal fatherhood of God and the universal brotherhood of man. The problem with Harnack's conclusion is that neither concept is taught in the Bible. While God is the Creator of all people, the father-hood of God is a radical concept in the New Testament. This is why John expresses an attitude of amazement when he says, "See what kind of love the Father has given to us, that we should be called children of God."

Another German scholar, Joachim Jeremias, did a study of the scriptural concept of the fatherhood of God. He noted that among the Jewish people of antiquity, children were instructed in the proper ways to address God in prayer. Conspicuously absent from the lengthy list of approved titles was "Father." By contrast, when we come to the New Testament, we see that in almost every prayer Jesus offered, He addressed God directly as "Father." Jeremias went on to say that out-side of the Christian community, the first printed reference he could find to a Jew addressing God as "Father" was from the tenth century AD in Italy. In other words, Jesus' addressing God as "Father" was a radical departure from Jewish custom, a fact that outraged the Phari-sees because they considered it to be a tacit claim to deity.

Today, praying to God as "Father" is no longer considered radi-cal. Even more astonishing is that Jesus, in giving the Lord's Prayer, instructed His disciples to direct their prayers to the Father (Matt. 6:9). So not only did Jesus address God as "Father," He extended the privi-lege to His disciples.

The New Age movement has had such an impact on the church in recent years that some ministers teach that any true Christian is as much an incarnation of God as Jesus was. Such teaching denies the uniqueness of Christ in His incarnation. Christians who espouse this idea have realized the significance of being children of God but have gotten carried away with it to such an extent that they obscure the uniqueness of the sonship of Christ.

Christ's sonship is central to the New Testament. There are three references in the New Testament to God the Father's speaking audibly from heaven, and on two of those occasions, He declares the sonship of Jesus: "This is my beloved Son, with whom I am well pleased" (Matt. 3:17; see also Matt. 17:5; John 12:28). Therefore, we must be careful to protect the uniqueness of Christ's sonship. Indeed, He is called the *monogenēs*, the "only begotten" of the Father. According to Jesus, we are not children of God by nature; we are children of Satan. The only one who can lay claim to being a child of God inherently, or naturally, is Jesus Himself.

> He was in the world, and the world was made through him, yet the world did not know him. He came to his own, and his own people did not receive him. But to all who did receive him, who believed in his name, he gave the right to become children of God, who were born, not of blood nor of the will of the flesh nor of the will of man, but of God. (John 1:10–13)

The Greek word translated as "right" in verse 12 is a powerful word for "authority." It is the same word that was used of Jesus by His contemporaries when they said, "He taught them as one who had authority, and not as the scribes" (Mark 1:22). Extraordinary authority has been given to us in being given the right to call God "Father."

So we learn here that to be the children of God is a gift. It is not earned or received by natural birth. How do we receive it? Paul tells us:

> So then, brothers, we are debtors, not to the flesh, to live according to the flesh. For if you live according to the flesh you will die, but if by the Spirit you put to death the deeds of the body, you will live. For all who are led by the Spirit of God are sons of God. For you did not receive the spirit of slavery to fall back into fear, but you have received the Spirit of adoption

as sons, by whom we cry, "Abba! Father!" The Spirit himself bears witness with our spirit that we are children of God, and if children, then heirs—heirs of God and fellow heirs with Christ, provided we suffer with him in order that we may also be glorified with him. (Rom. 8:12–17)

RIGHTS OF ADOPTION

We are children of God by adoption, which is a fruit of our justification. When we are reconciled to God, He brings us into His family. The church is a family with one Father and one Son, and everyone else in the family is adopted. This is why we look to Christ as our elder brother. We have been made heirs of God and joint heirs with Christ. The true Son of God makes available all that He received in His inheritance. He shares with His brothers and sisters His full legacy.

That is something we ought never take for granted. Whenever we pray, "Our Father," we should tremble with amazement that we, of all people, should be called "children of God." There is no second-class membership in God's family. We rightly distinguish between the natural Son of God and the adopted children of God, but once the adoption takes place, there is no difference in the status of membership in His family. He gives to all His children the full measure of the inheritance that belongs to the natural Son.

In our adoption as sons, we also enjoy the mystical union of the believer with Christ. When we describe something as "mystical," we are saying it transcends the natural and, in a certain sense, is ineffable. We can understand this through a study of two Greek prepositions, *en* and *eis*, both of which may be translated as "in." The technical distinction between these two words is important. The preposition *en* means "in" or "inside of," whereas the preposition *eis* means "into." When the New Testament calls us to believe in the Lord Jesus Christ, we are called not just to believe something about Him but to believe *into* Him.

If we are outside of a building, in order to get inside, we must go through a door. Once we make the transition, once we cross the threshold from the outside to the inside, we are inside. Entering is the *eis*, and once we are inside, we are *en*. The distinction is important, because the New Testament tells us that not only are we to believe *into* Christ, but also that those with genuine faith are *in* Christ. We are in Christ, and Christ is in us. There is a spiritual union between every believer and Christ Himself.

Additionally, we are all part of the mystical communion of the saints. This mystical communion is the foundation for the transcendent spiritual fellowship that each Christian enjoys with all other Christians. Additionally, it has a restraining impact upon us. If you and I are both in Christ, the union we share transcends our relational difficulties. This is not just a theoretical concept; the bond of that family is a stronger bond even than what we enjoy with our biological family. This is the fruit of our adoption.

Chapter 44

———•———

SANCTIFICATION

As a young believer, I listened frequently to the radio preaching of Robert J. Lamont. Later, while I was in seminary, I had an opportunity to meet Dr. Lamont, and on that occasion he jokingly asked me, "Now then, young man, what is on your partially sanctified mind?"

The good news of the Christian faith is not only that we are justified by the righteousness of someone else, but also that we do not have to wait until we are fully sanctified before God accepts us into His fellowship. Sanctification, as partial as it may be in this life, is real. It is the process by which those declared righteous are made holy. Our status before God is based on someone else's righteousness; however, the moment we are justified, a real change is enacted upon us by the Holy Spirit, so that we are increasingly brought into conformity with Christil. The change of our nature toward holiness and righteousness begins immediately.

SANCTIFICATION GUARANTEED

We noted earlier that justification is by faith alone, but not by a faith that is alone. In other words, if true faith is present, there is a change in one's actual nature that manifests itself in good works. The fruit of sanctification is both a necessary and an inevitable consequence of justification. This truth serves as a warning to those who hold the view that it is possible for people to be converted to Christ yet never bring

247

forth good fruit or change in behavior. This is the idea of "the carnal Christian."

Of course, in a certain sense, Christians *are* carnal throughout their lives; that is, we never in this life completely vanquish the impact of the flesh. We have to struggle with the flesh until we enter into glory. However, if someone is completely in the flesh such that there is no evidence of any change in the person's nature, then this individual is not a carnal Christian but a carnal non-Christian. Some are so zealous to keep the number of evangelistic converts high that they are loath to consider that some make false professions of faith. But if someone makes a profession of faith yet shows no fruit of it whatsoever, there was no real conversion. We are justified not by a *profession* of faith but by the *possession* of faith. Where faith is true, the fruit of that faith begins to appear immediately. It is impossible for a converted person to remain unchanged. The very presence of the new nature—the presence and power of the indwelling Holy Spirit—indicates that we are indeed changed and changing people.

At the same time, sanctification does not progress in a steady line from the starting point of conversion until we are home in glory. For the most part, there is steady growth in the Christian life, but there are peaks and valleys. There may be occasions when a Christian has a radical fall into protracted sin. In fact, Christians might fall into such egregious sin that they must undergo church discipline and perhaps even excommunication. Sometimes that last step of discipline, excommunication, is necessary to restore a backslider to faith. That being said, as we move from spiritual infancy to spiritual adulthood, the peaks and valleys tend to smooth out. Our spiritual highs are less intense, but so also are our plummets to the depths. We become more stable, as it were, in our Christian growth and fellowship.

WORKING OUT WHAT GOD WORKS IN

There are many churches that teach forms of perfectionism, and closely related to those views are the movements that promise an instantaneous leap of sanctification through a deeper-life experience or a deeper fellowship with the Holy Spirit. Even though many adherents of these movements fall short of teaching full-orbed perfectionism, they do talk about two kinds of Christians: those on a normal growth pattern and those who have a sudden advance in their sanctification through a deeper experience with the Spirit. I certainly do not want to dissuade anyone from pursuing a deeper walk with the Holy Spirit; that is something we should seek at all times. However, Scripture nowhere teaches that we should expect an instant cure for sin or a victorious Christian life by means of a special dose of the Spirit.

Thomas à Kempis, who wrote *The Imitation of Christ*, which remains a Christian classic on sanctification, said that it is a rare thing for a Christian to be able to break a single bad habit in the course of a lifetime. There are times when every Christian asks, "How can I be a Christian yet still struggle so with my flesh?" If we have been walking with God for a long time, we can find comfort in looking back over the course of our Christian lives and recognizing that God has been reshaping us and giving us real progress in the Christian faith. Nevertheless, to be shaped and brought into spiritual maturity is a long-term experience. We tend to seek instant gratification. We want to know how we can be sanctified in three easy steps, but there are no three easy steps. Sanctification is a lifelong process that involves an enormous amount of intensive labor.

Paul writes: "Therefore, my beloved, as you have always obeyed, so now, not only as in my presence but much more in my absence, work out your own salvation with fear and trembling, for it is God who works in you, both to will and to work for his good pleasure" (Phil. 2:12–13). Paul tells us to work out our salvation, which is really a call to be diligent in the pursuit of righteousness. This is work, and therefore a Christian seeking sanctification and spiritual maturity must be active. Paul also tells us to do so "with fear and trembling." He does not mean that we should be in a state of paralyzing anxiety. Rather, he is describing the atmosphere in which we are to work out our salvation. One cannot simply relax in the pursuit of sanctification, going along for the ride as the Holy Spirit carries us on. We are to try to please God.

The good news, as Paul points out, is that we can do so because God is at work within us both to will and to work. This is an area in which there is a genuine synergism, a cooperation. Sanctification is a cooperative process in which God works and we work. One of the chief tasks of the Holy Spirit is the application of our redemption; He brings to bear on our souls the fruit of our justification. He works in us to change our very nature, and we cooperate with Him.

HERETICAL VIEWS OF SANCTIFICATION

That raises the specter of two nagging sets of heresies that have threatened the church throughout history. The first of these sets is activism and quietism. Activism is the heresy of self-righteousness in which people attempt to obtain sanctification by their own efforts. The error of quietism was introduced by French mystics in the seventeenth century. Proponents of quietism hold that sanctification is exclusively the work of the Holy Spirit. Christians do not need to be exercised about it; they need only to be quiet and get out of the way while the Holy Spirit does all the work. They say, in essence, "Let go and let God." There are surely times when it is important to let go. If we hold too tightly to our own strength and do not rely upon the help of the Holy Spirit, then it is time to be quiet. Yet we must not embrace a kind of quietism that seeks to let God do all the work.

A second pair of heresies that follows the doctrine of sanctification is antinomianism and legalism. Very few churches have not been severely afflicted by one or the other, and sometimes even both, of these distortions. Legalists see the law of God as so important to sanctification that they add to the law. In order to assist in their sanctification, they try to legislate where God has left men free. They tend to create rules and regulations, such as forbidding Christians to dance or go to movies. Where God has not legislated, legalists put others in chains and inevitably substitute man-made laws for the real law of God.

The other extreme is antinomianism, which claims that the law of God has no bearing on the Christian life. Antinomians say that because Christians are under grace, they have no need to obey the law of God.

This heresy is rampant. In fact, we are living in a period of pervasive antinomianism in the church. A truly godly person understands he is no longer under bondage to the law, yet he still loves the law of God and meditates on it day and night because therein he discovers what is pleasing to God and what reflects God's character. Rather than fleeing from the law of God, one who is diligent in the pursuit of righteousness and sanctification becomes a serious student of it.

Chapter 45

———

PERSEVERANCE OF THE SAINTS

C an truly converted people lose their salvation? I am asked that
question regularly, often by those who observe young people
renouncing the faith in which they were raised. However, those who
have true faith can never lose it; those who lose their faith never had
it. As John wrote, "They went out from us, but they were not of us; for
if they had been of us, they would have continued with us. But they
went out, that it might become plain that they all are not of us" (1 John
2:19).

There are those who make a profession of faith and become deeply
immersed in the life of the church or in some Christian organization,
only later to leave the church and disavow the faith they professed. It is
easy to become converted to institutions but lack a genuine conversion
to Christ. There are ministries that are skilled in making Christianity appealing so that people join in droves, but those who join do so
without ever dealing with Christ or with sin. Jesus told a parable that
directly relates to this phenomenon:

A sower went out to sow. And as he sowed, some seeds fell
along the path, and the birds came and devoured them. Other
seeds fell on rocky ground, where they did not have much soil,
and immediately they sprang up, since they had no depth of

soil, but when the sun rose they were scorched. And since they had no root, they withered away. Other seeds fell among thorns, and the thorns grew up and choked them. Other seeds fell on good soil and produced grain, some a hundredfold, some sixty, some thirty. (Matt 13:3–8)

The point of the parable is that only seed sown in good soil will last, and that good soil is the transformed soul that has been regenerated by the Holy Spirit.

TWO VIEWS

The doctrine of the perseverance of the saints speaks directly to the question of whether Christians can lose their salvation. The answer given by the Roman Catholic Church is yes. Roman theologians hold that people can and do lose their salvation by committing mortal sin, which, as we noted in an earlier chapter, is a sin that kills or destroys justifying grace in the soul, making it necessary for the sinner to be justified afresh through the sacrament of penance. If the sinner is not justified afresh, he or she can lose salvation and go to hell. Many semi-Pelagians also believe that people can lose their salvation.

The Reformed believe in the perseverance of the saints as a logical deduction from the doctrine of election. If God elects people from all eternity, certainly the elect will remain elect forever. However, even though the doctrine of the perseverance of the saints is a corollary to the doctrine of election, it is dangerous to construct a theology only on the basis of logical inferences or conclusions from one doctrine.

To the Philippians, Paul wrote:

I thank my God in all my remembrance of you, always in every prayer of mine for you all making my prayer with joy, because of your partnership in the gospel from the first day until now. And I am sure of this, that he who began a good work in you will bring it to completion at the day of Jesus Christ. (Phil 1:3–6)

Here Paul expresses his Apostolic confidence that what Christ has started, Christ will finish. Christ is called "founder and perfecter of our faith" (Heb. 12:2). We are the craftsmanship of Christ, and when Christ crafts a person in conformity to His image, He does not have to throw away the product at the end.

CAN SALVATION BE LOST?

There are passages in Scripture, however, that seem to indicate that people can and do lose their salvation. Paul himself said, "But I discipline my body and keep it under control, lest after preaching to others I myself should be disqualified" (1 Cor. 9:27). Another important text in Scripture that relates to the possibility of losing salvation is found in the book of Hebrews:

> Therefore let us leave the elementary doctrine of Christ and go on to maturity, not laying again a foundation of repentance from dead works and of faith toward God, and of instruction about washings, the laying on of hands, the resurrection of the dead, and eternal judgment. And this we will do if God permits. For it is impossible, in the case of those who have once been enlightened, who have tasted the heavenly gift, and have shared in the Holy Spirit, and have tasted the goodness of the word of God and the powers of the age to come, and then have fallen away, to restore them again to repentance, since they are crucifying once again the Son of God to their own harm and holding him up to contempt. (Heb. 6:1–6)

Here we have a solemn warning: it is impossible to restore to salvation those who have crucified Christ once again. This text has caused no small amount of consternation. It seems to go against the grain of everything else the New Testament teaches about God's preserving His saints.

Many believe that the author of Hebrews has in mind unregenerate church members. Jesus said that His church would be filled with both wheat and tares, a mixed body (Matt. 13:24–30). People do join the church and later repudiate it; in that sense, they do become apostate. They fall away from their original profession of faith. Yet we are still left with the question of whether the author was speaking of those whose original profession was genuine or of those inside the visible covenant community who were never truly converted.

The people are described as "those who have once been enlightened," but enlightened to what degree? The enlightened could include the unconverted who attend church and hear Scripture read and preached there. Hebrews refers to the enlightened as those who "have tasted the heavenly gift, and have shared in the Holy Spirit, and have tasted the goodness of the word of God." That applies to churchgoers, regardless of conversion. Churchgoers literally taste the sacraments and hear the Word of God—they are immersed in the ways of the Christian faith. So the "enlightened" could have been members of the church who were never converted.

However, I believe that the author of Hebrews is not describing mere church members but actual believers, because anyone who repents in the true sense is a regenerate person. There is false repentance, such as the repentance of Esau in the Old Testament, but genuine repentance brings genuine renewal as a fruit of regeneration. So since the epistle says that it is impossible to renew people again to repentance, it clearly indicates that there was a time when these people *were* renewed by repentance, thereby indicating that believers are in view.

Nevertheless, I do not believe that this text demolishes the doctrine of the perseverance of the saints. We must consider why the author gave this solemn warning. We do not know who wrote the epistle to the Hebrews or why it was written, but the congregation to which it was written obviously faced a serious problem. Scholars have speculated that the problem was persecution, and because of that threat believers were denying the faith. That is a possibility. Additionally, the first-century church was confronted by the heresy of the Judaizers, which tore the early church apart. Paul's letter to the Galatians addresses this issue, as do other New Testament books. The Judaizers insisted that Gentile converts had to embrace Old Testament Judaism, including circumcision. Paul fought boldly against that teaching. He wrote to the Galatians:

> For all who rely on works of the law are under a curse; for it is written, "Cursed be everyone who does not abide by all things written in the Book of the Law, and do them." Now it is evident that no one is justified before God by the law, for "The righteous shall live by faith." But the law is not of faith, rather "The one who does them shall live by them." Christ redeemed us from the curse of the law by becoming a curse for us—for it is written, "Cursed is everyone who is hanged on a tree"—so that in Christ Jesus the blessing of Abraham might come to the Gentiles, so that we might receive the promised Spirit through faith. (Gal. 3:10–14)

The Apostolic community argued well in a *reductio ad absurdum* fashion; in other words, they took their opponents' premises to their logical conclusion to show that they led only to absurdity. If the Judaizing heresy is in view in Hebrews 6, the author of Hebrews is writing in a manner similar to the way in which Paul wrote to the Galatians. He is saying that if his readers wanted to go back to circumcision, they were, in effect, repudiating the finished work of Christ, and if they repudiated the finished work of Christ, how could they possibly be saved? They would have no way to be saved, because they were going back and embracing the old form, leaving no way to be restored. I think the writer of Hebrews is giving that kind of *reductio ad absurdum* argument; I think it can be detected in verse 9: "*Though we speak in this way*, yet in your case, beloved, we feel sure of better things—things that belong to salvation" (Heb. 6:9, emphasis added). The author makes clear here that his words concerning salvation are a manner of speaking. In the final analysis, he is confident of better things for them, things that accompany salvation, and what accompanies salvation is perseverance.

KEPT BY CHRIST

Any Christian is capable of a serious and radical fall. The question is whether a true believer can have a full and final fall. Judas was a member of the Apostolic community, a disciple of Jesus Christ, yet Judas betrayed Christ for thirty pieces of silver and went off and hanged himself. Jesus said that Judas was a devil from the beginning (John 6:70). He predicted His betrayal: "Truly, truly, I say to you, one of you will betray me" (John 13:21). Then He identified Judas as the betrayer, saying to him, "What you are going to do, do quickly" (v. 27). At that same time, He foretold Peter's denial, which Peter protested vehemently. Jesus looked at him and said, "Simon, Simon, behold, Satan demanded to have you, that he might sift you like wheat, but I have prayed for you that your faith may not fail. And when you have turned again, strengthen your brothers" (Luke 22:31–32). Jesus did not say to Simon Peter, "*If* you turn again"; he said, "*When* you have turned again." Simon belonged to Christ. He fell radically, but the intercessory work of Christ was in effect so that Simon was not lost.

In His High Priestly Prayer, Jesus prayed not only for His disciples but also for all who would believe—which includes us—that they would not be lost (John 17:11, 15, 24). Our confidence in the perseverance of the saints does not rest in the flesh. We should not be like Peter, who had such confidence in his own strength that he protested that he would never deny his Lord. The only reason we can persevere is because God preserves us. If left to ourselves, we could fall at any moment; Satan could sift us like wheat. Our confidence in the final chapter of our salvation rests in the promises of God to finish what He has started. It rests upon the efficacy of our Great High Priest, who intercedes for us every day. He will preserve us.

Part Seven

_____

ECCLESIOLOGY

Chapter 46

———

BIBLICAL IMAGES
OF THE CHURCH

E cclesiology is a subdivision of systematic theology. It concerns
the nature, function, and mission of the church. We can begin to
understand those aspects of the church by looking at the Greek word
kyriakon, from which we get the English word *church*. The words for
"church" in other languages—*kirk* in Scots, *kerk* in Dutch, and *Kirche*
in German—all derive from the same root. *Kyriakon* refers to those
who are possessed or owned by the *kyrios*, or Lord.

Ekklēsia is another Greek word translated as "church." The word
ekklēsia is made up of the prefix *ek-*, which means "out of " or "from,"
and a form of the verb *kaleō*, which means "to call." Thus, *ekklēsia*
means "the called-out ones."

The church does not always reflect what its name implies, however.
This is because, as Augustine said, the church is a *corpus per mixtum*,
a mixed body. The church in this world is made up of a combination of
wheat and tares, and while the church is called to pursue purity, Christ
warned against overzealous church discipline that, in seeking to root
out the tares, might do harm to the wheat (Matt. 13:24–30).

Jesus also said: "On that day many will say to me, 'Lord, Lord, did
we not prophesy in your name, and cast out demons in your name,
and do many mighty works in your name?' And then will I declare to

them, 'I never knew you; depart from me, you workers of lawlessness'" (Matt. 7:22–23). That is why Augustine made a distinction between the visible church and the invisible church.

THE INVISIBLE CHURCH

Theologians use the term *invisible church* to refer to those who make up the true church of Jesus Christ; that is, those who are truly regenerate. By contrast, the *visible church* is the body of all who claim to be in a state of grace and who identify with the church. The invisible church is so called because, according to Scripture, we can evaluate others' professions of faith and their commitment to Christ only on the basis of outward appearances. If someone tells me he is a Christian, I must assume he is telling the truth. I am not able to read his heart. The actual state of his soul is beyond my ability to penetrate.

Yet what is invisible to us is plainly visible to God. We are limited to the outward appearances; God can read the heart. For God, there is nothing invisible about the church; it is all plain and open to Him. We must avoid the assumption that the invisible church and the visible church are separate entities. As Augustine observed, the invisible church is found substantially within the visible church. Thus, the invisible church is made up of the true believers within the visible church.

Augustine also pointed out that there are true believers, members of the invisible church, who, for a variety of reasons, cannot be found on the rolls of institutional churches. Sometimes a believer is providentially hindered from joining a visible church. He might, for example, become a believer but die before he ever has a chance to join a church. Such was the case with the thief on the cross in Luke's gospel (23:32–43). Likewise, some might be hindered from joining a church because they are isolated from other believers.

Still others might be outside simply because they are derelict in their responsibility as Christians. For one reason or another, they willingly keep themselves from joining a church. Many Christians, particularly in our culture today, are so frustrated with the institutional church that they decide not to enter into church membership. However, in my judgment, that is a serious transgression against the Lord Jesus Christ, who established a visible church, gave it a mission, and called us to be part of it. Some who are young in their faith have not come to the realization that they belong in a visible church and that it is their duty to be there. They do not yet understand the importance of belonging to a church and therefore do not attend, yet they are still believers. However, if anyone learns that he is required to be in a church but persists in remaining outside, then we can rightly question whether that person is really a Christian.

Some Christians do not belong to a visible church because they have been excommunicated. Excommunication, the removal of someone from the fellowship of the church, is the final step in the process of church discipline. Once someone has reached this final step, he is to be regarded by the church as an unbeliever. In the final analysis, there is only one sin for which someone can be excommunicated, and that is impenitence. If a sinner repents during the earlier stages of church discipline, he can maintain his communion in the visible church. The last step, excommunication, is undertaken only if he refuses to repent. Theoretically, true Christians can fall into egregious sin and persist in it throughout the process of church discipline, such that the only thing that brings them to their senses is excommunication. This in fact is the very purpose of excommunication.

The point is that the invisible church, the corporate body of the true people of God, exists substantially within the visible church, and it is our duty as those who belong to the Lord to be a part of it.

CHURCH ROOTS

The church has its roots all the way back in the garden of Eden. Adam and Eve, in the direct worship they offered their Creator, were the church. Some have traced the church after the fall back to Abel. For instance, Yves Congar, a twentieth-century Roman Catholic theologian, wrote an essay titled *Ecclesia ab Abel*, that is, *The Church from Abel*. In that work, Congar argued that the church was not started in the New Testament; in reality, it began very early, as we see Cain and

Abel, the sons of Adam and Eve, at worship (Gen. 4), and the author of Hebrews indicates that Abel made his offering by faith (Heb. 11:4).

If I had written that essay, I would have titled it *The Church from Adam*, because I believe the concept of the church can be traced even further back to Cain and Abel's father and mother, who enjoyed fellowship in the immediate presence of God that certainly included worship. Wherever we find people who trust God for their salvation through Christ (or, in the case of the Old Testament saints, the promise of Christ), there we find the church.

Chapter 47

THE CHURCH: ONE AND HOLY

The church consists of those people whom God in Christ has gathered together. The New Testament does not endorse a rugged individualism. Of course, no one is saved by the faith of another, so in that regard, faith is highly individual. However, God saves individuals to establish a corporate body. Just as there was a corporate body, Israel, in the Old Testament, there is a body of people in the New Testament— the church.

The New Testament uses a variety of metaphors to describe the church. One is that of the human body, which we explored briefly when we studied the ministry of the Holy Spirit. The Apostle Paul used the image of the body to describe the unity and diversity found within the visible church of Christ. Not everyone has the same task and gifting; they vary in order to provide organic health to the whole body.

The church is also described in the New Testament as the *laos theou*, "the people of God." We get the word "laity" from the Greek word *laos*.

When Jesus and the Apostles spoke about the nature of the church, they sometimes used the metaphor of a building. The church is not a building, but the church is *like* a building that has a foundation, pillars, and walls. The vast majority of Christians believe that Christ is the foundation of the church, but that is incorrect. Christ is the cornerstone. The actual foundation is the Apostles and the prophets

(Eph. 2:20). The rest of the church is made up of individual stones (vv. 21–22; 1 Peter 2:5). Every believer in Christ who is part of the visible church is a building stone of the church of God.

The church has also formulated ways to describe itself. Chiefly, these are found in the Nicene Creed (see appendix), produced by the Council of Nicea (AD 325). The creed defines the church by four distinct attributes—one, holy, catholic, and Apostolic. Although those terms are rarely used today, particularly in evangelical Protestantism, they provide a wonderful description of the church. We will consider the first two, one and holy, in this chapter.

THE CHURCH IS ONE

The so-called ecumenical movement has made a passionate effort in recent decades to bring disparate denominations together into one worldwide Christian institution. This effort has been motivated by the fragmentation and the disintegration of the unified, visible church. In the United States there are more than two thousand distinct Protestant denominations. Because of that, many believe the church can regain its effectiveness only if it bands together to communicate to the world in unity.

The ecumenical movement finds additional motivation in Christ's prayer for the church: "The glory that you have given me I have given to them, that they may be one even as we are one, I in them and you in me, that they may become perfectly one, so that the world may know that you sent me and loved them even as you loved me" (John 17:22–23).

The fact that there is a lack of unity in the visible church today is all the more scandalous because it seems to fly in the face of the desire of the head of the church, Jesus Christ.

However, the lack of unity does not mean that there is no unity of the true church; neither does it mean that Christ as our Intercessor has failed. This is clear if we hold to the concept of the invisible church as Augustine explained it. There is indeed a genuine unity of the church, and it is found across denominational lines in the invisible fellowship, the communion of the saints. There is an unbroken fellowship, a spiritual unity, among all true Christians by virtue of their common union with Christ.

Therefore, Christ's prayer has been answered. All Christians enjoy a unity of mission in which we have one Lord, one faith, and one baptism (Eph. 4:4–5). There is surely disunity in the visible church, but that is not as important as the reality of the unity that we enjoy by virtue of our shared communion in Christ.

There are always dissatisfied individuals who want to break away from the main body and start something new. We must be conscientious about seeking to preserve unity with other professing Christians. Of course, there are times when we must break fellowship with other groups or institutions, but overall we should seek to be at one with as many professing Christians as we possibly can. Churches split far too easily over too many things, yet often they split over insignficant issues or remain together despite divisions over substantive issues. We are not to negotiate over the essentials of the gospel, but neither should we be at odds over minor matters.

THE CHURCH IS HOLY

The church is also holy, although from another perspective it is the most corrupt institution on earth. We can rightly see the church as corrupt if we consider how corruption is measured. We are told in Scripture, "Everyone to whom much was given, of him much will be required, and from him to whom they entrusted much, they will demand the more" (Luke 12:48). No institution has been as gifted as the Christian church. No institution has been given a more sacred mission. When we fail to obey that mission, corruption is the result.

The primary meaning of the word *holy* is "set apart" or "consecrated," which ties directly to the very meaning of the word *ekklēsia*, which means "the called-out ones." The church consists of those called out and set apart for a holy task. The church is holy insofar as it has a sacred vocation.

It is worth noting that the church is the only institution in the history of the world to whom God has given an absolute guarantee that, in the final analysis, it will not fail. The great institutions of the world come and go, but the church of Jesus Christ will remain. Jesus said of the church that "the gates of hell shall not prevail against it" (Matt. 16:18). In the ancient world, gates were defensive mechanisms, so, based on Jesus' reference, the church is called to attack the strongholds of Satan, and those strongholds cannot withstand the power that has been invested in the church.

The church is holy also because it is made up of people indwelt by the Holy Spirit. The church is the Holy Spirit's institution. Surely the Spirit works in the lives of people in a host of other institutions, but the church is the focal point of the Spirit's ministry. The means of God's divine grace are not restricted to the visible church, but they are concentrated there. Not everyone in the visible camp of Israel was saved; as Paul wrote, "Not all who are descended from Israel belong to Israel" (Rom. 9:6). Yet he also wrote: "Then what advantage has the Jew? Or what is the value of circumcision? Much in every way. To begin with, the Jews were entrusted with the oracles of God" (Rom. 3:1–2). The church has the preaching of the Word, the celebration of the sacraments, and the worship of God in corporate gatherings, and this is where Christians gather together in fellowship. Insofar as this is the principal domain of the Holy Spirit and the place where the saints gather, the church can be called "holy."

Chapter 48

THE CHURCH:
CATHOLIC AND APOSTOLIC

S ome years ago, while I was traveling with my wife and two friends
in Eastern Europe, our train was stopped as we entered Romania. A
customs official asked for our passports, which we handed over. When
he noticed a Bible among our belongings, he said, "You are not Ameri-
cans!" We were a bit confused because our passports clearly identified
us as American citizens. He asked for the Bible, which we handed to
him, and he opened it and read from Ephesians 2:19: "You are no longer strangers and aliens, but you are fellow citizens with the saints and
members of the household of God." He was a Christian, too, and once
he discovered the connection he had with us, he joyfully approved our
passage into Romania.

THE CHURCH IS CATHOLIC

That incident communicated to us the flesh-and-blood reality of a
third attribute of the true church—it is catholic, or universal. This is
the third of four attributes of the church set forth in the fourth century
at the Council of Nicea. The Nicene Creed (see appendix) declares that
the true church is one, holy, catholic, and Apostolic. We looked at the
first two attributes in the previous chapter; we will consider the third
and fourth in this chapter.

269

The catholic church—the church universal—is different from the Roman Catholic Church. In America, the term "Roman Catholic" is often shortened to simply "Catholic," so when people refer to "the Catholic Church," they mean the Roman Catholic Church. Technically, however, the term *catholic* does not refer to a specific institution but to the church of Jesus Christ that encompasses all nations, tribes, and peoples.

Many Protestant churches have national or regional boundaries, whereas the Roman Catholic Church does not. Its members worldwide are all united under the headship of Rome. Rome excludes Protestants from its view of the true church because of Protestant fragmentation. However, the universal church is the invisible church. The church of Jesus Christ extends around the world, just as I encountered at the Romanian border.

THE CHURCH IS APOSTOLIC

The true church is also Apostolic. We noted in the previous chapter that the foundation of the church is the prophets and the Apostles. When Christ established the New Testament covenant community, He gave first the office of Apostle (Eph. 4:11). The primary authority of the infant Christian community was vested in the Apostles. The title *Apostle* comes from the Greek word *apostolos*, which means "one who is sent." In ancient Greek culture, an apostle was an envoy or a delegate sent by a king or some other authority figure. The apostle carried with him the delegated authority of the king. He was a spokesman for the one he represented.

We tend to use the terms *Apostle* and *disciple* interchangeably, but there is a significant difference between them. With the exception of the Apostle Paul, all the Apostles in the New Testament were first disciples, but not all disciples became Apostles. Jesus had many more disciples than the twelve we know from the Gospels. At one point during His ministry, He sent seventy disciples on a particular mission (Luke 10). The Greek word for "disciple," *mathētēs*, means "student" or "learner." Disciples were those who gathered around Jesus to study in His rabbinic school. They called Him "Rabbi," following Him from place to place as He taught. However, toward the end of His earthly ministry, He chose from His body of disciples a select number to be Apostles (Matt. 10). To these He transferred His authority, saying, "Whoever receives you receives me, and whoever receives me receives him who sent me" (Matt. 10:40).

Early on in the church, heretical groups arose that tried to supplant the authority of the Apostles. One group, the Gnostics, tried to claim Apostolic authority for themselves while at the same time claiming allegiance to Jesus. But they were not genuine Apostles.

The first and primary Apostle of the New Testament was Jesus Himself. He was sent by the Father and authorized to speak for Him, as He testified: "All authority in heaven and on earth has been given to me" (Matt. 28:18) and "I have not spoken on my own authority, but the Father who sent me has himself given me a commandment—what to say and what to speak" (John 12:49). When the Pharisees tried to reject Jesus' authority, He told them:

> If I glorify myself, my glory is nothing. It is my Father who glorifies me, of whom you say, 'He is our God.' But you have not known him. I know him. If I were to say that I do not know him, I would be a liar like you, but I do know him and I keep his word. Your father Abraham rejoiced that he would see my day. He saw it and was glad. (John 8:54–56)

In other words, one cannot the love the Father and yet hate the Son, and it was the Son who vested His authority in the Apostles. Irenaeus of Lyon (AD 130–202), an early church apologist, made the same point against the heretics of his day when he said that those who rejected the Apostles were rejecting the One who had commissioned them, namely, Christ. There was a line of authority from God to Christ to the Apostles.

Apostolic authority has been under attack even more in our own day, chiefly by feminists who argue against the teachings of Paul, and also by the higher critics, who profess allegiance to Christ while rejecting the authority of sacred Scripture.

A minister I know was once flying home to Los Angeles, and while he was en route, an earthquake hit California. Once he arrived home, he went to his church to assess the damage. He was relieved to see that the building was still standing and everything inside seemed untouched. Not a single window was broken. Yet a short time later, when experts came to assess the damage, they discovered that the foundation had shifted under the building. As a result, the church was declared uninhabitable. Outwardly, the building appeared to be fine, but it was not. The foundation had moved, so the building was no longer stable.

That situation illustrates the issue concerning the Apostolic nature of the church. When people claim that the church has authority but reject the Bible, they are actually rejecting the church itself because they are rejecting one of the church's four attributes, namely, its Apostolic character. If we attack the authority of the word of the Apostles, we attack the very heart and soul of the church. As the psalmist said, "If the foundations are destroyed, what can the righteous do?" (Ps. 11:3).

Over the last two centuries, liberal theology, with its categorical rejection of the inspiration and authority of the Bible, has had such an impact on the visible church as to almost destroy it. In some countries, the churches are nearly empty; less than two percent of the population attends services. This is largely due to the abandonment of Apostolic authority in favor of a focus on social concerns, making the church indistinguishable from any number of other institutions. Apostolic authority, which means biblical authority, is the foundation of the church.

THE MARKS OF A TRUE CHURCH

During the Reformation, Protestantism fragmented into several groups. There were Reformed churches in Switzerland, the Netherlands, and Scotland; the Anglican church in England; Lutheran churches in Germany and Scandinavia; the Huguenots in France; and so on. All the while, Rome declared itself to be the true church. That is when Protestants began to refer to *a* true church rather than to *the* true church. The Reformers said that just as a particular congregation is a mix of tares and wheat, so no denomination is infallible; every one contains some degree of error or corruption. The Reformers then identified three essential marks of a true church.

The first is that the church professes the gospel. If a church denies any essential point of the gospel, such as the deity of Christ, the atonement, or justification by faith alone, it is no longer a church. The Reformers excluded the Roman Catholic Church because, although it embraced the deity of Christ and the atonement, it rejected justification by faith alone. Therefore, the Reformers said, Rome was no longer a true church.

The second mark is that the sacraments—baptism and the Lord's Supper—are duly administered. The Reformers recognized the differences among Christians over the presence of Christ in the Lord's Supper and the mode of baptism, but they said the basic celebration of the sacraments on a regular basis is a necessary element of a true church. Some so rejected the sacramental emphasis of the Roman Catholic Church that they sought to establish churches without the sacraments, but the Reformers argued that the sacraments were designed by Christ for the edification of God's people, and therefore it is the duty of the church to maintain the proper observation of them.

The third mark of a true church is discipline, which requires some form of church government. A church has responsibility for the spiritual nurture of its members, to see that people grow in their faith and become increasingly sanctified. Therefore, discipline is required to keep the church from becoming infected with impurities and corruption. If the clergy of a particular church continually deny the deity of Christ, yet the church does not censure or remove them, then that church has ceased to be a legitimate church.

Chapter 49

———

WORSHIP IN THE CHURCH

The New Testament gives us a glimpse into the inner sanctum of heaven itself, and we hear the song of the living creatures, the elders, and the angelic host. John describes the scene:

> "Worthy is the Lamb who was slain, to receive power and wealth and wisdom and might and honor and glory and blessing!"
>
> And I heard every creature in heaven and on earth and under the earth and in the sea, and all that is in them, saying, "To him who sits on the throne and to the Lamb be blessing and honor and glory and might forever and ever!"
>
> And the four living creatures said, "Amen!" and the elders fell down and worshiped. (Rev. 5:12–14)

In this text, we encounter something extraordinary, yet it is something to which all Christians should be able to relate—pure worship. As creatures made in the image of God, we were designed to worship our Creator, yet we depart from this purpose due to our sinful human nature. Nevertheless, once the Spirit of God quickens people, imparting to them spiritual life, they have a new capacity for worship. Deep within, all Christians have a hunger to find a way to express worship of God.

It is no accident, therefore, that worship is one of the central purposes of the church. When the people of God gather in a common assembly, the purpose is to worship. People often go to church primarily for fellowship, Christian education, or edification, but the primary reason we should be there is to join with other believers in worshiping the Lord.

WITH HONOR AND ADORATION

To worship is to assign worth or value to God. For example, the song in Revelation attributes worth to the person of Christ and what He accomplished. We call the attributing of worth "honor." We honor those who have proven themselves worthy of particular notice and affirmation. They have achieved something that we regard as valuable.

Conversely, in Romans 1, Paul speaks of the revelation of God's wrath against the human race. The world is exposed to the wrath of God because, even though He has manifested His eternal power and deity to all creatures, man refuses to honor God as God. In our fallen state, we refuse to worship God; we withhold from Him the honor that He deserves. Paul writes that instead of honoring God, we exchange the truth about God for a lie, and worship and serve the creature rather than the Creator (vv. 18–25). We love to receive honors ourselves and to be at celebrations where human beings are honored for prodigious achievements. People are glad to bestow all kinds of honor and glory upon other people, but they balk when it comes to giving honor where it is most due—to God, the being of supreme value and worth.

We describe the worship experience with words such as *exaltation* or *praise*. We talk about praise music and the offering of praise, which has its roots in biblical history, particularly in the Old Testament, where a primary element of worship was the offering of sacrifices. Even before the offering of animal sacrifices for sin, there was the offering of sacrifices to God simply to honor Him. We tend to think that since the Old Testament sacrificial system was fulfilled in Christ, the era of sacrifice is finished. The era of sin offerings is indeed over because Christ fulfilled that demand for us once and for all, yet Paul tells that we are to present our bodies as living sacrifices to God, which is our "spiritual worship" (Rom. 12:1). Sacrifice is still to be given—the sacrifice of praise to God (Heb. 13:15)—and it is to be given with the substance of our entire lives.

275

Closely connected to the concept of praise is *adoration*, a term we have cheapened in our day. We describe people as "adorable," meaning that they are cute or attractive, and in romantic situations, it is not uncommon to hear that one lover "adores" the other. Properly speaking, adoration is more than that. It is one thing for me to love my wife but quite another for me to worship her, which I am most certainly not to do. The sort of affection associated with the concept of adoration is meant to be given to God alone.

From a biblical standpoint, adoration takes place in the innermost recesses of our souls; it is of a spiritual nature that defies precise definition, yet we know when we experience it. We are aware of a spiritual connection between the nonphysical aspect of our humanity and the very character of God in which we praise Him with our lips or with our thoughts such that our spirits overflow with affection, admiration, reverence, and awe for Him. Adoration includes placing ourselves in a lowly position so that the One being reverenced is thereby exalted.

IN SPIRIT AND TRUTH

Jesus had a conversation with a woman at a well in the town of Sychar, and during that conversation, the subject of worship came up. She was a Samaritan. The Samaritans worshiped God at Mount Gerizim, whereas the Jews concentrated their worship at the central sanctuary in Jerusalem. After Jesus revealed that He knew she had had five husbands, the woman said to Him, "Sir, I perceive that you are a prophet. Our fathers worshiped on this mountain, but you say that in Jerusalem is the place where people ought to worship" (John 4:19–20). Jesus replied:

> Woman, believe me, the hour is coming when neither on this mountain nor in Jerusalem will you worship the Father. You worship what you do not know; we worship what we know, for salvation is from the Jews. But the hour is coming, and is now here, when the true worshipers will worship the Father in spirit and truth, for the Father is seeking such people to

worship him. God is spirit, and those who worship him must worship in spirit and truth. (vv. 21–24)

Here Jesus said two things about proper worship, the kind of worship God wants from His people. He said that worship that is pleasing to God is given in spirit and truth. The second of these descriptions of proper worship is not difficult to understand. Truthful worship precludes all forms of idolatrous worship, which is to substitute something for God that is not the true God. False worship is also hypocritical worship, that which is insincere.

Jesus' words about worshiping "in spirit" are a bit more difficult to interpret. The Bible speaks of "spirit" in two distinct ways. The most frequent reference is to the Holy Spirit, but Scripture also speaks about the spirit of a man. We give little attention to the human spirit. In fact, we have almost abandoned our belief that there is such a thing as a spirit or a soul that is an integral aspect of our humanity. In His conversation with the woman of Sychar, I think Jesus had in mind soulful worship, the sort that flows from the heart. God desires that people worship Him from that deep core of being that no one else can see or measure, because it is unique to each person. In fact, it is the very essence of what we call "personality." No one can deny this nonphysical aspect of what it means to be a person; without it, we would be soulless, brutish creatures. Yet because we have it, we have the capacity for spiritual connection with God.

John Calvin's all-consuming passion for reformation in the sixteenth century was focused on worship because he knew that the greatest enemy to the health of God's people is their proclivity toward idolatry. Idolatry creeps into the life of the church in countless ways, which is why Calvin was driven to offer pure worship to God—something lost in our day. We tend to be more interested in entertainment than in expressing worship in spirit and truth.

OLD TESTAMENT WORSHIP
If we examine the patterns of worship found in the Old Testament, we find that God Himself directed and authorized those patterns, and

277

from them we learn the basic principles of what pleases Him.

One key feature of Old Testament worship is that the whole person was engaged in the act of worship. It was certainly not mindless worship; in fact, the mind was very much involved. Yet there is more to worship than the mind. All five human senses were engaged in Old Testament worship.

The sense of sight was engaged by the design of the tabernacle and the beauty of the temple, which was filled with beautiful things that God Himself had designed "for glory and for beauty" (Ex. 28:2, 40). Everything in the sanctuary, down to the garments that the priests wore, excited the eye with a sense of the transcendent beauty of God.

We know that the sense of hearing also was an important part of the worship service because music was given a central place in the Old Testament. The psalms are basically hymns that were used in worship.

The sense of smell was also part of worship, which is why incense was used. A pleasing aroma became associated with the presence of God; it was a delightful sensory aspect of their worship. I am not advocating that we must bring incense into our worship services today. The point is that the olfactory sense was integral to Old Testament worshipers' response.

The sense of taste had a place also, as shown by the Passover meal, which was transferred in the New Testament to the Lord's Supper. Also, in one of the Old Testament worship hymns we hear, "Oh, taste and see that the LORD is good!" (Ps. 34:8).

Finally, there was the tactile dimension, the laying on of hands by which the priest touched the worshiper to indicate God's blessing or benediction. In the early church, a minister laid his hands on each member and pronounce God's blessing. Today, when a minister raises his hands and pronounces the benediction, he is replicating that practice. As congregations grew larger over time, the raised hand of the minister came to symbolize the touch of the minister bestowing the blessing of God.

If we look at the Old Testament, we find dynamic worship principles that can teach us to offer the kind of honor, adoration, and praise that God requires.

Chapter 50

THE SACRAMENTS
OF THE CHURCH

One area of Christian theology that has provoked endless controversy and about which there has been very little agreement among
Christians is the sacraments. This remains true today. As the word
sacrament implies, sacraments are sacred, and that is the underlying
reason for the intensity of the debates. The controversies involve the
mode in which the sacraments are given, who is allowed to participate,
and who can administer them. A significant debate is over the number
of sacraments. The Roman Catholic Church believes there are seven
sacraments, whereas the vast majority of Protestant churches identify
only two.

THE ROMAN CATHOLIC VIEW

The Roman church sees each of the sacraments as a means of grace.
Thomas Aquinas said that the seven Roman Catholic sacraments prepare the communicant member for various stages of life. Thus, the first
sacrament is baptism, which is administered to infants. When a child is
baptized, the grace of justification is seen as being infused or poured into
the child's soul. Subsequently, if the child cooperates with that grace, he
is brought into a state of righteousness and declared just by God.

This grace is said to operate *ex opere operato*, which means "through the working of the works." This formula applies to all the sacraments in the Roman Catholic Church. The idea is that sacramentally imparted grace provides automatic efficacy so long as no hindrance is brought about by the recipient.

Baptism is the beginning of the way. Upon baptism, the recipient receives not only an infusion of grace but also an indelible mark upon the soul, the character *indelebilis*. This spiritual mark is so imprinted upon the baptized child that even if he should subsequently lose the grace he gained from the sacrament, he is not rebaptized. The original baptism sufficiently marks his soul.

The second sacrament in the Roman Catholic system is confirmation, at which time the grace received at baptism is confirmed. This sacrament occurs at the transition from childhood to adulthood. It reflects the concept of *bar mitzvah* in Old Testament Israel, when a boy became a man, responsible for his own keeping of the law.

There is also the sacrament of penance, which is defined by the church as "the second plank" of justification for those who have made "shipwreck" of their souls. The saving grace conferred at baptism can be lost through the commission of mortal sin, but the sinner can be restored to a state of grace by means of penance or confession. This is the second sacramental source of justifying grace. Once again, the grace of Christ is supposedly infused into the soul, giving the individual an opportunity to be restored to a state of justification.

Matrimony is also a sacrament in the Roman Catholic Church. Of course, not everyone in the church receives the sacrament of matrimony because not everyone gets married. However, when two people enter into the sacred union of marriage, that union is blessed by the church, and new grace is administered sacramentally to the couple to provide them with the necessary strength to grow in the marital union.

The sacrament of holy orders corresponds to ordination in other denominations. When a man is elevated to the priesthood, he receives the sacrament of holy orders, through which he is empowered to administer grace to others through these same sacraments. Apart from receiving the grace of holy orders, one lacks the power to offer the prayer of consecration, by which the elements of bread and wine are transformed into the body and blood of Christ during the Roman Catholic Mass.

Also found in the Roman Catholic Church is the sacrament of the anointing of the sick, previously called extreme unction or last rites. It is designed to impart grace to someone on the brink of death to prepare him or her to come before the judgment seat of God. Originally, the anointing of the sick was based upon James' instruction in his epistle: "Is anyone among you sick? Let him call for the elders of the church, and let them pray over him, anointing him with oil in the name of the Lord. And the prayer of faith will save the one who is sick, and the Lord will raise him up" (5:14–15). This was originally a healing rite in the church, but as time progressed, it developed into a final healing rite, as it were, to heal the soul as it is leaving the world.

The sacrament deemed most important by the Roman church is the Eucharist or the Lord's Supper, in which the sanctifying grace and nurturing power of Christ are again communicated to those who receive it.

THE PROTESTANT VIEW

One of the most inflammatory writings of the Protestant Reformation was Martin Luther's booklet *The Babylonian Captivity of the Church*. In it, he lashed out against the Roman system of sacraments, calling it "sacerdotalism," which is the belief that salvation is communicated through a priesthood. Luther objected vigorously to the Roman Catholic Church's sacramental system, which had developed to the degree that it had begun to usurp the central importance of the Word of God.

By contrast, the Reformers tried to reconstitute a proper balance between Word and sacrament, believing that the two must be distinguished but never separated; that is, that the sacraments should never be distributed or administered without the preaching of the Word. For example, in the church where I preach, I am not allowed to celebrate the Lord's Supper without also offering a proclamation of the Word of God. The Reformers were also concerned about those who sought to do away with the sacraments altogether. Some were so radically opposed to the Roman sacramental system that they thought the Word should stand alone without the sacrament. The Reformers reminded this faction that Christ Himself had instituted and authorized the sacraments, and therefore they ought never be neglected.

Contrary to the Roman church, the Reformers stressed two sacraments—baptism and the Lord's Supper. These rites qualify as sacraments in the Reformers' view because they were instituted explicitly by Christ. In the upper room, Jesus clearly instituted the celebration of the Lord's Supper (Matt. 26:26–29), and in the Great Commission, He commanded His disciples to baptize those brought into the Christian faith (28:19). The Reformers viewed the remainder of the Roman sacraments as special ordinances of the church that fell short of this qualifying mark.

The Reformers also rejected *ex opere operato*, adopting instead the idea of *ex opere operantis*, or "through the work of the worker." The simple difference in the Latin has to do with the efficacy or the benefits that flow from the sacraments; they are efficacious only for those who receive them in and by faith. So, for example, even though infants receive the sacrament of baptism, the benefits promised by that sacrament do not occur automatically. Just because one is baptized does not mean one is saved—all are justified only by faith. When one has faith, then everything communicated through the sign and seal of baptism is fully received. Likewise, one who comes to the celebration of the Lord's Supper without faith runs the risk of Christ's judgment, which Paul warned about in 1 Corinthians 11:27–32. The issue for the Reformers was not the validity but the efficacy of the sacraments, which was inextricably tied to the presence of genuine faith.

SIGNS AND SEALS

The sacraments are seen as signs and seals. In a sense, the sign character of the sacrament is the Word dramatized, something we see God doing frequently in the Old Testament. God's prophets not only spoke God's words, at times they dramatized them, sometimes in bizarre ways. Additionally, God instituted practices and ceremonies that contained symbolic significance, such as circumcision and the Passover. These were visible, outward signs of invisible, transcendent, divine operations. This is the same manner in which human beings communicate. We do not merely speak words; we gesture and move around when we talk. We enhance our words with bodily actions. The sacraments operate in the same manner. God communicates to our senses through the dramatization of His Word by these visible signs, the sacraments.

The sacraments are also seals. In the ancient world, a seal was used to guarantee the authenticity of someone's word. If a king issued a decree, he would press his signet ring into wax on the edict, verifying that it was from him. In so doing, he communicated the authority behind the decree. In like manner, the sacraments represent God's sealing of His promises of redemption. They are His visible guarantees to all who believe that they will receive all the benefits offered to us in Christ.

Chapter 51

BAPTISM

B aptism is clearly a sacrament that was established by Jesus Christ. He commanded His followers: "Go therefore and make disciples of all nations, baptizing them in the name of the Father and of the Son and of the Holy Spirit, teaching them to observe all that I have commanded you" (Matt. 28:19–20).

However, there are sharp differences between Christians over baptism. For instance, many Christian communities will not baptize people until they are adults and have made a profession of faith, whereas other communities baptize babies shortly after they are born. Given this and other differences of opinion, how are we to understand this important Christian rite?

THE BAPTISM OF JOHN

Many believe that baptism was initiated by John the Baptist, but the baptism of John and the New Testament rite that we celebrate in the Christian community are not identical. The baptism inaugurated by John was directed specifically to the Jewish nation, and it was initiated during the period of the Old Testament.

For centuries, God had promised the coming of the Messiah, so when the Savior was about to make His entrance into the world, just as the Old Testament had foretold, God sent a prophet out of the wilderness to prepare for His coming. John was that prophet, and he came to proclaim the Messiah's advent to a people who were unprepared.

During the period between the Old Testament and the New Testament, a practice emerged among the Jews called "proselyte baptism." This was a purification rite for Gentiles, a bathing that symbolized the cleansing of people considered to be unclean. If a Gentile wanted to become a Jew, he was required to do three things. He had to make a profession of faith in Judaism. Then, if he was a male, he had to undergo circumcision. Finally, he had to undergo the purification rite of proselyte baptism because he was considered ceremonially unclean.

John the Baptist scandalized many when he declared that *Jews* needed to be purified in the same manner. It was not only the Gentiles who were in need of repentance and preparation for the coming of the Messiah; the Jews also needed to prepare themselves. This is why John cried to the Jewish people, "Repent, for the kingdom of heaven is at hand" (Matt. 3:2). The Pharisees were outraged by John's message because they found their security in the old covenant.

When Jesus came, He instituted a new covenant and a new covenantal sign along with it. In the Old Testament, God ratified His covenants with signs. The sign of the covenant God made with Noah was the rainbow, signifying that He would never again destroy the world with water. When God entered into a covenant with Abraham and his seed, He established it with the sign of circumcision. At that time, circumcision became the sign of God's promise.

In time, many, including the Pharisees, came to think of circumcision as the means to salvation. Paul argues against that view in his epistle to the Romans: "For no one is a Jew who is merely one outwardly, nor is circumcision outward and physical. But a Jew is one inwardly, and circumcision is a matter of the heart, by the Spirit, not by the letter. His praise is not from man but from God" (2:28–29).

Paul adds that although the sign of circumcision does not save, the sign is not meaningless. Circumcision signified God's covenantal promise to all who put their trust in Him. Circumcision illustrated the validity of the promise of God, but the promise of God was to be realized only through faith.

Circumcision was not the sign of the new covenant. This was the subject of Paul's dispute with the Judaizers, who insisted that all converts to Christianity must be circumcised. Paul wanted the Judaizers to understand that circumcision was a sign not only of the promise of the covenant but also of its curse. All those who failed to fulfill the terms of the old covenant were cut off from God's presence. On the cross, however, Christ fulfilled the curse. Therefore, those under the new covenant who insisted on circumcision were falling back to the terms of the old covenant.

THE BAPTISM OF JESUS

So the sign of the new covenant is not the baptism of John; it is the baptism of Jesus. Jesus took the rite of cleansing and identified it not with Israel but with His new covenant. As a result, baptism replaced circumcision as the outward sign of inclusion in the new covenant community. Those who are baptized are not necessarily saved; however, they have God's promise that all the benefits of Christ are theirs if and when they believe.

Martin Luther experienced difficult sessions of satanic attack. When subjected to such a siege, he would say aloud to Satan, "Be gone from me! I am baptized!" In other words, Luther was holding by faith to the promises of God that are communicated to His people in this covenant sign. That is the significance of baptism; it is a dramatized word. It is God's word of promise to all who believe. Paul wrote:

See to it that no one takes you captive by philosophy and empty deceit, according to human tradition, according to the elemental spirits of the world, and not according to Christ. For in him the whole fullness of deity dwells bodily, and you have been filled in him, who is the head of all rule and authority. In him also you were circumcised with a circumcision made without hands, by putting off the body of the flesh, by the circumcision of Christ, having been buried with him in baptism, in which you were also raised with him through faith in the powerful working of God, who raised him from the dead. (Col. 2:8–12)

Here Paul speaks of the circumcision not made with hands; he sees a direct link between the circumcision of the Old Testament and the baptism of the New Testament.

Baptism is a sign of our regeneration, that we have been raised from spiritual death and made new creatures. The sign itself does not accomplish that; it simply points to what does—the Holy Spirit. Just as we are baptized with water, so God promises to baptize with His Holy Spirit those who are in Christ. Additionally, baptism indicates our participation in the death and resurrection of Christ. In a very real sense, we died with Christ on the cross because it was our sins He bore there.

Paul emphasizes that we are called to participate in the suffering of Christ, not to gain merit but to identify with our crucified Lord by participating willingly in His humiliation. That, too, is signified by baptism. Paul wrote that unless we are willing to participate in the afflictions of Christ, we will not participate in His exaltation. Christ promised that His faithful disciples will be persecuted (Luke 21:16–17). His people will be called upon to suffer in that way, yet those afflictions are not worthy to be compared to the glory that God has stored up for His people in heaven (Rom. 8:18). Baptism signifies our participation in Christ's death, His resurrection, His suffering, His humiliation, and His exaltation.

A MEANINGFUL PROMISE

Some churches argue that only adults who make a conscious profession of faith can be baptized. Historically, however, the majority has believed that just as the Old Testament covenant promise was given to Abraham and to his seed, the New Testament covenant promise has been given to believers and to their seed; and just as the old covenant sign was given to believers and their children, the new covenant sign is given to believers and their children. Just as baptism is a sign of faith, so circumcision was a sign of faith, and we cannot argue that a sign of faith cannot be given to one's children. The primary point is that neither circumcision nor baptism confers faith. What they confer is the promise of God to all who believe.

John Calvin argued that the efficacy of the sacrament is never tied to the time that it is given; salvation may come before, during, or after the administration of the sign, even as was the case with circumcision. Neither does the validity of baptism rest upon the one who receives or administers it. It rests instead on the character of the One whose promise it signifies.

Chapter 52

——

THE LORD'S SUPPER

When we study the book of Acts and the life of the early Christian community, we discover that the people placed great value on coming together to celebrate the Lord's Supper. Throughout church history, this has been the central sacrament. It has its roots in the New Testament, but we see a precursor of it in the Old Testament ordinance of Passover.

PASSOVER CHANGED

Before Jesus died, He asked His disciples to make arrangements for them to celebrate the Passover one final time in a borrowed place, an upper room. When they came together, He told them that He had earnestly desired to celebrate the Passover with them one final time (Luke 22:7–15). There, as they were celebrating the Passover, Jesus changed the words of the liturgy and told His disciples that the bread was His body, which was about to be broken for them (v. 19). In so doing, He changed the significance of the Old Testament Passover. Then He took the wine for the Passover meal and declared that it was His blood (v. 20). So He instituted a new dimension of redemptive history. There in the upper room, the New Testament was born.

We tend to think that the New Testament era began where the writings of the New Testament begin—with the announcement of the coming of John the Baptist. But the historical period of the New

289

Testament actually began when the new covenant was established. It began in the upper room, when Jesus instituted the Lord's Supper. As God had used the Old Testament Passover as a remembrance of the people's deliverance from the plague of the death of the firstborn in Egypt, so Christ instituted the Lord's Supper as a remembrance for the church of His death for redemption.

MAJOR VIEWS

Because the death of Christ is central to the Christian faith, the celebration of the Lord's Supper is of extreme importance, and for that reason it has been yet another source of controversy throughout church history. A tragedy of the sixteenth century was that the Reformers could not come to agreement on the meaning of the Lord's Supper. As close as John Calvin and Martin Luther were in terms of their theology, they held different views on critical aspects of the Supper.

Mode of the Presence

The central debate then and now has to do with the mode of the presence of Christ in the sacrament. The major views on the nature of the Lord's Supper include those of Roman Catholics, Lutherans, and Calvinists.

The Roman Catholic view is called "transubstantiation." In simple terms, the Roman church believes that a miracle takes place when the priest blesses the bread and wine during the Mass. The ordinary elements of bread and wine are transformed into the actual body and blood of Jesus Christ. This doctrine was shaped using the philosophy of Aristotle. In his attempts to define reality, Aristotle made a distinction between the *essential* and *accidental* properties of an object. I can identify a piece of chalk by its color and cylindrical shape, but I cannot penetrate into its innermost core of being. According to Aristotle, the innermost core of a piece of chalk is its substance; its external qualities are merely its *accidentia*, the physical properties of the chalk.

Applying this framework to the Lord's Supper in the formula of transubstantiation, Rome said that the inner core of the bread and the wine changes to the body and blood of Christ even though the *accidentia* of the bread and wine, its appearance and such, remain the same. Following the language of Aristotle, then, there is a double miracle, because the *accidentia* of any object are related to its substance. Chalk looks like chalk because chalk has the *accidentia* of chalk. There is always a perfect relationship between the substance of a thing and its external qualities. However, in the miracle of the Mass, we find the *accidentia* of bread without its substance and the substance of the body of Jesus without its *accidentia*—a double miracle.

Luther objected to this theory, saying that the presence of Christ does not take the place of the elements but instead is added to the bread and wine, albeit invisibly. In other words, Christ is physically present in, with, and under the elements. This view is called the "sacramental union," and is sometimes called "consubstantiation." The prefix *con-* means "with," and it indicates how the body and blood of Jesus attend the physical elements of bread and wine. So Luther insisted that Christ's body is physically present in the Supper, a conviction he based on Jesus' words upon instituting the sacrament: "This is my body." Luther argued that Jesus would never have said that the bread was His body if, in fact, it was not.

Calvin stressed that a physical body, such as the one Jesus has, can be in only one place at a time, and since Jesus' body is in heaven, He cannot be physically present in the sacraments. However, the divine nature of Jesus can be everywhere at once; therefore, He is truly present at the Lord's Supper, albeit spiritually.

In sum, Roman Catholics, Lutherans, and Calvinists all agree that Christ is truly present in the Lord's Supper; the debate concerns *how* He is present, whether physically or spiritually.

The Time Factor

The time factor involved in the Lord's Supper is threefold. With respect to the past, the Lord's Supper is a remembrance of the Lord's death for sinners. The Apostle Paul recounts Jesus' words when the Supper was instituted:

For I received from the Lord what I also delivered to you, that the Lord Jesus on the night when he was betrayed took bread, and when he had given thanks, he broke it, and said, "This is my body which is for you. Do this in remembrance of me." In the same way also he took the cup, after supper, saying, "This cup is the new covenant in my blood. Do this, as often as you drink it, in remembrance of me." (1 Cor. 11:23–25)

When Jesus instituted the Supper, He also said, "I will not drink of the fruit of the vine until the kingdom of God comes" (Luke 22:18). From that we see that the Lord's Supper also causes us to think of the future when we will sit at the table of the Lord in heaven, at the marriage feast of the Lamb. There is a future orientation to the Lord's Supper.

At the same time, there is the present benefit of meeting the risen Christ in person at His table every time we participate in the Supper. So there is a present reality, a remembrance of things past, and an anticipation of the blessed future that God has promised for His people.

Part Eight

ESCHATOLOGY

Chapter 53

———•———

DEATH AND
THE INTERMEDIATE STATE

With this chapter, we begin our study of the subdivision of systematic theology called "eschatology." This term comes from the Greek word *eschaton*, which refers to so-called last things. One of the initial aspects of eschatology is the afterlife and that dreaded event that takes us there—death.

Death is the greatest problem human beings encounter. We may try to tuck thoughts of it away in a far corner of our minds, but we cannot completely erase our awareness of our mortality. We know that the specter of death awaits us.

THE ORIGIN OF DEATH

The Apostle Paul writes: "Therefore, just as sin came into the world through one man, and death through sin, and so death spread to all men because all sinned—for sin indeed was in the world before the law was given, but sin is not counted where there is no law. Yet death reigned from Adam to Moses" (Rom. 5:12–14). We see that there was sin even before the law was given through Moses, and this is shown by the fact that death occurred before the law was given. The fact of death proves the presence of sin, and the fact of sin proves the presence of law, which has been revealed inwardly to human beings from the beginning. So, death came into the world as a direct result of sin.

The secular world views death as part of the natural order, whereas the Christian sees death as part of the fallen order; it was not the original state of man. Death came as God's judgment for sin. From the beginning, all sin was a capital offense. God said to Adam and Eve, "You may surely eat of every tree of the garden, but of the tree of the knowledge of good and evil you shall not eat, for in the day that you eat of it you shall surely die" (Gen. 2:16–17). The death God warned about was not only spiritual but also physical. Adam and Eve did not die physically the day they sinned; God granted them grace to live for some time before exacting the penalty. Nevertheless, they eventually perished from the earth.

HOPE IN DEATH

Every human being is a sinner and therefore has been sentenced to death. We are all waiting for the sentence to be carried out. However, for Christians, the penalty has been paid by Christ. Christians see death as the moment of transition from this world to the next. Paul was in prison when he wrote:

I know that through your prayers and the help of the Spirit of Jesus Christ this will turn out for my deliverance, as it is my eager expectation and hope that I will not be at all ashamed, but that with full courage now as always Christ will be honored in my body, whether by life or by death. For to me to live is Christ, and to die is gain. If I am to live in the flesh, that means fruitful labor for me. Yet which I shall choose I cannot tell. I am hard pressed between the two. My desire is to depart and be with Christ, for that is far better. But to remain in the flesh is more necessary on your account. (Phil. 1:19–24)

Many of us are staggered by Paul's words in this text. Although we rejoice in Christ's victory over the grave, we nevertheless fear death. To the best of my knowledge, I am not afraid of death, but I tend to be afraid of the dying process. Christians are not guaranteed exemption from a painful death; our guarantee is the presence of God with us in the midst of it and where we will go when we die. In the face of that, Paul wrote, "For to me to live is Christ, and to die is gain." He lived an extraordinary life, and he was able to endure great suffering because he was passionately convinced of the truth of his eternal life. He gladly risked life and limb because every minute of his life was about Christ. Life on this earth was a means to serve Christ, and death was the means to be with Christ. Death for the Christian falls on the positive side of the ledger.

Paul reinforces his conviction about life and death: "I am hard pressed between the two. My desire is to depart and be with Christ, for that is far better. But to remain in the flesh is more necessary on your account." Paul desired to continue his earthly ministry, but his heart was in heaven. He loved those to whom he ministered, but he was eager to go home, "to depart and be with Christ, for that is far better."

We have a tendency to view the difference between life and death as the difference between good and bad, but that was not how the Apostle viewed it. He saw the difference as between good and better. Living is good. Yes, there is much pain in life, and some are reduced to such a level of suffering that they long to die; but most of us, despite the pains, heartbreaks, and disappointments, want to live. There is joy in living, so we hold on to life with a passion. Yet for Christians, death is even better, because we go immediately to be with Christ, a hope verified by Christ's resurrection.

The Bible teaches that there is both death and a final resurrection. When we recite the Apostles' Creed and say, "I believe in the resurrection of the body," we are expressing our confidence that our bodies will be raised. Someday our bones will rise again, just as Christ came out of the tomb with the same body with which He went into the tomb, although His body had been dramatically altered. Jesus' body had been glorified, changed from mortal to immortal. Paul writes:

But in fact Christ has been raised from the dead, the firstfruits of those who have fallen asleep. For as by a man came death, by a man has come also the resurrection of the dead. For as in Adam all die, so also in Christ shall all be made alive. But each in his own order: Christ the firstfruits, then at his coming those who belong to Christ. (1 Cor. 15:20–23)

We do not know what we will look like in heaven, but there will be recognition. We will have recognizable bodies. The best state in the future is the glorified body. Living in the body here on earth is good, but the best is yet to come.

BETWEEN NOW AND THEN

Theologians refer to "the intermediate state," by which they mean the time between our deaths and the final resurrection. When we die, our bodies will go into the grave, but our souls will go directly to heaven and be immediately in the presence of Jesus Christ. In the intermediate state, each of us will have a soul without a body, but the best of all possible situations will occur later, in the consummation of the kingdom of Christ, when our souls will take on imperishable and glorified bodies.

Upon death, we do not, as some heretics have taught, enter into some kind of soul sleep, existing in a state of personal unconsciousness and separated from Christ. The biblical view is that we experience an unbroken continuity of personal, conscious existence such that immediately upon death we are actively in the presence of Christ and of God. We are often unaware of the physical aging going on in our bodies, because we actually live inside ourselves—in our minds, spirits, and our souls. It is that personal continuity of consciousness that will continue, only in a much greater state because we will be living in the presence of Christ.

Paul's dilemma was answered with the victory of his death, at which time he went home to experience the gain of being with Christ.

Chapter 54

THE RESURRECTION

The Greek word that we translate as "resurrection," *anastasia,* literally means "to stand again" or "to rise again." We often tend to think of our future resurrection as simply the continuity of personal existence, of the soul continuing in a conscious state in the presence of God in heaven while the body disintegrates in the grave. However, the resurrection is really about the physical body, which experiences decay in the grave before rising up to life anew.

THE FIRSTFRUITS

Since the first century, the church has affirmed the resurrection of the body, the *resurrectionis carnis,* which includes the bodily resurrection not only of Christ but also of His people. This truth is treated in numerous places in the Scriptures. Paul wrote:

> You, however, are not in the flesh but in the Spirit, if in fact the Spirit of God dwells in you. Anyone who does not have the Spirit of Christ does not belong to him. But if Christ is in you, although the body is dead because of sin, the Spirit is life because of righteousness. If the Spirit of him who raised Jesus from the dead dwells in you, he who raised Christ Jesus from the dead will also give life to your mortal bodies through his Spirit who dwells in you. (Rom. 8:9–11)

Some say this text refers only to the renewal or regeneration of our inner man, of being raised from spiritual death to spiritual life. That concept is certainly included in Paul's thinking, but he adds that the same Spirit who raised Jesus' mortal body from the dead will also raise our mortal bodies from the dead. Paul teaches this principle repeatedly, particularly when he makes a contrast between Adam and Christ, the last Adam. As death came into the world through the first Adam, so triumph over death comes as a result of the ministry of the last Adam. Paul sees Christ's physical resurrection from the dead not as a single event but as the first of many to come. Christ became the firstfruits of those who are raised from the dead (1 Cor. 15:20).

Scripture recounts the resurrections of several people before that of Christ, including the son of the widow of Zarephath (1 Kings 17:17–24) in the Old Testament and the son of the widow of Nain (Luke 7:11–15), Jairus' daughter (Luke 8:41–42, 49–56), and Lazarus (John 11:1–44) in the New Testament; however, each of those resurrected people later died again. Jesus' resurrection was distinct from those examples. The resurrection of Christ was more than simply a return to life; it also involved a significant transformation of His body. There was continuity between the body laid to rest in the tomb and the body that came forth from the tomb; the same body that was buried was also raised. That was also true of the earlier resurrections. However, in Jesus' resurrection, there was also an element of discontinuity. His body experienced a dramatic change. He was the same person with the same body, but His body had been glorified.

AN ESSENTIAL DOCTRINE

In his first epistle to the Corinthians, Paul gives a lengthy explanation and defense of the resurrection of Christ. He addresses those who are skeptical about resurrection in general by means of a *reductio ad absurdum* argument, which, as we noted earlier, is the technique of taking the premise of one's opponent to its logical conclusion in order to prove its absurdity. In this epistle, Paul reasons from the premise that there is no resurrection, and he concludes that if there is no resurrection, then Christ was not raised (1 Cor. 15:13). Where there is a universal negative, there can be no particular affirmative.

Paul then goes on to say that if Christ was not raised, we are still in our sin (v. 17). So there is no Christian faith without resurrection. The concept of resurrection is absolutely essential to the whole of the Apostolic faith.

A host of contemporary theologians have come to the conclusion that we can have a vibrant Christianity without the supernatural aspects that attend it, such as the death and resurrection of Christ. Rudolf Bultmann, for example, who gave a precise and insightful exegesis of 1 Corinthians 15, set forth clearly what the Apostle said, but then he claimed Paul got it wrong. Bultmann concluded, along with many in the contemporary church, that the Apostolic testimony of the central significance of the resurrection is false.

People can have a religion without believing in the resurrection, and they can even call it a Christian religion, but it has nothing to do with the biblical message of Christ and the original Christian faith. Paul said that there is no Christian faith apart from the resurrection, and if there is no resurrection, Christians are of all people the most to be pitied for placing their hope in what is false (v. 19).

That being said, Paul does not rest his case for the truth of Christ's resurrection on these negative implications. He points to the manifold witnesses of the resurrection—to the testimony of the Apostles, including his own, and the five hundred people who saw Christ after He was raised (vv. 3–8).

Paul goes on to say that Christ was raised and given a glorified body, and what God has done for Him, He has promised to do for all Christians: "For as in Adam all die, so also in Christ shall all be made alive. But each in his own order: Christ the firstfruits, then at his coming those who belong to Christ. Then comes the end, when he delivers the kingdom to God the Father after destroying every rule and every authority and power" (vv. 22–24).

RESURRECTION BODIES

Then Paul addresses the nature of our resurrection bodies: "But someone will ask, 'How are the dead raised? With what kind of body do they come?'" (v. 35). In other words, what will our resurrected bodies look like? Will we look as we did at the time of death? Here is how Paul answers: "You foolish person! What you sow does not come to life unless it dies. And what you sow is not the body that is to be, but a bare kernel, perhaps of wheat or of some other grain. But God gives it a body as he has chosen, and to each kind of seed its own body" (vv. 36–38). Paul appeals to nature for an analogy, using an argument of Plato's. In order to grow fruit, a seed must first be planted, and before the seed can bring forth life, it has to undergo a certain decay. When the fruit finally comes forth, it does not look anything like the seed. In terms of the resurrection, the body that goes to the grave is like the seed; we have to die. Yet in death, the body is transformed. There will be continuity, just as there is continuity between the seed and the fruit, but there will also be significant discontinuity between the seed of our earthly bodies and our glorified bodies.

Our resurrection bodies will be human and recognizable. Mysterious things occurred at the appearances of Jesus in His resurrected body. He was not always immediately recognized; we see that in the example of those who encountered Him on the Emmaus road (Luke 24:13–31). We do not know whether their failure to recognize Jesus was due to changes in Jesus or to God's hiding Jesus' identity from them. Likewise, Mary Magdalene did not recognize Jesus until Jesus addressed her (John 20:11–16). Yet when He appeared to the disciples in the upper room, they recognized Him instantly. So there will be changes, but we do not know what will be the extent of those changes. In fact, we do not know whether the body in which Jesus appeared in the upper room was in its final state of glorification or whether changes were still occurring. He had said to Mary, "Do not cling to me, for I have not yet ascended to the Father" (John 20:17), which some see as an indication that Jesus was still in the process of being reconstituted in His glorified body. That is only speculation, however.

In terms of our resurrected bodies, we can assume that our basic human faculties will be present; we will still have minds, wills, and affections. The basic difference will be that the new body will not be capable of dying; we are sown mortal and will be raised immortal (1 Cor. 15:53), but not because we will be inherently immortal. The Greeks believed that souls are eternal and therefore incapable of destruction, whereas Christians believe that souls are created, not eternal. We will live forever in heaven, not because we will have an inherently indestructible existence but because we will be rendered immortal by the decree of God. God will not allow us to perish. What guarantees our immortality is the preserving grace and love of God.

In his treatise on the resurrection, Paul makes analogies from nature:

> For not all flesh is the same, but there is one kind for humans, another for animals, another for birds, and another for fish. There are heavenly bodies and earthly bodies, but the glory of the heavenly is of one kind, and the glory of the earthly is of another. There is one glory of the sun, and another glory of the moon, and another glory of the stars; for star differs from star in glory. (vv. 39–41)

Paul is telling us to look around and observe life in its variety of forms that we might realize that there is much more to come:

> So is it with the resurrection of the dead. What is sown is perishable; what is raised is imperishable. It is sown in dishonor; it is raised in glory. It is sown in weakness; it is raised in power. It is sown a natural body; it is raised a spiritual body. If there is a natural body, there is also a spiritual body. Thus it is written, "The first man Adam became a living being"; the last Adam became a life-giving spirit. But it is not the spiritual that is first but the natural, and then the spiritual. The first man was from the earth, a man of dust; the second man is from heaven. As was the man

of dust, so also are those who are of the dust, and as is the man of heaven, so also are those who are of heaven. (vv. 42–48)

Paul then makes his key point: "Just as we have borne the image of the man of dust, we shall also bear the image of the man of heaven" (v. 49). That is the hope of the final resurrection—we will be like Christ, for He will grant to us the same glory of resurrection that He received.

Chapter 55

———

THE KINGDOM OF GOD

When Jesus' disciples asked Him to teach them to pray, He gave them a model prayer, the Lord's Prayer (Matt. 6:9–13). As part of that prayer, He instructed them to request, "Your kingdom come, your will be done, on earth as it is in heaven" (v. 10). Jesus here established a priority for the people of God to pray for the coming of the kingdom.

The question is whether the kingdom for which we pray is already being made manifest or is yet to be revealed. This is a matter of debate in the Christian community, and it is important because of the central importance in Scripture of the concept of the kingdom. In his book *The Kingdom of God*, Old Testament scholar John Bright said that the kingdom is the theme that ties the Old Testament to the New Testament. Early in the Old Testament, God began to promise a future realm where His sovereignty would be universal and eternal. This promise, however, was not a denial of God's sovereign reign over the universe now. God has reigned from the moment He created. Instead, the promise has to do with the voluntary submission of all creatures to the lordship of God. At present, the kingdom of this world, over which God has reigned from the moment of creation, is fundamentally in rebellion against its King.

So the promise in the Old Testament was of a universal, eternal kingdom. It is universal not in the sense that all will be redeemed but that all will obey. Some will obey willingly; they will bow the knee in sincere devotion. Others will be forced into submission. A day will come when people of all nations will submit to God's anointed King, the Messiah.

The New Testament writers refer to both the kingdom of God and the kingdom of heaven. The phrase "kingdom of heaven" is found in Matthew's gospel, whereas the other gospel writers, particularly Luke, refer to "the kingdom of God." The difference is due to the fact that Matthew was writing as a Jew to a Jewish audience. The Jews were protective of the sacred name of God and therefore used *periphrasis*, which is the use of a roundabout form of expression to paraphrase. As we noted in an earlier chapter, Jews in the Old Testament used the title *Adonai* ("Lord") as a substitute or periphrastic reference to God. Matthew does the same thing in his references to the kingdom; "heaven" was simply a Jewish substitute for "God."

ALREADY AND NOT YET

Many professing evangelicals today believe the kingdom of God is strictly in the future, although there is no biblical foundation for that. This view robs the church of important teachings concerning the kingdom that are clearly set forth in the New Testament. In fact, the New Testament opens with John the Baptist's announcement of the kingdom: "Repent, for the kingdom of heaven is at hand" (Matt. 3:2). The Old Testament prophets spoke of the kingdom to come at some point in the future, but at the time of John the Baptist, it was about to burst onto the scene. It was "at hand." If we examine John's message carefully, we see that his announcement of the kingdom contained urgent warnings: "Even now the axe is laid to the root of the trees" (Matt. 3:10) and "His winnowing fork is in his hand" (Luke 3:17). Time was running out, and people were not ready.

Christ came on the scene just a short time later with the same message: "The time is fulfilled, and the kingdom of God is at hand; repent and believe in the gospel" (Mark 1:15). However, there were differences between the behavior of John the Baptist and that of Jesus. John was an ascetic; he lived a life of radical self-denial. He ate locusts and wild honey, and dressed like the Old Testament prophets. Jesus, on the other hand, was accused of being "a glutton and a drunkard" (Matt. 11:19). He went to the wedding feast at Cana and ate at a banquet with tax collectors, which caused some of John's disciples to ask Him, "Why do we and the Pharisees fast, but your disciples do not fast?" (Matt. 9:14). Jesus replied, "Can the wedding guests mourn as long as the bridegroom is with them? The days will come when the bridegroom is taken away from them, and then they will fast" (v. 15).

Another time the Pharisees asked Him when the kingdom of God would come, and Jesus replied, "Behold, the kingdom of God is in the midst of you" (Luke 17:21). The kingdom was in their midst became the King was there. On another occasion, He said, "But if it is by the finger of God that I cast out demons, then the kingdom of God has come upon you" (Luke 11:20).

So John came first with his warning of the radical nearness of the kingdom. Then Jesus came announcing the presence of the kingdom. This was followed by the acme of His redemptive work in the ascension, when He left earth to go to His coronation, where God declared Him King. As Jesus stood on the Mount of Olives, ready to depart, His disciples asked him, "Lord, will you at this time restore the kingdom to Israel?" (Acts 1:6). They had been waiting for Jesus to make His move, to drive out the Romans and establish the kingdom, but Jesus replied, "It is not for you to know times or seasons that the Father has fixed by his own authority. But you will receive power when the Holy Spirit has come upon you, and you will be my witnesses in Jerusalem and in all Judea and Samaria, and to the end of the earth" (vv. 7–8).

In answer to their question about the kingdom, Jesus gave the fundamental mission of the church. Men would be blind to His kingship, so His disciples were given the task of making it visible. The fundamental task of the church is to bear witness to the kingdom of God. Our King reigns now, so for us to put the kingdom of God entirely in the future is to miss one of the most significant points of the New Testament. Our King has come and has inaugurated the kingdom of God. The future aspect of the kingdom is its final consummation.

KINGDOM PARABLES

Jesus taught frequently through parables, and the primary theme of those parables was the kingdom of God. Many of the parables begin, "The kingdom of God is like . . ." The parables make clear that the kingdom has a progressive character. The kingdom started small, but over time it began to expand, and it will continue to grow until it encompasses all things. Jesus said that the kingdom is like a mustard seed, the smallest of seeds (Matt. 13:31–32; Mark 4:30–32; Luke 13:18–19). He also likened it to leaven, which spreads through the dough so that the lump enlarges (Matt. 13:33; Luke 13:20–21). The Old Testament foretold that the kingdom would be a stone cut without hands, which would become a great mountain (Dan. 2:35).

Jesus also made clear that we, as His disciples, are to pursue the kingdom. He said, "But seek first the kingdom of God and his righteousness, and all these things will be added to you" (Matt. 6:33). The priority of the Christian life, according to Jesus, is seeking the kingdom. The Greek word translated as "first" here is *prōtos*. The word means more than first in a series; it means first in order of importance. According to Jesus, seeking the kingdom is the most important task of the Christian life.

CHRIST REIGNS

Christ reigns now as the Lamb who is worthy to receive the kingdom of God. That kingdom has begun and is growing, but it will not be consummated until Christ comes at the end of human history to subdue all kingdoms. At that time, the kingdom, which is now invisible, will become visible. But although the kingdom is now invisible, it is not unreal. At the consummation, there will be a complete renovation of the created order as we know it, and Christ will establish His kingdom in its full glory forever.

Chapter 56

THE MILLENNIUM

The concept of the millennium is a highly debated aspect of eschatology because of the nature of eschatological literature. The first
reference to the millennium, a period of time that extends for one thousand years, occurs in Revelation 20, and there it is mentioned with
respect to the binding of Satan:

> Then I saw an angel coming down from heaven, holding in his
> hand the key to the bottomless pit and a great chain. And he
> seized the dragon, that ancient serpent, who is the devil and
> Satan, and bound him for a thousand years, and threw him into
> the pit, and shut it and sealed it over him, so that he might not
> deceive the nations any longer, until the thousand years were
> ended. After that he must be released for a little while.
>
> Then I saw thrones, and seated on them were those to whom
> the authority to judge was committed. Also I saw the souls
> of those who had been beheaded for the testimony of Jesus
> and for the word of God, and those who had not worshiped
> the beast or its image and had not received its mark on their
> foreheads or their hands. They came to life and reigned with
> Christ for a thousand years. The rest of the dead did not come
> to life until the thousand years were ended. This is the first
> resurrection. Blessed and holy is the one who shares in the first

resurrection! Over such the second death has no power, but they will be priests of God and of Christ, and they will reign with him for a thousand years.

And when the thousand years are ended, Satan will be released from his prison and will come out to deceive the nations that are at the four corners of the earth, Gog and Magog, to gather them for battle; their number is like the sand of the sea. (Rev. 20:1–8)

INTERPRETING ESCHATOLOGICAL LITERATURE

When considering the millennium, theologians are concerned with its nature and its chronological relationship to the consummation of the kingdom of God. The way in which those concerns are answered determines whether one holds to premillennialism, amillennialism, postmillennialism, or another end-times view. The prefixes in the names of those views reflect what their adherents believe in terms of when the millennium occurs.

Revelation 20 is the only place in the Scriptures where the millennium is mentioned. The fact of this solitary reference does not detract from its importance, but what makes it problematic is that it occurs in a book of the Bible that is highly symbolic. Literature of this genre necessitates rules of interpretation that differ from those used to interpret other types of literature.

The basic principle of biblical interpretation established by the Reformers was literal interpretation, *sensus literalis*, which means that responsible interpreters of Scripture always interpret the Bible in the sense in which it was written. Poetic literature should be interpreted as poetry, didactic literature should be interpreted as didactic, and so on. A verb remains a verb, a noun remains a noun, a simile is a simile, and a metaphor is a metaphor.

Conversely, the style of interpretation called "literalism" involves applying a wooden interpretation, which does not work well for poetic literature. For example, when the psalmist says that the rivers clap their hands (98:8), we do not take that to mean that rivers somehow grow hands and begin clapping. We do not interpret such poetic images in an overly literalistic way.

When it comes to interpreting prophetic literature, the question is whether the language is figurative or ordinary prose, and there is widespread disagreement about that. Some believe that we must interpret the prophecies of the future literally in order to be faithful to the Bible, but that can lead us in circles.

MILLENNIAL POSITIONS

Let us look briefly at the main features of the various millennial positions.*

Premillennialism

Premillennialism teaches that after Christ returns there will be a literal, earthly millennial kingdom. The prefix here, *pre-*, indicates the conviction that Christ will return before the millennium is established. There are two popular forms of premillennialism today: dispensational premillennialism and historic premillennialism.

Dispensational theology is a complete system of doctrine. It is most noted for its particular scheme of understanding the prophecies of the Bible. Dispensational premillennialists believe that the prophecies of the kingdom given to Israel in the Old Testament will be literally fulfilled in the contemporary Jewish state. They look for a literal rebuilding of the temple and a reinstitution of the sacrificial system.

Foundational to the eschatological position of dispensationalists is the belief that God has two separate plans of redemption, one for Israel and one for the church. Traditional dispensational premillennialism teaches that Christ offered the Jews the kingdom of David, but the Jews rejected it, so the coming of David's kingdom, a Jewish kingdom, was postponed until sometime in the future. They also believe that the church as we know it exists in "the church age," one of several major periods or dispensations of biblical history. The church age is a

---

* For a fuller treatment, see R.C. Sproul, *The Last Days according to Jesus: When Did Jesus Say He Would Return?* (Grand Rapids, Mich.: Baker, 2000).

parenthesis between the advent of Christ and the future coming of the kingdom. Dispensational premillennialists believe that the church ultimately will lose influence in the world and become apostate toward the end of the church age, and will not be restored until after the return of Christ. Finally, Christ will return to rapture His saints before the great tribulation.

This return of Christ to rapture His people is seen as the first of His two returns. Upon His first return, He will translate His people up into the clouds, thereby delivering them from the pain and persecution of the tribulation. Then Christ will come back again to establish His kingdom. He will administer a Jewish political kingdom that will be headquartered in Jerusalem, and that kingdom will last for exactly one thousand years. During that time, Satan will be bound, the temple will be rebuilt, and the sacrificial system of the Old Testament will be reinstituted. Near the end of the millennium, Satan will be released, and Christ and His followers will be attacked at Jerusalem. At this point, Christ will call down judgment from heaven and destroy His enemies, judgment of the wicked will occur, and the final eternal order will be initiated.

This version of dispensational premillennialism, where the church is raptured before the tribulation, is the most popular version among evangelicals. There are other versions that place the rapture at other times relative to the tribulation while keeping the rest of the system essentially the same. But while the pretribulation rapture is popular because it provides Christians with hope of avoiding the great tribulation at the end of the age, I find not a shred of evidence in Scripture to support it.

Historic premillennialism is a bit different. It teaches that the church is the initial phase of Christ's kingdom, as prophesied by the Old Testament prophets. The church gains occasional victories in history but ultimately will fail in its mission. It will lose influence and become corrupt as worldwide evil increases toward the end of the church age. The church will eventually pass through an unprecedented worldwide time of travail known as "the great tribulation," which will mark the end of history as we know it. At the end of the tribulation, Christ will return to rapture His church, to resurrect deceased saints, and to conduct the judgment of the righteous, all in the twinkling of an eye. Christ will then descend to earth with His glorified saints, fight the battle of Armageddon, bind Satan, and establish a worldwide political kingdom, in which Christ will reign from Jerusalem for a thousand years. At the end of the millennium, Satan will be loosed, and a massive rebellion against Christ's kingdom will occur. Finally, God will intervene with fiery judgment to rescue Jesus and the saints, which will be followed by the resurrection and judgment of the wicked.

Amillennialism

The amillennial position, which holds some points in common with both of the premillennial positions, believes that the church age is the kingdom age prophesied in the Old Testament. The New Testament church has become the Israel of God. Amillennialists believe that the binding of Satan took place during Jesus' earthly ministry; Satan was restrained while the gospel was preached to the world, and this restraint continues today. Insofar as Christ presently rules in the hearts of believers, they have some influence in the culture in which they live, but they will not transform the culture. Toward the end, the growth of evil will accelerate, resulting in the great tribulation and a personal Antichrist. Christ will return to end history, resurrect and judge all men, and establish the eternal order. In eternity, the redeemed may be either in heaven or in a totally renovated earth.

Postmillennialism

Postmillennialism has several distinctive features. First, it holds that the messianic kingdom of Christ was founded on earth during His early ministry in fulfillment of Old Testament prophecy—the church is Israel. Second, the kingdom is essentially redemptive and spiritual rather than political and physical. Third, the kingdom will exercise a transformational influence in history, a belief that some have called the most distinctive characteristic of postmillennial eschatology. It is optimistic that the influence of the church of Jesus Christ will have a positive, redeeming influence on culture and on the world over time.

Despite times of weakness and corruption, the church will ultimately triumph over the wickedness of this world, such that the kingdom will gradually expand on earth. This will be accomplished with Christ's kingly power but without His physical presence on earth. Finally, postmillennialists believe that the Great Commission will succeed. What distinguishes postmillennialists from amillennialists and premillennialists is the belief that Scripture teaches the success of the Great Commission in the age of the church.

There are differences among postmillennialists, just as there are among those of the other convictions. There is also a debate over a view known as preterism, which occurs in both full-preterist and partial-preterist forms.

Preterism

Partial preterism holds that many of the prophecies of the future were fulfilled in the first century—chiefly in the events surrounding the destruction of Jerusalem in AD 70. Most partial preterists say that the first twenty chapters of Revelation have taken place while the last two chapters have yet to be fulfilled. Partial preterists tend to be postmillennial in their thinking, holding that the millennium (not a literal one thousand years) began with the first advent of Christ.

By contrast, full preterism teaches that *all* the prophecies regarding the coming of Christ—including the millennium and the last judgment— were fulfilled in the first century. Full preterism is regarded as heretical, as it denies an essential truth of Scripture: the return of the King.

Whichever eschatological view we hold, we must hold it humbly because we do not know the future. We can all look backward, but we do not know God's agenda for what's to come. We must be humble and acknowledge that our eschatological view might not be accurate. At the same time, much of the doctrinal teaching in the New Testament has to do with future things, so how we understand God's promises about the future has a dramatic impact on our personal confidence and involvement in the mission Christ gave to the church.

Chapter 57

———

THE RETURN OF CHRIST

After the creation of the state of Israel in 1948, many Christians began to follow the advice of the Swiss theologian Karl Barth to hold a Bible in one hand and a newspaper in the other. The restoration of the Jewish state and the Jews' recovery of Jerusalem in 1967 provoked heightened interest in the end times and especially the return of Jesus. The reason for this lies in Jesus' prediction in the Olivet Discourse of the destruction of the temple and the city of Jerusalem, which He concluded this way: "Jerusalem will be trampled underfoot by the Gentiles, until the times of the Gentiles are fulfilled" (Luke 21:24).

THE TEACHING OF SCRIPTURE

That text is the only place in the Gospels where we find the phrase "the times of the Gentiles." However, a similar phrase in Paul's epistle to the Romans piques great interest in future things: "A partial hardening has come upon Israel, until the fullness of the Gentiles has come in" (Rom. 11:25). Here Paul is writing about Jewish people who have rejected the Messiah and about Gentiles being grafted in to the holy root that is Israel. He goes on to say that God has not cast off the Jews forever but will do a future work among them when the times of the Gentiles are fulfilled.

In light of these biblical texts, the events in the Middle East in 1948 and 1967 led many to conclude that we are on the threshold of the final days of redemptive history and that the return of Christ is near.

315

Compounding the speculation was the approach of the new millennium. Expectation of Jesus' return reached a fever pitch then, and His coming continues to be a subject of intense interest today.

We observed earlier that much of the doctrinal material in the New Testament relates to future aspects of the kingdom of God, and there is no element of prophecy more important to the people of God than the return of Jesus. The Lord's promised return is the Christian's blessed hope, yet the time of Jesus' return and the manner in which He will come are highly debated issues.

At the beginning of Acts, we read of Jesus' departure from this world:

> And when he had said these things, as they were looking on, he was lifted up, and a cloud took him out of their sight. And while they were gazing into heaven as he went, behold, two men stood by them in white robes, and said, "Men of Galilee, why do you stand looking into heaven? This Jesus, who was taken up from you into heaven, will come in the same way as you saw him go into heaven." (Acts 1:9–11)

There are many predictions in the New Testament of the return of Jesus, and there are particular elements that accompany these predictions. First, we are assured that the return of Christ will be personal; in other words, He will return in person. Second, His return will be visible. Third, His return will be in glory; it will be attended by majestic fanfare. We see all three elements here in Acts 1. Verse 11 affirms that "this Jesus"—the very one whose departure the Apostles had witnessed—would come again "in the same way." In other words, the mode of Jesus' return will parallel the mode of His departure. His departure was visible, and He ascended on clouds of glory; therefore, His return at the end of the age will be just as visible and just as glorious.

THEORIES OF CHRIST'S RETURN

However, despite these clear prophecies, the subject of Christ's personal, visible, glorious return is a topic of controversy, which is due most especially to the influence of higher criticism. In my book *The Last Days according to Jesus*, I provide a summary of the critical theories that have emerged along with the unprecedented assault against the reliability of the New Testament documents and the teaching of Jesus.* For example, Albert Schweitzer, in his quest for the historical Jesus, claimed that Jesus expected the consummation of the kingdom to occur during His lifetime, which is why He sent the seventy disciples on their mission (Luke 10), and was disappointed when it did not happen. According to Schweitzer, in Jesus' mind, the pivotal moment for the coming of the kingdom was likely to be His entry into Jerusalem, and when the kingdom did not arrive, Jesus allowed Himself to be taken to the cross. His subsequent cry, "My God, my God, why have you forsaken me?" (Matt. 27:46), indicates Jesus' disillusionment.

Other scholars have argued that the New Testament writers and Jesus Himself expected and taught Jesus' personal return within the lifetime of the first generation of Christians. Because it did not happen, they say, we can safely discard the New Testament documents as unreliable and understand Jesus as merely a model of love. In response to this critical theory, C.H. Dodd spoke of "realized eschatology," meaning that all the New Testament prophecies about the future and Christ's return were in fact fulfilled in the first century. Concerning certain remarks made by Jesus, such as "There are some standing here who will not taste death until they see the Son of Man coming in his kingdom" (Matt. 16:28), Dodd said that Jesus was referring not to a future return but to the visible manifestations of His glory that took place at the transfiguration, the resurrection, and the ascension.

The most contested text is found in the Olivet Discourse, particularly the rendering in Matthew's gospel, in which Jesus describes future events, including the destruction of the temple and of Jerusalem, as well as His return. Jesus' disciples asked him: "Tell us, when will these things be, and what will be the sign of your coming and of the end of the age?" (Matt. 24:3). In direct response to the disciples' inquiry,

---

* R.C. Sproul, *The Last Days according to Jesus: When Did Jesus Say He Would Return?* (Grand Rapids, Mich.: Baker, 2000).

Jesus said, "Truly, I say to you, this generation will not pass away until all these things take place" (v. 34). Christ seems to have been saying clearly that these things would take place within the span of a single human generation, which, in Jewish terms, was approximately forty years. If Christ's crucifixion took place sometime around AD 30, one would expect fulfillment of that prophecy around AD 70, which happens to be the date of the destruction of the temple and the fall of the city of Jerusalem to the Romans.

Critics argue that although the temple was destroyed and the city was captured, Jesus did not come back, which renders Him a false prophet. Yet nothing more clearly proves the identity and integrity of Jesus Christ than these specific prophecies. The events He predicted were utterly unthinkable to Jewish people, who assumed that the temple and the holy city of God were indestructible. Yet Jesus specifically predicted these events before they took place. It is ironic that the very text that should function as irrefutable proof of the trustworthiness of Christ and the biblical documents has become the one critics have used to repudiate the trustworthiness of the New Testament and of the integrity of Jesus.

Concerning this text, evangelicals say that *generation* in the Olivet Discourse does not refer to a life span or to a particular time frame but to a type of people. In other words, *generation* in this context means that the same kind of people who were living in Jerusalem at the time of Jesus would still be around at the time of all these future events. That is a possible interpretation of the text but an unlikely one, because the term *generation* is used consistently throughout the Gospels with specific reference to a particular group of people.

Others argue that "all these things" included only the first two elements, the destruction of the temple and of Jerusalem. Full preterism teaches that Jesus did return in AD 70, and all the future prophecies concerning the coming of Christ took place invisibly when He executed His judgment on Jerusalem. Full preterists argue that the biblical language of prophecy makes frequent use of catastrophic imagery. In the Old Testament, for example, the prophets describe God's visiting

His justice on wicked cities in terms of the moon turning to blood (Joel 2:31), and the same type of language is used with respect to the return of Jesus (Matt. 24:2). Full preterists believe that Jesus came in judgment on the Jewish nation in AD 70, and that was the end of Judaism. That was the last judgment. It was the end not of history but of the Jewish age, but it was the beginning of the age of the Gentiles.

The problem for full preterism is that there are other texts in the New Testament that indicate we have every reason to hope for a future, personal, visible return of Jesus. However, I do think that partial preterism has to be taken seriously—that a significant event did take place in AD 70. I am convinced that in the Olivet Discourse, Jesus was, in fact, speaking of His judgment coming upon Israel, but I do not think He was referring to the final consummation of His kingdom.

In the final analysis, no one knows for sure when Jesus is going to come. Nevertheless, we, as the people of God, have a blessed hope and every reason to believe in the integrity of Jesus' word. His promises are without fail, and we look forward to His personal, visible, and glorious return.

Chapter 58

THE FINAL JUDGMENT

In the nineteenth century, the German philosopher Friedrich Nietzsche announced the death of God. When he did so, an unprecedented spirit of optimism emerged in the intellectual world, which had a tremendous impact on European and American culture. Many people welcomed Nietzsche's announcement. The news heralded a major victory for humanism, freeing mankind—so it was thought—from reliance upon a supernatural deity and allowing reliance upon technology and education instead. People anticipated ridding the world of disease, warfare, ignorance, and all the things that plague human civilization.

Auguste Comte, the nineteenth-century French philosopher, said that history is divided into three stages: infancy, adolescence, and adulthood. In describing the development of Western civilization, he said that in its infancy, people defined their lives in terms of religion, but as civilization grew into adolescence, they replaced religion with metaphysical philosophy. Adulthood did not begin, he said, until the age of science, and it was the optimistic anticipation of what science would produce that provoked such joy in people. World War I was seen as a tremendous stumbling block to this evolutionary optimism, but even those disappointed by the onset of war held on to their man-centered hopes, declaring the conflict to be "the war to end all wars." Of course, they did not anticipate the Holocaust of World War II or the pessimistic philosophies of atheistic existentialism in the writings of Jean-Paul

Sartre, Albert Camus, and others. At the heart of nineteenth-century optimism was the perceived good news that since God does not exist, there is no need to fear a final judgment, and since there is no judgment, there is no moral accountability.

A SCORNFUL AGE

When we consider the pessimism of our day, we recognize that there has been a radical shift away from the optimism of the nineteenth century. Man is now seen as a cosmic accident moving inexorably to the bottomless pit of nothingness. The thinking of today's nihilistic existentialist is that if man is not ultimately accountable for his life, that can only mean that ultimately his life does not count. The optimism has turned to bitter gloom, so the culture has turned to drugs and other means of escape to avoid the horrible idea that our lives are an exercise in futility.

Over against all this is the clear teaching of the New Testament and of Jesus that our lives do count and that we are accountable—truths that every human being knows apart from philosophical investigation and reflection. People have a sense of God within their hearts. They were given consciences by their Creator and know they will be held accountable for how they live their lives. There will come a day when God will judge every man and woman by the standards of His sacred law.

While in Athens, the Apostle Paul noticed that a temple had been erected to an unknown god, so, in the presence of the philosophers of his day, he said, "What therefore you worship as unknown, this I proclaim to you. . . . The times of ignorance God overlooked, but now he commands all people everywhere to repent" (Acts 17:23, 30). Paul's command was universal in scope. God had long been patient with man's manifold disobedience, but a critical moment in redemptive history had taken place, and the need for repentance was urgent. Paul continued, "He has fixed a day on which he will judge the world in righteousness by a man whom he has appointed; and of this he has given assurance to all by raising him from the dead" (v. 31).

This was the response to Paul's words: "Now when they heard of the resurrection of the dead, some mocked. But others said, 'We will hear you again about this.' So Paul went out from their midst. But some men joined him and believed, among whom also were Dionysius the Areopagite and a woman named Damaris and others with them" (vv. 32–34).

Things have not changed. When we tell people that God has appointed a day on which He will judge the world in righteousness, people laugh. There in Athens, only a few took Paul seriously, and few believe today.

Integral to this Apostolic testimony was the declaration that God has appointed a day of judgment. Such a day was not initiated by the Apostles; in fact, it was not initiated even by Jesus, although Jesus spoke about it frequently. It has its roots deep in the Old Testament, which warned people of the day when the Judge of heaven and earth would bring all things into account.

Year ago, while I was teaching philosophy at a university, I lectured on Immanuel Kant's critique of the traditional arguments for the existence of God alongside his substitute argument, which was based on Kant's understanding of "the categorical imperative." Kant said that every human being has a sense of "oughtness" built into his conscience, which is what drives ethics. Kant raised the question as to whether this sense of oughtness is meaningless. If there is no foundation for a moral sense of oughtness, then any attempt to construct a meaningful ethic perishes, and without a meaningful ethic, civilization cannot be preserved. In order for this sense of right and wrong to be meaningful, Kant said, there has to be justice; in other words, righteousness must be rewarded and wickedness must be punished. However, it is clear that justice does not always prevail, which led Kant to ask why the wicked prosper and the righteous suffer. He concluded that since justice does not occur in this life, there must be some kind of survival beyond the grave so that justice can be distributed. To my surprise, I later learned that one of the students in the class was converted to Christianity just by listening to Kant's speculation about a last judgment.

For Jesus, however, the last judgment was not a matter of speculation but of divine declaration, and He warned people regularly about this certain reality, saying, for example, "I tell you, on the day of judgment people will give account for every careless word they speak" (Matt. 12:36). That brings to mind the prophet Isaiah, who, when confronted with the holiness of God, was immediately overwhelmed by his unworthiness and said, "Woe is me! For I am lost; for I am a man of unclean lips, and I dwell in the midst of a people of unclean lips" (Isa. 6:5). If our idle words will be brought into judgment, how much more our every intentional word?

Years later, I ran into a student who had been in that class I had taught and who had gone on to study neuroscience. During our encounter, he recalled the lecture I had given on Kant and the last judgment. He went on to tell me from a scientific viewpoint how the brain functions. He explained that every experience we have is recorded in the brain. In fact, he said, it would take a computer the size of a building to be able to hold all the data that can be recorded in a single human brain. He then tied his scientific understanding to the last judgment, saying that he pictures God on judgment day replaying all the experiences recorded in each human brain—every thought, word, and deed—such that the clarity of the evidence will render man incapable of argument. The point of my former student's metaphor is that, whether we have a conscious brain record or not, God is aware of everything we have ever thought, said, and done.

JESUS' TEACHING

Most sermons are constructed with a climactic point, and that is true of Jesus' Sermon on the Mount. At the end of that sermon, Jesus said:

Beware of false prophets, who come to you in sheep's clothing but inwardly are ravenous wolves. You will recognize them by their fruits. Are grapes gathered from thornbushes, or figs from thistles? So, every healthy tree bears good fruit, but the diseased tree bears bad fruit. A healthy tree cannot bear bad fruit, nor can a diseased tree bear good fruit. Every tree that does not bear good fruit is cut down and thrown into the fire. Thus you will recognize them by their fruits. (Matt. 7:15–20)

Many evangelicals are unaware that Jesus spoke of the final judgment, but He clearly did, and He said that every person will be judged according to his works. We press hard on the biblical doctrine of justification by faith alone, but sometimes our excitement over redemption by faith rather than by works leads us to think that works do not matter to God. Yet here we read that judgment will be according to works. The rewards that God will distribute to His people at the last judgment will be according to works. We are encouraged as Christians that rewards will be distributed according to our degree of obedience. So works are extremely important, both good and bad, because they will all be brought into the judgment.

Jesus went on to say:

Not everyone who says to me, "Lord, Lord," will enter the kingdom of heaven, but the one who does the will of my Father who is in heaven. On that day many will say to me, "Lord, Lord, did we not prophesy in your name, and cast out demons in your name, and do many mighty works in your name?" And then will I declare to them, "I never knew you; depart from me, you workers of lawlessness." (vv. 21–23)

On the day of judgment, people will claim to know Jesus, emphatically addressing Him as "Lord." They will claim to have performed good works and engaged in church activities, yet Jesus will state categorically that He never knew them.

Later in Matthew's gospel, Jesus tells a parable about the kingdom of heaven:

Then the kingdom of heaven will be like ten virgins who took their lamps and went to meet the bridegroom. Five of them were foolish, and five were wise. For when the foolish took their lamps, they took no oil with them, but the wise took flasks of oil with their lamps. As the bridegroom was delayed, they all became drowsy and slept. But at midnight there was a cry, "Here is the bridegroom! Come out to meet him." Then all those virgins rose and trimmed their lamps. And the foolish said to the wise, "Give us some of your oil, for our lamps are going out." But the wise answered, saying, "Since there will not be enough for us and for you, go rather to the dealers and buy for yourselves." And while they were going to buy, the bridegroom came, and those who were ready went in with him to the marriage feast, and the door was shut. Afterward the other virgins came also, saying, "Lord, lord, open to us." But he answered, "Truly, I say to you, I do not know you." Watch therefore, for you know neither the day nor the hour. (Matt. 25:1–13)

Our Lord gives to us and to the world these sober warnings. God has appointed a day, and He has appointed a Judge, and the Judge is the Lord Himself. When we stand before that judgment, we had better be ready.

Chapter 59

ETERNAL PUNISHMENT

In the previous chapter, we examined the last judgment as it is set forth in the New Testament, specifically from the lips of Jesus Himself. The last judgment will be no casual evaluation of people; rather, it will be in the context of a heavenly courtroom, where the Judge of all will take into account everything we have done. At the end of the trial, there will be a verdict of "guilty" or "not guilty" that will hinge on whether the one on trial is covered by the righteousness of Christ. For those who belong to Christ, there will be reward, but for those who do not, there will be punishment.

The last judgment will be administered by a perfectly just and righteous Judge, so there will be nothing arbitrary or unjust about it. We will face the judgment of God either on the basis of our works or on the basis of Christ's work. If we have committed even one sin, one offense against the holiness of God—which we all certainly have—then we desperately need Christ. As the psalmist prayed so many centuries ago, "If you, O Lord, should mark iniquities, O Lord, who could stand?" (Ps. 130:3). The answer is obvious: no one. The bad news is that the Lord *does* mark iniquities. The blessed person is the one to whom the Lord does not impute guilt. This is the core of the gospel.

ACCORDING TO REVELATION

Since the judgment will be perfectly just, the Scriptures make clear that it will be rendered according to the light we have. What happens,

326

then, to the innocent person who has never heard the gospel of Jesus Christ? The answer is that God never punishes innocent people. Those who are innocent have no need to worry about the judgment of God. Yet according to the New Testament, there are no innocent people. No one can come before the judgment seat of God and say, "I had no light of revelation"; that is the significance of Romans 1. There, Paul writes of God's wrath being poured out against evildoers because they have suppressed the knowledge of God that is clear through nature. They have turned away and refused to honor God as God. Therefore, no one can stand at the judgment seat of God and claim he did not know that there was a God.

In the last judgment, people who have never heard of Jesus will not be punished for rejecting Jesus. God judges according to the light that each one has, and it would be unjust for Him to hold people responsible for rejecting Jesus if they have never heard of Him. That being said, Jesus came to people who were already under God's indictment—not for rejecting Jesus, whom they did not know, but for rejecting the Father, whom they did know by the revelation that He had given in nature. Even if we did not have the Bible, the heavens declare God's glory (Ps. 19:1; Rom. 1:20). Indeed, our very consciences bear witness that we know who God is and that we have violated His law (Rom. 2:15).

The destiny to which we will be subject at the last judgment is unalterable. Many hope for a second chance after death, even if it is a mythical purgatory where they can pay off their debts and then enter heaven, yet nothing in Scripture gives the slightest hope of that. The Bible tells us that "it is appointed for man to die once, and after that comes judgment" (Heb. 9:27).

HELL

That which makes us most squeamish about the last judgment is the doctrine of hell. When I was in seminary, another student once asked our professor, John Gerstner, how we will be able to rejoice in heaven if we get there only to find that some of our loved ones are in hell. Dr. Gerstner replied that we will not be sad about that but instead will rejoice, for it will bring glory to God and vindicate His holiness. There was a collective gasp from the students, but as I reflected upon his words, I understood what he was saying. While we are in our mortal flesh, even though we have some affection for Christ, our basic affections are rooted in this world. We care more about the well-being of our family members and friends than about the vindication of the righteousness of God, but that will not be the case when we arrive in heaven in our glorified state.

If we were to picture Jesus standing on one side of a room, representing utter righteousness, and Adolf Hitler standing on the other, representing utter evil, where on that scale would we place a friend we consider righteous? We would have to place our friend right next to Hitler, as far away from Christ as possible; in fact, in this illustration, the room would have to be infinitely large. Because Jesus is sinless, the gulf between Christ and sinners is immeasurable. Given our fallen frame of reference, we can understand Hitler, but Jesus baffles our imagination by His perfect righteousness. That is why we have trouble considering that God, in the execution of His justice, would send our loved ones to hell.

The New Testament speaks of hell as darkness, as a lake of fire, and as a prison. For instance:

> They marched up over the broad plain of the earth and surrounded the camp of the saints and the beloved city, but fire came down from heaven and consumed them, and the devil who had deceived them was thrown into the lake of fire and sulfur where the beast and the false prophet were, and they will be tormented day and night forever and ever.
>
> Then I saw a great white throne and him who was seated on it. From his presence earth and sky fled away, and no place was found for them. And I saw the dead, great and small, standing before the throne, and books were opened. Then another book was opened, which is the book of life. And the dead were judged by what was written in the books, according to what

they had done. And the sea gave up the dead who were in it, Death and Hades gave up the dead who were in them, and they were judged, each one of them, according to what they had done. Then Death and Hades were thrown into the lake of fire. This is the second death, the lake of fire. And if anyone's name was not found written in the book of life, he was thrown into the lake of fire. (Rev. 20:9–15)

I doubt that hell is a literal lake of fire, but whatever it is, those who are there would give everything they had and do everything they could not to be there. A symbol is always exceeded in intensity by the reality to which it points, and because of that we can take no comfort in the idea that the New Testament language about hell is symbolic. If it is symbolic, then the reality must be worse than the symbol.

We hear people say, "My life is a hell on earth," but that is mere hyperbole, because as terrible as one's life might be, it is not close to being as bad as hell. Someone in a most abysmal state of suffering still enjoys many benefits of the common grace of almighty God, which are removed entirely from those in hell. Hell is separation from God in a certain sense but not in an absolute sense. It is separation from the grace, care, and love of God, but not from God Himself. The biggest problem for those in hell is not the devil; it is God. God is in hell, actively punishing the wicked. When we are saved, we are saved from God. We are saved from exposure to His fierce wrath and punishment.

The New Testament also teaches that there are degrees of punishment in hell, just as degrees of reward are distributed to people in heaven. Someone once said that in heaven everyone will have a full cup, but not everyone will have a cup of the same size. Jesus made a frequent distinction between those whose reward will be great and those whose reward will be small.

When a murderer is sentenced to multiple life sentences, we find that redundant. After all, people have only one life. In terms of the law, however, each count is a separate offense and therefore worthy of a separate punishment, and that principle applies eternally. We may not be able to punish criminals seven times for seven murders, but God can, and the person who murders one person will receive a punishment seven times less than the person who murders seven. God's punitive, retributive justice will be perfect, such that the punishment will always fit the crime, which is why Paul warns us against storing up wrath on the day of wrath (Rom. 2:5). Jesus calls us to store up treasures in heaven; in contrast, Paul says that people who are not storing up heavenly treasure are storing up punishments in hell, compounding the degree of judgment they will receive.

In recent years, there has been a revival within evangelical circles of the heretical doctrine called annihilationism, which holds that at the last judgment believers are raised from the dead and rewarded, whereas the wicked are merely annihilated. In other words, they cease to exist, and that is their punishment—the loss of life. Historically, Christians have believed that, according to Scripture, the punishment of hell is conscious and unending. Sinners in hell yearn to be annihilated, to pass out of existence, because anything is better than standing daily before the punishment of God.

In the final analysis, we do not know the details of hell, and if we are honest, we must admit that we do not *want* to know. However, if we take the words of Jesus and the Apostles seriously, we need to take hell seriously. If we really believed the biblical testimony about hell, it would change not only the way we live but the way we work in terms of the mission of the church.

Chapter 60

———

HEAVEN AND EARTH
MADE NEW

Many today doubt that there is life after death. They scorn those who believe in eternal life, saying that our hope of heaven is merely the projection of our desires. They question the basis for our confidence that the next world will be better than this one.

Our answer as Christians is the testimony of Christ, both that of His resurrection and of His teaching. Jesus said, "I am the resurrection and the life. Whoever believes in me, though he die, yet shall he live" (John 11:25). In the Upper Room Discourse, on the night of His betrayal, Jesus said, "Let not your hearts be troubled. Believe in God; believe also in me" (John 14:1). He began the discourse with an imperative: "Let not . . ." An imperative implies an obligation. We are commanded not to have troubled hearts regarding our future in heaven. Jesus also said:

> In my Father's house are many rooms. If it were not so, would I have told you that I go to prepare a place for you? And if I go and prepare a place for you, I will come again and will take you to myself, that where I am you may be also. And you know the way to where I am going." (vv. 2–4)

Jesus was with His disciples but was about to be removed from their midst, and they were anxious. Jesus offered them comfort, backing up His reassurances with these words: "If it were not so, would I have told you that I go to prepare a place for you?" In other words, if heaven were a false hope to which the disciples were clinging, Jesus would have corrected their error. However, it is all true, and Jesus was going ahead of them to prepare their place there. That is the promise of Christ to His people: for everyone who trusts in Christ, a place in His Father's house is prepared. Therefore, we have every reason to be confident of heaven's reality.

PROMISED JOY

In John's first epistle, we are given some insight into our future state:

> See what kind of love the Father has given to us, that we should be called children of God; and so we are. The reason why the world does not know us is that it did not know him. Beloved, we are God's children now, and what we will be has not yet appeared; but we know that when he appears we shall be like him, because we shall see him as he is. And everyone who thus hopes in him purifies himself as he is pure. (1 John 3:1–3)

This is one of the most important, if not the most important, eschatological texts in the New Testament. It promises believers that we will enjoy the zenith of felicity in heaven, "the beatific vision" or the *visio Dei*. The word *beatific* comes from the same root word from which we get the word *beatitude*. The beatitudes are the sayings of Jesus from His Sermon on the Mount, in which Jesus pronounces oracles of blessing (Matt. 5:3–12). They are promises of blessedness, a degree of happiness that transcends any earthly pleasure or happiness. When God gives blessedness to the soul, it is a supreme joy and fulfillment. That blessedness is in view here in 1 John in the beatific vision. It is so wonderful that the vision itself brings with it the fullness of the blessing.

The beatific vision is the vision of God. John states that we do not know yet what we are going to be in heaven, but one thing we do know is that we will be like Him, for we shall see Him *as He is*. We will see Him as He is in Himself. We are going to be able to see not merely an indirect manifestation of God—a burning bush or a pillar of cloud and fire—but His unveiled being. Moses was allowed a glimpse of God's passing glory, but he could not see God's face (Ex. 34:5–7). An intimate, face-to-face look at God is absolutely forbidden to every mortal in this world. We are called to dedicate ourselves in holiness to a God we have never seen. We serve a Master who is invisible to us. Yet we are promised that someday we will see Him. In the Beatitudes, it is not the merciful, the poor, or the peacemakers who are promised the sight of God. Instead, Jesus says, "Blessed are the pure in heart, for they shall see God" (Matt. 5:8). The reason we cannot see God has nothing to do with our eyes. It has to do with our hearts. Yet when we enter into glory and receive the fullness of our sanctification, the barrier to a direct and immediate perception of God will be removed.

When I watch a basketball game on television, am I really watching the basketball game? I am not present at the event; the game is taking place miles away. I am watching an electronic broadcast, a reproduction. There is a medium between the game and me so that I am made aware of the plays of the game through the medium. A medium is an intermediary; in this case, it communicates images of something from one place to another. When I watch the game on television, I see only pictures of the game. If I were actually at the game, the light of the arena would communicate those images to my eyes. Yet even if I had perfect vision, if I were locked in a room without any light, I would see nothing. We need both light and images to be able to see.

Even our present sight is mediated. Jonathan Edwards said that in glory our souls will have a direct apprehension of the invisible God. How that will occur we do not know, but we do know by means of God's Word that the delight of our souls in heaven will be seeing Him as He is.

THE NATURE OF HEAVEN

In the book of Revelation, the Apostle John records the vision he received on the island of Patmos. In that vision, Christ showed John many things, including the new heaven and the new earth:

> Then I saw a new heaven and a new earth, for the first heaven and the first earth had passed away, and the sea was no more. And I saw the holy city, new Jerusalem, coming down out of heaven from God, prepared as a bride adorned for her husband. And I heard a loud voice from the throne saying, "Behold, the dwelling place of God is with man. He will dwell with them, and they will be his people, and God himself will be with them as their God. He will wipe away every tear from their eyes, and death shall be no more, neither shall there be mourning, nor crying, nor pain anymore, for the former things have passed away." (Rev. 21:1–4)

We read that in heaven there will be no sea, which, if taken literally, might disappoint beach lovers. However, for the Hebrew, the sea was a symbol of violence. The seacoast in Israel was rocky and rough. Moreover, it was an entry point for attacking marauders, and violent weather came in off the Mediterranean. In all of Hebrew poetry, the sea is a negative symbol; the river, the fountain, and the well serve as positive images. So we understand John's vision as indicating that there will be no more violent natural catastrophes.

Tears will also be absent in heaven. We associate tears with sorrow and grief. Many of us recall how, when we were children, our mothers comforted us when we were sad, wiping away our tears with her apron. We usually were brought to tears again the next day, and needed comfort all over again. However, when God wipes away our tears, they will never come back, because the things that now make us cry will be removed. There will be no more death, sorrow, or pain. These former things will have passed away.

As John continues his description, we encounter some startling dimensions of what heaven will be like and what it will not be like (vv. 18–21). We are told what will be there and what will not be there. We find streets of gold that is so fine and pure that it is translucent. We are told of gates constructed of magnificent pearls and a foundation adorned with precious jewels. Apocalyptic literature is imaginative, so we assume that these are symbolic representations of heaven, but I would not put it past God to construct a city just like the one described here.

John tells us more: "And I saw no temple in the city, for its temple is the Lord God the Almighty and the Lamb. And the city has no need of sun or moon to shine on it, for the glory of God gives it light, and its lamp is the Lamb" (vv. 22–23). There will be no temple, sun, or moon. On this earth, a temple, or church, is the visible symbol of the presence of God, but in heaven there will be no need for a temple, because we will be in God's actual presence. There will also be no need for created sources of light—sun, moon, or stars. The radiance of the glory of God and of the Lamb will illumine the whole city, and there will never be night because the glowing, brilliant, radiant glory of God never stops. Heaven will be aglow with the unvarnished, unveiled radiance of God.

What do we live for? By way of illustration, Jonathan Edwards described someone who saves money for years in order to go on a vacation. To get to his destination, he must travel, so the first night he stays at a wayside inn. However, the next day, instead of continuing on the journey to his desired destination, he decides to forgo it all and stay at the inn. We live our lives just that way. We hold on tenaciously to life in this world because we are not really convinced of the glory that the Father has established in heaven for His people. Every hope and joy that we look forward to—and then some—will abound in this wonderful place. Our greatest moment will be when we walk through the door and leave this world of tears and sorrow, this valley of death, and enter into the presence of the Lamb.

Appendix

———

THE CREEDS

THE APOSTLES' CREED

I believe in God the Father Almighty, Maker of heaven and earth.

And in Jesus Christ His only Son our Lord; who was conceived by the Holy Ghost, born of the Virgin Mary, suffered under Pontius Pilate, was crucified, dead, and buried; He descended into hell; the third day He rose again from the dead; He ascended into heaven, and sits on the right hand of God the Father Almighty; from where He shall come to judge the quick and the dead.

I believe in the Holy Ghost; the holy catholic church; the communion of saints; the forgiveness of sins; the resurrection of the body; and the life everlasting. Amen.

THE NICENE CREED

We believe in one God,
the Father, the Almighty,
maker of heaven and earth,
of all that is, seen and unseen.

We believe in one Lord, Jesus Christ, the only Son of God, eternally begotten of the Father, God from God, light from light, true God from true God, begotten, not made, of one Being with the Father; through Him all things were made. For us and for our salvation He came down from heaven, was incarnate of the Holy Spirit and the Virgin Mary and became truly human. For our sake He was crucified under Pontius Pilate; He suffered death and was buried. On the third day He rose again in accordance with the Scriptures; He ascended into heaven and is seated at the right hand of the Father. He will come again in glory to judge the living and the dead, and His kingdom will have no end.

We believe in the Holy Spirit, the Lord, the giver of life, who proceeds from the Father and the Son, who with the Father and the Son is worshiped and glorified, who has spoken through the prophets. We believe in one holy catholic and Apostolic church. We acknowledge one baptism for the forgiveness of sins. We look for the resurrection of the dead, and the life of the world to come. Amen.

THE CREED OF CHALCEDON

We, then, following the holy fathers, all with one consent teach men to confess one and the same Son, our Lord Jesus Christ, the same perfect in Godhead and also perfect in manhood; truly God and truly man, of a rational soul and body; coessential with the Father according to the Godhead, and consubstantial with us according to the manhood; in all things like unto us, without sin; begotten before all ages of the Father according to the Godhead, and in these latter days, for us and for our salvation, born of the Virgin Mary, the mother of God, according to the manhood; one and the same Christ, Son, Lord, Only-begotten, to be acknowledged in two natures, without confusion, without change, without division, without separation; the distinction of natures being by no means taken away by the union, but rather the property of each nature being preserved, and concurring in one person and one subsistence, not parted or divided into two persons, but one and the same Son, and only begotten, God the Word, the Lord Jesus Christ; as the prophets from the beginning have declared concerning Him, and the Lord Jesus Christ Himself has taught us, and the creed of the holy fathers has handed down to us.

SUBJECT INDEX

Aaron, 116
Abel, 263–64
Abraham, 33, 68, 79, 115–17, 121,
    130–31, 157
absurdity, 197–98, 256, 300–301
accommodation theory, 136
activism, 250
Adam, 104–5, 108–9, 113–15, 118–19,
    123–24, 161, 296, 300
Adonai, 141–42, 306
adoption, 240, 242–46
adoration, 276
adultery, 105, 203
advocate, 184–85
affections, 102, 103, 328
AIDS, 218
alcohol, 203
alienation, 104–6
already and not yet, 306–7
ambiguity, 110
amillennialism, 313
Amos, 22
analogia entis, 101
analogical speech, 51
analogy of being, 102–3
analytical justification, 233, 236
Ancient of Days, 131, 142
angels, 93–98
annihilationism, 330
anomalies, 9
Anselm of Canterbury, 154, 156
anthropology, 3, 4
anthropomorphism, 48–49
antichrist, 107, 313

antinomianism, 203, 237–38, 250–51
anxiety, 79
Apocrypha, 39
apostasy, 254–55, 312
Apostles, 21–23, 37
    and the church, 270–72
    succession of, 42
    testimony of, 131
Apostles' Creed, 144, 148, 153, 337
archaeology, 9
Arianism, 133
Aristotle, 234, 290–91
Arminianism, 226, 231
ascension, 147–48
aseity, 62–64, 79–81
assensus, 238
assurance, 76
atheism, 87
atomism, 10, 17
atonement, 154–59
    extent of, 166–69
    as substitution, 160–65
Augustine, 11, 14–15, 30, 109, 112,
    117, 222, 261–62, 266
authenticity, 37, 209–10
authority
    of angels, 95–96
    of Apostles, 270–72
    of Scripture, 25–29, 40–44
authorship, 26–27

Balaam, 176
baptism, 234, 273, 279–80, 282
    of Holy Spirit, 188–93

SCRIPTURE INDEX